CONSTITUTIONAL STUDIES
State and Federal

Da Capo Press Reprints in

AMERICAN CONSTITUTIONAL AND LEGAL HISTORY

GENERAL EDITOR: LEONARD W. LEVY

Claremont Graduate School

CONSTITUTIONAL STUDIES

State and Federal

By James Schouler

DA CAPO PRESS • NEW YORK • 1971

A Da Capo Press Reprint Edition

This Da Capo Press edition of
Constitutional Studies, State and Federal,
is an unabridged republication of the first
edition published in New York in 1897.

Library of Congress Catalog Card Number 76-124894
SBN 306-71993-2

Published by Da Capo Press, Inc.
A Subsidiary of Plenum Publishing Corporation
227 West 17th Street, New York, N.Y. 10011

Manufactured in the United States of America

CONSTITUTIONAL STUDIES
State and Federal

CONSTITUTIONAL STUDIES,

STATE AND FEDERAL.

BY

JAMES SCHOULER, LL.D.,

PROFESSOR OF LAW, AND AUTHOR OF "HISTORY OF THE UNITED
STATES UNDER THE CONSTITUTION."

NEW YORK:
DODD, MEAD AND COMPANY.
1897.

UNIVERSITY PRESS:
JOHN WILSON AND SON, CAMBRIDGE, U.S.A.

PREFACE.

THIS volume contains the substance of lectures delivered before the graduate students of Johns Hopkins University during the years 1893–1896. The author, pursuing his own investigation of the primary documents, has sought to trace the origin and progress of those political ideas which have become dominant and fundamental in American government. His order of study embraces: (1) Early colonial charters and the constitutions of the old thirteen States; (2) documents of Union, whose full fruition is the Constitution of the United States; (3) State constitutions since the adoption of this full Federal system. Such a study brings many important facts into new relief which pertain to American democracy and its progression,[1] and should be found both interesting and suggestive. Even in the more trite and familiar analysis of our Federal Constitution, the author has sought to impart some freshness of treatment by employing historical illustration drawn from the national experience of a century.

J. S.

AUGUST 10, 1897.

[1] See, *e. g.*, as to methods of constitutional adoption, p. 211 *et seq.*; oral voting and the ballot, p. 231 *et seq.*

CONTENTS.

PART I.

EARLY CHARTERS AND CONSTITUTIONS.

I.

II.

III.

IV.

PART II.

THE FEDERAL UNION.

I.

II.

III.

IV.

V.

VI.

VII.

VIII.

IX.

X.

XI.

XII.

PART III.

STATE CONSTITUTIONS SINCE 1789.

I.

VII.

VIII.

CONSTITUTIONAL STUDIES.

PART I.

EARLY CHARTERS AND CONSTITUTIONS.

I.

INTRODUCTORY.

IF we examine the Revised Statutes of any well-ordered commonwealth, — a work prepared and published under authority of the legislature as the full and systematized expression of written law at a given date, — we shall find printed there the State constitution, followed or preceded by the great mass of general enactments condensed and arranged by titles and chapters. And the same may be said correspondingly of the Revised Statutes of our Federal Union. In such a huge bound volume, which exhibits only what still remains enforceable in the community as a code, we perceive that the constitution occupies but a few pages comparatively, while perhaps nineteen-twentieths of the whole bulk comprise public statutes, the periodical efflux of legislation. Here and there, perhaps, if the codifying work be scholarly, we shall find citations from the judicial reports, indicating that this vast array of mandatory text has received from time to time the comment and construction of the courts as to its fundamental force and meaning.

Sovereign precepts are in these modern days publicly set forth; and from such an open book we

1

gather in detail the institutions of a modern American State, so far as the people's organic text, supplemented and expanded by the variable but consistent enactments of popular representatives in the legislature from time to time, may display them at a certain epoch. To the former, and more constant as well as more comprehensive class of written institutions in America, this volume will confine itself.

Charters and constitutions, the framework and fundamental expression of American government, whether in a State or Federal sense, furnish, in fact, the primary ideas of our political system, the organic institutions to which legislation, and, indeed, the whole practical conduct of public affairs, must be purely subsidiary, like water conducted through some prearranged channel. Every statute, every act of the legislature, must conform to the basic mould of our local constitution, else the judiciary, when invoked, will check its operation. Not that American constitutions and legislative acts progress historically together and change together, but that the constitution of any given date acquires supremacy, and each constitutional change is radical. Herein consists the great difference between constitutional government in the mother country and our own. In Great Britain the struggle of centuries has been between King and Parliament, the predominance of executive or legislature; in the United States of to-day, public authority, whether of executive or legislature or judiciary, is but representative in theory, an authority of co-ordinate departments, and the people alone are sovereign and predominant. Thus, men learned in British law assert to-day that Parliament has at length triumphed, by virtue of a representative popular authority irrevocable; and that throughout the realm of Great Britain no fundamental limit can be set to whatever Parliament may choose at any time to ordain. Settlers from the old country, at an age when the old struggle for royal prerogative merged into civil war, regicide, and the protectorate of Cromwell, our early American colonists ripened in the belief that there existed, even in the parent country, an English constitutional law, a "law of the land" for the people, which such documents as *magna charta* had formulated for individual protection in life, liberty, and property, and which neither a monarch nor Parliament could rightfully transgress. Such views had been upheld at home by the sturdy Coke, that Gamaliel of our pre-Revolutionary lawyers. For America, for these United States, at all events, no law, no system, can, since 1776, be deemed obligatory in a commonwealth but what originates in convention with the popular sanction; and upon the solid pillars of such law, such a system, rests the whole fabric of sovereignty. A written constitution, therefore, whether rigid or elastic in expression, determines and defines the scope of all departments of government, of all government. That idea sprang from the primitive condition of American settlements, which was settlement under the constraints of a written charter.

It is fit, then, that those written institutions should be studied and understood which are at the very base of American life and manners. But equally basic, by presumption, at least, in the spread of the Anglo-Saxon race, is that accretion of customs, shrouded as to origin in the darkness of the middle ages, which Blackstone pronounces "the first ground and chief corner-stone of the laws of England." [1] This English common law was brought from Great

[1] Bl. Com. 73.

Britain to America, and propagated by our early colonists wherever their settlements extended. Some famous men of our Revolutionary era contended that such consuetudinary law existed in these colonies only by force of early colonial legislation which expressly recognized its operation; others, with perhaps the better reason, that as originally liege subjects of Great Britain we brought that law to the new world, subject only to such express changes as might afterwards be found needful for adapting it to our new condition.[1] But all have agreed that by the time independence of Great Britain was declared in 1776, the English common law, with some such local variance and adaptation, had overspread the surface of American society, for the presumptive regulation of private rights; and one great patriot, at least, is said to have declared that he would never have drawn sword against King George had he not believed that the common law still remained his birthright.[2]

Hence originates case-law, as it is termed, which, in its mighty accumulation of judicial precedents historically preserved for reference through the authentic reports of England and America, constitutes the first layer, so to speak, of our common State and Federal jurisprudence. Unwritten law, it was formerly termed, as distinguished from the written law of positive enactment, which we first discussed, — unenacted, we should rather term it to-day, since in modern times reports of the appellate courts are nearly as accessible and as widely printed and circulated as statutes or the organic constitution itself. Modern reports are not, strictly speaking, the technical transcripts of court records; but prepared in a more readable shape, they supply, by way of narra-

[1] And see the language of colonial charters on this point, II. *post.*
[2] A remark attributed to John Adams.

tive, a summary of the facts, in each decided case (which narration is often the court's own statement in the opinion rendered), together with a judicial opinion at full length disclosing the grounds upon which the decision was rendered. *Leges et consuetudines regni* was the accepted title of the English common law in early times. No body of law can have developed so easily and so smoothly as that founded upon the customs of a homogeneous people by the gradual accretion of precedents. Customs make manners and shape manners. Custom or usage, in business or the household, for determining private rights and wrongs, precedes usually the law, though fundamental maxims were earlier; a test case in the courts determines the full scope and legality of such usage; and the precedent as recorded and published gives force and expansion to the custom, or else denies it on consideration of sound policy. Legislation, to be sure, may interpose with more violence and radical effect to change that custom, and with it the existing course of judicial precedents or procedure; but, whether it be under court or legislative direction, innovation or its suggestion must have begun usually in the ingenuity of society, feeling its own way over the surface of human existence and among the pitfalls of public sovereignty, towards some new combination of circumstances where former analogies are to be applied. And thus do judicial precedents, which, by their sequence, confirm principles in the course of an extended and novel application, come to supply society with a jurisprudence so wise, so tolerable, and so methodically progressive, that we of England and the United States may well wonder how civilized nations, professing popular institutions, could ever have got on well without them. Scholars have asserted that there was more of the *a priori* assertion of law in the Roman methods of Justinian's age; but, be that as it may, our Anglo-Saxon system prevails readily in modern application. Foreign jurists tell us that in colonies such as Canada, which have come from other nations under English influence and authority, the English system of reporting judicial cases and of developing the law from such reports has come into easy predominance. So is it, we might add, with Louisiana, Florida, Texas, and those other annexations to the United States where the law of continental France or Spain once shaped the rights of society.

Precedents, like cobble-stones, pave the pathway of our common law, and that pathway stretches far back into time immemorial. So natural is the habit of relying upon precedents for smoothing out consistently the broadening avenue of human achievement that we find them, not for judicial development alone, but in ceremonial observances, in holiday celebrations and memorials, whether as concerning the State, the community of neighbors, or the family circle. Precedents take strong lodgment in the simplest mind; and the simpler the people, the more conclusive, as well as irrational, becomes their expression. Sir Frederick Pollock, in one of his essays on jurisprudence, observes how readily a young child will cite precedents to justify conduct for which he is yet unable to allege a sound motive. "Why, father (or A) did so," is his excuse; or, if pushed still more closely for a plea, "I did so yesterday, and you let me." Tribes and families living remote from civilized society pursue their peculiar customs, because such was the tribal or parental custom before; as we see in the quaint dress or festivities which keep up old manners. With some simple village peasantry who have seen little of the enlightened world, novelties find little favor; such folk are content to bake and brew and to pursue their sports as the generations did before them. Precedents thus relied upon are of course not conclusively just and reasonable. But those precedents which in our own mosaic-work of the common law become established by the judgment of some intelligent tribunal, learned in what has been judicially established already, and skilful to apply, — of a tribunal fairly and honestly disposed to do justice according to the merits of each case, and composed of men selected for their superior legal wisdom and aptitude, who hear the arguments of both sides before deciding, and who have power to enforce the decision, — ought surely to carry the greatest weight as authority for a custom in any specified jurisdiction.

Of public institutions, therefore, in an American modern State, any comprehensive study must take a threefold range : (1) There is the common or consuetudinary law as the first stratum, that most particularly which prevailed at the original colonization of this country; (2) There is the legislative enactment or positive statute which displaces such common law, regulating and modifying so far as may be ; (3) There is the further written fundamental State constitution, primitive enough in charter origin to control common law at the colonial outset, which " as the act of the people speaking in their original character " [1] overrules and supersedes whatever in either custom or contemporaneous statute law proves inconsistent with its mandate, giving to local government and society a new progression. To this may be added (4) that the constitution of the United States and the acts and statutes of Congress and treaties pursuant

[1] 1 Kent Com. 449.

thereto are the supreme law of this land, and paramount in authority to custom, State statutes, or even
the State constitution itself. American institutions,
both State and Federal, we now proceed to examine
in their consecutive order so as to trace out American
ideas of government in their historical origin and
development, as embodied in these third and fourth
classes only of fundamental law. It should be observed, however, in passing, that many of those ideas
which State constitutions usually put forward to-day
as fundamental have in certain other States, whose
organic law comprises less detail, worked into practical expression as the less positive fiat of a State legislature, exercising its own unfettered discretion over
the subject.

II.

THE COLONIAL GOVERNMENTS.

1607–1776.

BLACKSTONE has classified the governments of our American colonies as follows : (1) Provincial ; (2) Proprietary ; (3) Charter Governments.[1] Such was doubtless their condition when he published his Commentaries, or shortly before the Revolution. Seven of these colonies, and in fact the majority, were of the first or Provincial class, — New Hampshire, New York, New Jersey, Virginia, North Carolina, South Carolina, and Georgia ; that is to say, in each of them a royal governor who was appointed by the British Crown served as royal deputy within the jurisdiction, under instructions which usually accompanied or followed his commission. Of Proprietary governments there were Maryland, Pennsylvania, and Delaware ; and here some favored individual or family — that of Lord Baltimore, in the first named, and of William Penn in the other two — ruled with sub-royal dominion and subordinate powers of legislation. The Charter governments proper comprised at this late period only Massachusetts, Connecticut, and Rhode Island.

Historically speaking, however, most of these thirteen American colonies had been originally settled and established under a fundamental charter or grant of some sort from the British Crown, which served as

[1] 1 Bl. Com. 108 ; 1 Story Commentaries, § 159.

a parchment basis of government; most of their inhabitants had become habituated to a written fundamental polity to which all local legislation had to
conform, very much as in the by-laws of a chartered
business corporation of to-day; nor did the primitive
government in such cases differ very greatly from
that of our modern private corporation in committing
the main general management of affairs to a President
or Governor with a Board of Directors or Assistants,
all of whom, under the most favoring circumstances,
were chosen by the body of freemen or stockholders.
In fact, the complaint against the Winthrops and Dud-
leys of Massachusetts Bay and their followers had
been that what the Crown originally intended as a
mere civil corporation within the realm had been perverted across the ocean by the corporators into a full
political establishment. Proprietary governments,
moreover, were conducted by virtue of royal grants
or charters. During the eighteenth century and for
a long time prior to 1775, we find only Connecticut
and Rhode Island possessed of charters which conferred a liberal authority upon the people, while
Massachusetts lived under a royal charter which
made its government scarcely less in practice of the
provincial sort than that of Virginia. Both Virginia
and Massachusetts had, in fact, experienced various
charter vicissitudes since their earliest settlement;
and the Massachusetts charter from William and
Mary, dated 1691, was reserved and cautious in its
allowance of self-government. On the other hand,
the charters of Connecticut and Rhode Island from
Charles II. — the one granted in 1662 and the other
in 1663 — were so manifestly liberal in popular privileges that each served essentially through the Revolution and even beyond the eighteenth century as
the fundamental constitution of an American State,

though not democratic enough to stand long the popular test of this nineteenth century.

These early American charters afford a curious and interesting study. In the earliest of them we shall find ideas and expressions which have immensely influenced the development of manners and politics in this new world, not through the colonial era alone, but for all time. The idiosyncrasies of the several British monarchs who granted them appear moreover in their composition. James I. leads the list of grantors with that prolix, diffuse, and wordy style of expression so common in his age, recounting marvellous " providences " of a special cast; Charles I. follows with a more concise style, as befitted a monarch of greater personal dignity; through the times of Cromwell and the Commonwealth we find these colonies singularly neglected; after which Charles II., — from whose reign, frivolous though he was, so much excellent legislation takes its rise, — granted presently the most liberal, and indeed the only thoroughly liberal and popular, American charters of this whole colonial age. From the final expulsion of the Stuarts, British policy held the American colonies well in check, so as to afford a rich market for British manufactures and commerce, and, while encouraging colonial resources, to repress all tendencies to independence or disloyalty. All these charters or grants for American colonization were English in expression, except for the Maryland charter of 1632, which employed the Latin tongue, — a royal recognition, most likely, of rank and scholarship in Lord Baltimore, the beneficiary of Charles I., who was a devout Roman Catholic.[1]

---

[1] Sir George Calvert, first Lord Baltimore, was the applicant for this charter, but, as he died before its execution, it was intrusted to his son, Cecil Calvert, the second Lord Baltimore.

The first charter of Virginia, which James I. issued in 1606, shortly before the primitive Jamestown settlement, granted the lands along our northern Atlantic coast to which Great Britain laid claim, between the 34th and 45th degrees of north latitude, to two distinct companies, one of which had its headquarters at London and the other at Plymouth, in the mother country. Organizing at once under this charter of 1606, the London Company sought and obtained by 1609 a new and enlarged charter as the " Virginia Company," for prosecuting its practical work of American settlement. Under the simple reign of James I. there were three different charters granted to this oldest of American colonies. The Plymouth Company reorganized in 1620 for the more northerly colonization of our American coast, and received that year from James I. another charter for " the planting, ruling, ordering, and governing of New England in America." Under this " New England charter " came the Pilgrims of the " Mayflower " to their new Plymouth of Massachusetts Bay; and the agreement signed by them off Cape Cod before they came ashore bound the new settlers by common consent into a body politic, — a memorable transaction. Next came the charter of Massachusetts Bay, granted in 1629 under Charles I., which by 1684, after the establishment of a most thriving colony, was cancelled by the English Chancery during the reign of James II., for alleged infractions of the royal grant. The new charter of William and Mary in 1691, to which we have alluded, annexed Plymouth finally to Massachusetts Bay and erected Massachusetts into a single colony. Unlike the previous Massachusetts charters, that of 1691 designed a full political government.

The Pennsylvania colony, whose proprietary charter to William Penn passed the seals in 1682, exhibits various fundamental documents which testify to the prudent and thrifty management of this excellent Quaker and his philanthropic and statesmanlike views. By virtue of his legal supremacy, Penn as Governor prescribed from time to time a frame of government with increasing liberality, and under the document of 1701 granted broad political powers with the specific approbation of the Pennsylvania General Assembly, and of the Governor's Council, under an express proviso that no change should be made in these fundaments without the joint assent of the Governor and six-sevenths of the Legislature. This famous document of 1701, known as Penn's "Charter of Privileges," declared full liberty of religious conscience, in an article pronounced inviolable and forever incapable of amendment. Among other provisions it enlarged the English common law by according to criminals the same privilege of witnesses and counsel as their prosecutors,[1] and abolished the common-law forfeiture which attached to suicides and death by the "deodand."[2] William Penn's charter of 1701 to Delaware is of a similar scope; and this latter domain which came to William Penn as proprietor in 1682 and by quitclaim from the Duke of York was known in early colonial times as "The Territories."

The first of the so-called Carolina charters — for North and South Carolina were long colonially united — antedates the permanent English settlement of this Atlantic coast, having been granted to Sir Walter Raleigh in 1584 by Queen Elizabeth. That charter really constitutes the first step in the work of

---

[1] See Article VI., amendments to the Constitution of the United States, embodying this same feature.

[2] This provision, in essentially the same language, found its way into several early State constitutions.

British colonization in America; and five voyages, all of them unsuccessful in planting a colony, were made under it. The charter of 1663 for Carolina was granted by Charles II. to various English peers as lords proprietors, and John Locke's fundamental constitution, drawn up at the instance of these privileged owners for the settlers, followed in 1669 to last only for a brief and turbulent period. Although this scheme of the broadest political philosopher of his age proved a practical failure, as history has recorded, setting prerogative, as it did, high above self-government in the new world, seeking to establish a feudal tenure in the primeval soil, avowing the absolute power and authority of every freeman over his slaves, and declaring the Church of England the orthodox religion of the colony, it had some good points in minor details. Probably much of this ill-adapted constitution was made by its framer to order, and did not embody Locke's personal views.

With some of these colonial charters went out spontaneously the good-will of the sovereign who granted it. The grants of Charles II., in particular, breathed loving-kindness to his beneficiaries. In the charter to William Penn he recounts that love and philanthropy of the latter to the native Indians which his own royal ancestors had enjoined; and the monarch gave and confirmed the name "Pennsylvania" to the colony after the family surname, — a token of royal favor towards a private subject without an American parallel. Charles II. had granted the popular charters of Connecticut and Rhode Island, nearly twenty years earlier, in affectionate language. To our "loving subjects" is the expression of the Connecticut charter. In that of Rhode Island (1663) the monarch makes special mention that these settlers, Roger Williams and his com-

panions, had been harshly treated for their religious
views by the other New England colonies; he recognizes "their peaceable and loyal minds," "their sober,
serious, and religious intentions," their self-exile, and
their prosperity and preservation "by the good Providence of God, from whom the Plantations have taken
their names." [1]   And to these good subjects the King
plainly offers himself to be their champion, promising
to protect them against all molestation from their
neighbors; and in all controversies between Rhode
Island and the other New England colonies which
might arise, this colony is specially invited to appeal
to the Crown for redress.[2]

Emanating from the same national source, and
embodying a single national purpose, we may expect
to find these English colonial governments closely,
on the whole, resembling one another in essentials;
at the same time that differences of local origin and
development give rise to local differences in their
public management.

1. As to the structure of colonial government.
There was not in these earlier days any marked separation of fundamental powers such as Montesquieu
has inculcated.   But the British monarchs after 1688
strongly favored the establishment of a strong royal
executive or vicegerent in each colony, with powers
commensurate for holding the settlers in allegiance
to Great Britain, and an appointment immediately
dependent upon the Crown.   Such was the royal governor in those provincial governments which constituted a majority of the American colonies; and such,
too, regardless of her former usages, or of the favor

[1] " Rhode Island and Providence Plantations " was the early style
of this colony.
[2] See Poore's Charters and Constitutions, *passim.*

still accorded to her neighbors, Rhode Island and Connecticut, was the governor imposed upon Massachusetts under the William and Mary charter. Lieutenant-Governor and Secretary were for Massachusetts, and in most, if not all, such provinces as recognized these lesser officials, appointed directly by the British Crown; while in certainly eight colonies the King commissioned the Governor, or chief executive, as his own immediate representative or deputy, styling him captain-general and commander-in-chief over the jurisdiction, as well as chancellor, vice-admiral, and ordinary. In our American provinces the Crown also appointed, directly or indirectly, a "Council," whose chief function, resembling more or less that of a board of directors, was to advise and assist the Governor in his executive duties. This council held secret sessions and possessed often a share in legislation, like an upper House. But the Massachusetts charter of 1691 so far respected ancient local usage as to permit the Council of that colony to be appointed annually from the representative assembly (or "Great and General Court"), and thus operate somewhat as a popular check upon the royal governor's action.[1] With advice of Council,[2] a provincial governor had usually the power to establish local courts, and to appoint judges and other colonial magistrates and officers; and each provincial capital tended to become the seat of a court and official circle which reflected with paler brilliancy the ceremonials of a London monarch.[3]

---

[1] The Governor had, however, a negative upon this choice of a Council. 1 Story, Commentaries, § 171.

[2] Under the Massachusetts charter (1691) all appointments by the Governor required confirmation by the Council upon seven days' notice, — a practice preserved in that State to this day.

[3] See Poore's Charters and Constitutions; 1 Story, Commentaries, § 159 and citations.

As a popular offset to all this, representative government and the legislature bloomed out early in each American colony, and the British Crown made no effort to eradicate it. On the contrary, the royal governor's commission gave him authority usually to convene, at stated times, a general assembly of representatives of the freeholders and planters; and under such authority Provincial Assemblies, composed of the Governor, the Council, and the Representatives, were constituted; the Council serving perhaps as a separate branch or upper house for such legislation, while the Governor possessed a negative upon all legislative proceedings, and very considerable latitude, besides, to prorogue, adjourn, and dissolve the Legislature, or to convene it whenever and wherever he might think fit.[1]

While colonial legislation would thus seem vested usually in two houses, one body only, like the English House of Commons, came close to the heart of the local constituency, — as in Virginia, for instance, whose "House of Burgesses" struck the early chord of revolution, reckless of governor and royal councillors alike. That phrase, "General Court," so long applied to this representative assembly in Massachusetts, did not originate locally even in its earlier charters;[2] but for both Virginia and Massachusetts the old "General Court" had its terms or sessions defined like those of an English court of justice; and in its operations it blended judicial, legislative, and even executive authority as a final appellate tribunal of the colony in all matters. In Massachusetts, as in most other colonies, the Legislature was authorized[3] to levy taxes,

[1] See Poore's Charters and Constitutions; 1 Story, Commentaries, § 159 and citations.

[2] See Virginia charter of 1611–12, in Poore, 1905, which prescribes a "General Court" for that primitive colony.

[3] And so expressed under the charter of 1691.

and otherwise pass laws for the common interest; and yet so great was her royal governor's power, on the one hand, as specified in the charter of William and Mary, and so ill-defined, on the other, that of the " General Court," that two constitutional doubts had to be resolved in 1726, by a supplementary charter from George I. That sovereign did not incline strongly to the side of the local colonists in this controversy; for he ruled (1) that, as to choosing a speaker, the General Court might make such choice subject to the approval of the Governor, and (2) that, as to its right to adjourn, the General Court might adjourn for two days, but no longer, without the Governor's consent.[1]

In Connecticut and Rhode Island, however, the two favored jurisdictions of royalty, legislation, the choice of a governor, and the whole business of constituting courts and bestowing official patronage were confided fully by royal grace to the free settlers; and those two colonies, under their respective charters, organized local government, as they were permitted to do, upon a popular and republican basis. Here the Governor, Council, and Assembly continued annually chosen by the freemen down to the American Revolution, and all other officers were appointed by their authority.[2]   Annual elections prevailed here as elsewhere in America, so far as there were popular elections at all, — whence the maxim, familiar a century ago, that " wherever annual elections end tyranny begins," — and the colonial assembly moreover held annually its wonted sessions.   But the circum-

---

[1] Poore's Charters and Constitutions (Massachusetts).

[2] 1 Story, Constitutions, § 161, observes that while the Statutes of 7 and 8 William III. required that all governors appointed in charter or proprietary governments should be approved of by the Crown, this statute was, " if at all, ill observed," and produced apparently no change in the colonial policy.

stances of original settlement in Connecticut and Rhode Island had produced the anomaly of double capital towns and rivals; so that under their respective charters the legislature regularly met twice a year, rotating in the one colony from Hartford to New Haven, and in the other, from Providence to Newport, — a condition which long outlasted this colonial era.

In the three proprietary governments — Maryland, Pennsylvania, and Delaware — the grand proprietor exercised his sub-royal prerogative of appointing governors answerable to himself, as likewise of bestowing the colonial patronage, and defining legislative authority. Hence we find Penn's "Charter of Privileges" in 1701 proclaiming freely that henceforth there shall be an annual Assembly in Pennsylvania, with power to choose its own speaker and other officers, to judge of the qualifications and elections of its own members, to prepare and pass bills, to impeach criminals, to redress grievances, and to exercise "all other powers and privileges of an assembly according to the rights of the free-born subjects of England, and AS IS USUAL in any of the King's Plantations in America." [1] And in certain appointments to office, a compromising expedient is set forth in that document, long traceable in the fundamental law of Pennsylvania as a State, which empowered the freemen to choose a double number, leaving the Governor to select one or the other for the office. Here, as in all our other American colonies except Connecticut and Rhode Island, legislation by the popular branch required the Governor's specific approval, and his veto of a measure was absolute.

Some minor differences may be observed in respect to the mode of enacting laws in the several colonies;

---

[1] Poore's Charters and Constitutions (Pennsylvania).

and yet the legislature, of which at least one branch the people might freely choose to represent and defend their collective interests, became early a palladium of the American system inseparable from popular liberty, though in the earliest of these American charters no such provision was clearly set forth. For free-born Britons were not likely to endure long the exercise of arbitrary power by king or incorporators in this new world.[1] By the eighteenth century, therefore, this right of colonists to participate by their representatives in all local legislation was fairly conceded by the home government; but as to provincial governments there continued a controversy. For provincial colonists contended that such representation was a matter of right; but the Crown and its legal advisers, that representation was a privilege only, subject to the pleasure of the parent government. In the political struggles from time to time which culminated under George III. in bloodshed, the royal governor would harass the colonial legislature to the extent of his ample authority, or would long neglect to convene it, — practical mischiefs which our Declaration of Independence boldly denounced, and which many a bill of rights or constitution in the revolting States of America took care to guard against for the future.[2]

---

[1] Mr. Hutchinson, in his Colonial History of Massachusetts, 94 (cited 1 Story, Constitution, § 166), sketches admirably the progress made in all these early colonies, except Maryland (whose charter made express provision), before the reign of Charles II., in establishing a representative legislature of some sort and forcing its recognition upon the chartered proprietors or incorporators. "After the restoration (1688)," he adds, "there is no instance of a colony settled without a representation of the people, nor any attempt to deprive the colonies of this privilege, except in the arbitrary reign of King James the Second."

[2] In the colony of New York (and *semble* in Virginia also) the British Crown before the middle of the eighteenth century succeeded in

The germ of popular government in the earlier colonial charters consists, like that of all private guilds or corporations at the common law, in bringing the whole body of stockholders or those immediately concerned with affairs into an annual meeting for the election of managing officers. Such is the component element of government in that admirable system of New England towns, whose inhabitants came together once a year to discuss and arrange local affairs and to choose their selectmen. And to some extent any colony newly planted and small in numbers might conveniently assemble at stated times for the general regulation and control of affairs; but as new settlers scatter over the territory and extend as well as localize their interests and population, either the proxy or the representative principle comes soon into play. Representation serves the convenience of modern civil government popularly conducted, as does the proxy in private corporations. According to the expression of the Connecticut charter of 1662,[1] an option was given the settlers to hold either "a general meeting" of the freemen or a representative assembly, and the colonists naturally enough chose the latter. But popular representation as sanctioned by Charles II. and the seventeenth century was too crude to last, based as it was in Connecticut upon precise town equality; while in Rhode Island, Newport was allowed the permanent precedence over all other towns of the colony, Providence included, which

establishing septennial assemblies, in imitation of the septennial Parliaments of the parent country, "which was a measure so offensive to the people that it constituted one of their grievances propounded at the commencement of the American Revolution." 1 Story, § 167.

[1] "A body corporate and politic by the name of the governor and company of the English Colony of," etc., is the title employed in the Connecticut and Rhode Island charters of Charles II., the best fruition of these royal American charters.

were classed in political power by two set grades. Some towns grow into great cities, while others decline or become stagnant; and such a fixed basis of town representation, which left no chance to apportion by population, doomed at length these most lasting of all colonial charters more than any other defect in them; for being charters and royal ones, there was left no chance to amend them. Representation by towns instead of numbers was long the British fashion on either side of the Atlantic; but the Massachusetts charter (1691) from William and Mary provided with a wiser foresight that the colonial legislature might alter later at its discretion the basis of town representation drawn up in the instrument. And, in fine, the flexibility of provincial over charter governments in all such fundamental matters was doubtless a reason for preferring them upon experience in the colonial policy of the parent country.[1]

2. As to the fundamental safeguards of allegiance to Great Britain. Besides the practical constraint which any royal governor might have exerted while clothed with the ample powers we have enumerated, were certain fundamental expressions in these colonial charters, which bound grantees and the colonists to both legal and moral compliance. All thirteen of these American colonies lived under fundamental restrictions that no laws should be made repugnant to those of England, or that as nearly as convenient the laws should be consonant with and conformable thereto; and either expressly or by necessary implication it was provided that the laws of England should be in force in the colony so far as applica-

---

[1] As already shown (p. 13), Penn's "Charter of Privileges" (1701) was made capable of amendment under certain stringent conditions.

ble.[1] In the latest and most liberal charters this written reservation was still expressed as in the early Virginian document of 1609.

Thus were our American colonists nurtured and brought up in the knowledge of a fundamental restraint upon local legislation; and this, aside from that other written constraint upon local government which the charter itself imposed. Some power external to the colonial legislature must have existed for determining the validity of its enactments; and that paramount power the parent government naturally claimed as its own. Besides the royal governor's vigilant exercise of a negative upon such local colonial legislation, the British monarch reserved his own right to approve or disapprove, — a prerogative exercise from which Maryland, Connecticut, and Rhode Island alone were exempt.[2] Parental supremacy was still further aided by the judicial appeal which lay from the decisions of all colonial courts to the English privy council, — a practice which, on the whole, seems to have been deemed by our colonists a privilege rather than a grievance.[3] Except, however, for repugnant enactments, the colonial legislatures in America exercised a broad local authority, particularly in matters of

---

[1] Such a declaration was conclusive and could not afterwards be abrogated by the Crown, being a fundamental rule of the original settlement. 1 Story, § 156.

[2] "In all the other colonies [except Maryland, Connecticut, and Rhode Island] the King possessed the power of abrogating them [the laws], and they were not final in their authority until they had passed under his review." 1 Story, § 171. See also statute 7 and 8 William III. c. 22, declaring expressly that all colonial laws, by-laws, usages, and customs repugnant to any law of the kingdom, shall be utterly void. 1 Story, § 164.

[3] About the year 1680, Massachusetts, Rhode Island, and Connecticut inclined to dispute this right of appeal, but the contention subsided.

local taxation.[1] Oaths of allegiance, finally, or the "freeman's oath," were much relied upon for binding a subject in conscience to his British sovereign, under penalties of perjury.

3. As to civil rights. Except for Pennsylvania, the charters under which these colonies were first settled are found to contain an express royal declaration that all subjects and their children inhabiting therein shall be deemed natural born, and shall enjoy all the privileges and immunities of such subjects.[2] In some of them the King furthermore concedes expressly the right of his grantees to transport to the new colony all such British subjects and strangers as are willing to go.[3] The Virginia charter of 1606 set the example of a royal guaranty of indemnity to all English subjects and those of allied powers, against robbery and spoliation by his colonists.

Under the Connecticut and Rhode Island charters, self-government was freely committed to the "freemen" of the colony; while other royal grants less democratic confined suffrage to "freeholders" or men of specified property among the colonists.

4. As to inter-colonial rights. All British dwellers in the American colonies were fellow-subjects of the mother country, and for many purposes were to be deemed one people; each one might lawfully inhabit other colonies, or inherit lands in them by descent.[4] Charters themselves, however, were gen-

[1] For the issue of taxation as an inherent right in the colonial legislatures (which more than any other provoked the American Revolution) see 1 Story, Constitutional Law, §§ 166–170.

[2] 1 Story, § 156.

[3] See, e. g., Massachusetts charter of 1629; Connecticut charter of 1662.

[4] 1 Story, § 178; Jay, C. J., in 2 Dall. 470.

erally silent on such points ; but we find Charles II.,
out of his special solicitude for the persecuted Rhode
Islanders, asserting expressly in their charter of 1663,
that they may repass and trade with his other English colonies. Commercial intercourse, not, of course,
without some rivalry and collision, began very early
among these colonies ; [1] and the regulation of such
intercourse, as well as of extradition and other reciprocal conveniences, soon engaged their peculiar attention, as we shall show later.[2]

5. As to religious freedom and philanthropy.
Colonies as to matters of faith differed both in
tenets and practice, being Protestant, however, in
the main, and imbued with the prevalent spirit of the
English Reformation. Liberal religion, or rather
the desire to escape conformity to church establishments at home and to enjoy freedom of religious
faith in the new world after some new method,
operated as a powerful incentive to American emigra-
tion, even where the mind might not yet have been
open to full religious tolerance. Yet the genius of
these new world institutions tended unquestionably
to religious liberty, and in the Pennsylvania and
Rhode Island colonies guaranties for the rights of
conscience were already promulgated, very broad for
the age. "All confessing one God in any way shall
live unmolested," declares in substance Penn's Charter of 1701, "and all professing belief in Christ shall
be capable of serving in office in the colony." In the
Massachusetts charter of 1691, on the other hand,
granted while the expulsion of a Roman Catholic
dynasty was fresh in the British mind, William and

---

[1] See the arrival of a Maryland vessel in Massachusetts Bay, chron-
icled in Winthrop's Journal, October 14, 1634.

[2] See Tendencies to Union, Part II., *post.*

Mary gave direction that liberty of conscience be allowed to all inhabitants "except Papists."

The Stuarts had cherished the laudable wish of converting the American Indian to civilized arts and Christianity; and James I., in his first charter to Virginia (1606), zealously commended "so noble a work" in the propagating of Christian religion to such people as yet live in darkness and miserable ignorance of the true worship of God, so as in time to "bring the infidels and savages living in those parts to human civility and to a settled and quiet government." Little practical success, it is well known, attended such humane efforts by the Anglo-American except in Pennsylvania; and philanthropic sentiment towards the red race prevailed most strongly in this colonial age among benefactors whose hearts dilated at a safe distance.

6. As to trade and business occupation. British policy towards these American colonies developed, as history shows, in opening up on this western Atlantic coast a grand market for home manufactures, while stimulating the loyal and industrious settlers to cherish and supply the natural productions of this new region in return, thus giving scope to a lucrative British commerce. That the southern colonies, with their plantations of tobacco, rice, and indigo, were fostered differently from the northern cannot be doubted. Charters, to be sure, had little to promulgate for an economic policy; but those of New England, whose hardy inhabitants pursued the cod and whale into distant waters, repeatedly commend and encourage the "trade of fishing" towards the close of the seventeenth century; the Rhode Island charter in 1663 containing sundry royal details as to "the business of taking whales."

It is curious to observe that, in emulation of Spain, these English charters of the seventeenth century, beginning with Virginia, reserved specifically to the crown one-fifth of all such gold and silver as the chartered colony might produce. That of Massachusetts, in 1691, added one-fifth of all precious stones; while Penn's charter, which passed the seals ten years earlier, required two beaver skins a year, besides the talliage of gold and silver. Had the King levied upon Pennsylvania coal and iron, it might have been more to the purpose; for the present exaction could have yielded very little to the King's treasury.

7. As to land tenure. Under all our colonial charters, — James I. setting for Virginia the earliest example, — the new soil in America was to be held from the Crown in free and common socage, completely divested of all feudal burdens such as continued to encumber land tenure in the mother country until after the restoration of Charles II. An inestimable privilege this to America; for it encouraged these Atlantic settlers to become freeholders, owners severally of the soil they cultivated in fee and independently, without lease or manorial encumbrance at all.[1] "Partly from the cheapness of land, and partly from an innate love of independence," observed Judge Story from his native standpoint, more than fifty years ago, "few agricultural estates in the whole country have at any time been held on lease for a stipulated rent. The tenants and occupiers are almost universally the proprietors of the soil in feesimple. Strictly speaking, therefore, there has never

[1] Manorial estates were permitted under some charters, as in New York, but they soon faded into insignificance. The almost total absence of leasehold estates in our colonial history is a remarkable circumstance. 1 Story, § 172.

been in this country a dependent peasantry." The yeomanry, he adds, are absolute owners of the soil on which they tread, and their character has from this circumstance been marked by a jealous watchfulness of their rights and by a steady spirit of resistance against every encroachment.[1]

Connected with such simplicity of tenure, a simple real-estate system was seen to prevail in the American colonies from the earliest times, both with regard to the language of the deed itself which made conveyance and the public record of land titles. We find John Locke's charter of 1669 establishing in the Carolinas a registry of deeds for each convenient precinct; and the same registry system sprang up so spontaneously in the other colonies, north and south, as to have become general here a century before Blackstone was seen doubtfully commending a scheme of public records for general adoption at home in evincing real-estate title, in place of the time-honored family chest crammed with old parchments.[2]

[1] 1 Story, 173.
[2] 2 Bl. Com. 343. Pennsylvania's Frame of Government in 1683 is seen (§§ 20–23) providing for an extensive registry system in the colony, for wills, births, marriages, etc., as well as the record of conveyances.

REVOLUTIONARY BILLS OF RIGHTS.

1776–1783.

WHEN in 1776 these American colonies shook off
the British yoke and proclaimed independence, their
leading statesmen were familiar with the English
"Declaration" or "Bill of Rights," that glorious
enactment under which in 1689 the crown was settled
upon William and Mary to the final exclusion of the
Stuarts. These statesmen knew also the fundamental precepts of *Magna Charta* and of the "Petition of Right" and *Habeas Corpus* act, — documents
dear to a British ancestry that had contended stoutly
for individual freedom. Other maxims they formulated by experience, and while brooding over America's immediate wrongs sustained in the vexation of
her colonial legislatures by the royal governors and in
the tyranny of standing armies imported to overawe
the people. Other shining truths of political government had been embodied from early colonial times in
local codes and documents, such, for instance, as the
Massachusetts "Body of Liberties" of 1641. Montesquieu, whose "Spirit of the Laws" had lately been
translated into English and widely circulated, was
the new political oracle of an age not too far remote
from the times of Locke, Sidney, and Vane to
cherish their precious remembrance. Hence, without the need of tracing back an origin to times or
countries more remote, those bosom truths of politics

which found expression, during this revolution of
the thirteen colonies, in what their several constituencies were wont to style a "Bill of Rights," basic
as the structure of constitutional government itself.

"Bill of Rights" may be thought a less appropriate
phrase here than in England, to denote these fundamental maxims of life, liberty, and property, essential to civil liberty; for while the English "Bill of
Rights" is an act of legislation (or bill) proceeding
from the omnipotent Parliament (though not without
some special royal sanction), a "Bill of Rights" for
an American State originates in popular convention
and forms part of that written body of fundamental
law to which all legislative, all executive, and all
judicial authority must submit and be held subject.
Nor with America is it even a constitutional contract
(as in one sense perhaps was the English legislation of 1688) between sovereign and representatives
of the people, two great departments of government;
since the same people and their representatives in
convention who declare these rights may separate and
define at their discretion all the departments of all
the powers of government, whether executive, legislative, or judicial, and clothe them with their several
functions. A "Declaration of Rights," like a "Declaration of Independence," is for America the fitter
phrase; and both the United Colonies in Congress
and various individual colonies were seen in 1776
setting the precedent of declaring such primitive
and fundamental truths before essaying the more
formidable work of framing a practical scheme of
government.

Nor is this "Declaration" or "Bill of Rights"
easily distinguishable in all respects from that scheme
of practical government with which a written constitution should be mainly occupied. Various leading

truths essential to liberty are enjoined among the chartered particulars of government, which a philosophic mind would look for rather in the blazing introduction. When the Federal constitution, fresh from Philadelphia, was opposed for its want of a formal "Bill of Rights," several such safeguard maxims were pointed out as they glittered among the details of national authority proposed by that original instrument. And State experience for more than a century shows besides that, however well-drawn may be our schedule of civil rights, other precious generalities, equally fundamental, appropriate, and obligatory, are likely to be found scattered conveniently enough among the main provisions of the charter.

Virginia, first in years and influence among these American colonies, led off, that memorable year, in preparing the platform of human freedom, after the Continental Congress had given its momentous warning to the States that independence approached and that self-government must be provided for. The Virginia "Bill of Rights" (styled originally a Declaration of Rights "pertaining to the people and their posterity" as the basis and foundation of government) preceded by nearly a month the "Declaration of Independence" at Philadelphia, though framed for concurrence and designing full harmony with Congressional action anticipated. A representative convention, comprising many members of the Virginia House of Burgesses, met at Williamsburg, May 6, 1776, and unanimously adopted this Declaration of Rights on the 12th of June, as preliminary to the work of framing a State constitution. The instrument was drawn up by that friend of freedom, the illustrious George Mason, and the convention only slightly amended it. Its preamble and introductory

clauses, taken from a draft which Jefferson had sent
from Philadelphia, where he was composing the more
famous document of these United Colonies, proclaim
those same immortal rights of life, liberty, and the
pursuit of happiness, in the individual, and that
same institution of all government for the benefit and
security of the governed, who have the unalienable
right to reform, alter, or abolish as may most con-
duce to the general weal.

All power, declared further the Virginia Bill of
Rights, is vested in and derived from the people, and
magistrates are their trustees and servants. No
man or set of men is entitled to exclusive emoluments or privileges from the people, but in consideration of public services, which are not descendible,
so that office should not be hereditary. Elections
of representatives ought to be free,[1] with a right of
suffrage here broadly stated; nor should those of
the community "be taxed or deprived of their property for public uses without their own consent or
that of their representatives."[2] There should be
no suspension of laws or of their execution without
consent of the representatives of the people.[3] In all
criminal prosecutions, a man has a right to know the
cause and nature of his accusation, to be confronted
with the witnesses and accusers, to call for evidence
in his favor, and to be tried by an impartial jury of
the vicinage, without whose unanimous consent he
cannot be found guilty. He cannot be compelled to
give evidence against himself; nor can he be deprived
of his liberty except by the law of the land and the

---

[1] From English Bill of Rights, 1689 (Right 8).

[2] A protest against the colonial stamp and excise acts of Parliament.

[3] From English Bill of Rights (Rights 1 and 2); and see abuses by
royal governors in these colonies, recited in Declaration of Independence.

judgment of his peers.[1] Excessive bail ought not to be required, nor excessive fines imposed, nor cruel and unusual punishments inflicted.[2] General search-warrants ought not to be granted, but only specific ones.[3] Even in civil suits the ancient trial by jury is the preferable mode, and ought to be held sacred. Freedom of the press is one of the great bulwarks of liberty.[4] A well-regulated militia is the natural and safe defence of a free state; standing armies in time of peace are dangerous to liberty; and in all cases the military should be strictly subordinate to the civil power.[5] People have the right to uniform government, and no government separate from Virginia ought to be erected within its limits.[6] No free government can be preserved, "but by a firm adherence to justice, moderation, temperance, frugality, and virtue, and by frequent recurrence to fundamental principles." Of the sixteenth and final clause, advocating religious toleration, we shall make further mention presently.

Expressed in concise and admirable language, the Virginia Bill of Rights (whose sixteen sections we have thus condensed) was broad and universal in sentiment, breathing the spirit of human brotherhood, without a hint of race or class subjection. The

---

[1] Last clause is from *Magna Charta* (A. D. 1215), the famous § 45, whose general idea was aided by the recollection of wrongs under George III. (see Declaration of Independence), in depriving colonists of jury trial and transporting them to be tried across the seas.

[2] From English Bill of Rights, *verbatim* (Right 10).

[3] Recalling abuse of "writs of assistance" under George III.

[4] A new maxim in its present expression. But cf. English Bill of Rights (Right 9) as to freedom of speech in Parliament.

[5] See standing army grievances under the King recited in Declaration of Independence, also English Bill of Rights (Rights 6 and 7). Dependence upon a militia is more strongly asserted than hitherto.

[6] This seems to have had a local and immediate reference to the Revolution of 1776. The separation of West Virginia during 1861–65 suggests a thoughtful commentary.

declaration served well for example to the other
twelve States; and so proud of this instrument have
Virginians remained that they affixed it unchanged
to their new constitution of 1830, and, amending it
but slightly for the constitution of 1850, incorporated
it once more intact in the new framework of 1864.
With such further sections as civil war and the forcible abolition of slavery next compelled (though not
for changing a single sentence) that "Bill of Rights"
remains to this day, permanent in its original
assertions.

Among other American "Bills of Rights" of the
Revolutionary era, that of Pennsylvania next deserves
attention. From the State and city whose liberty
bell proclaimed independence through all the land,
emanated, soon after the adjournment of our Continental Congress, a novel scheme of State government, preceded by its own "Declaration of Rights."
This was the work of a State convention which sat
from July 15 to September 28, 1776. The Pennsylvania "Declaration," like that of Virginia, consisted
of sixteen articles, which adopted most of that earlier
document, with slight variations of language. "All
elections ought to be free" is the happier Pennsylvania assertion, enlarging the English and Virginia
formulas;[1] and all freemen having a common public
interest (the document adds) have the right to elect
or be elected to office. Again (improving upon the
Virginia expression) the accused in criminal prosecutions "hath a right to be heard by himself and his
counsel."[2] Quaker sentiment is honored by an

[1] Pennsylvania Declaration, No. 7. See *supra*, page 32.
[2] Penn's Charter of Liberties, art. v. (1701) expressly concedes to
all criminals "the same privileges of witnesses and counsel as their
prosecutors," — a decided gain upon the common law of England.

express pecuniary exemption for such as are con-
scientiously scrupulous of bearing arms. That frequent recurrence to fundamental principles which
Virginia enjoins is reinforced by a hortatory sentence
which does not add dignity to the article. In the
fifteenth and sixteenth Pennsylvania articles are
found new maxims which embody floating ideas of
the Revolution. The former claims for all mankind
the "natural inherent right" of going from one State
to another, and forming new States in vacant countries, — an idea which we have seen suggested through
royal favor in some early charters,[1] though not even
here stretched so far as to claim expatriation and the
renouncement of allegiance as a natural right of individuals. The latter and the unique article claims
the inherent right of the people "to assemble together, to consult for their common good," and to
instruct and petition the Legislature for redress of
grievances. This "right of petition" maxim is the
great glory of the Pennsylvania "Bill of Rights"
which seems to have formulated it first for the fundamental law of free America.[2] The suicide and
deodand clause from Penn's Charter of Privileges [3] is
here overlooked, but revolutionary New Jersey (and
perhaps Delaware) adopted it, and it reappeared in
the Pennsylvania constitution of 1790.

In the framework proper of this Pennsylvania constitution occur various other provisions of a "bill of
rights" character, — a primary instance of the uncer-

---

[1] See page 25.

[2] This excellent clause, since so widely copied into American constitutions, has a germ in the English Bill of Rights (Right 5 as to
petitioning the King). But this Pennsylvania expression gives the
maxim its fitter and more popular scope. Yet the idea was not new
in these colonies; for in the Massachusetts "Body of Liberties"(1641),
in broad, though less forcible language, appears (No. 12) an assertion
of the right of petition.

[3] See page 13.

tainty in classifying such political maxims. Excessive
bail and immoderate fines are there prohibited;[1]
printing-presses are declared free to examine the
proceedings of the Legislature; public offices of profit
are pronounced not useful, though reasonable compensation may be allowed men called into the public
service; entails and perpetuities are discouraged;
penal laws are to be reformed, and punishments made
less sanguinary and more proportionate to the crimes.
So, too, imprisonment for debt after the debtor has
surrendered all his property is thus early denounced;
and yet crimes not capital are to be punished by hard
labor for the public benefit, and the public moreover
shall be admitted to see the prisoners at work. By
way of general homily we further find in Pennsylvania's first constitution liberality enjoined towards
foreigners; law and good reason required for laying
taxes;[2] private liberty granted to fowl and hunt in
seasonable times and to fish "in all boatable waters;"
and finally the pious encouragement of virtue and
the prevention of vice and immorality.[3]

Maryland's "Bill of Rights," once more, formulated
early for the old thirteen States these maxims of liberty. The convention which framed the first constitution of Maryland sat at Annapolis from August 14
to November 11, 1776. The "Declaration of Rights"
for that instrument, which, together with the constitution, passed in convention on the 14th of August, consisted of forty-two articles, and covered more ground
than Virginia and Pennsylvania had already occupied, employing its own energetic paraphrase.[4] All

[1] See *supra*, page 33.

[2] No taxation except by Parliament. English Bill of Rights, No. 4;
and see *supra*, page 17.

[3] Pennsylvania constitution of 1776. Poore's Constitutions.

[4] Here, too, the "right of petition" is asserted, in different language
from that of Pennsylvania.

government, this Declaration asserted, originates of right from the people, "is founded in compact only," [1] and is instituted simply for the good of the whole. Sole right to their internal government is claimed for the people of Maryland, — a States' rights *caveat*, — together with an inheritance of the English common law with its trial by jury, and all local grants derived under the Calvert charter. The doctrine of non-resistance against arbitrary oppression is denounced as "absurd, slavish, and destructive of the good and happiness of mankind." Especial confidence is reposed in a legislative body as "the best security of liberty and the foundation of all free government." [2] And besides frequently assembling, the Legislature should meet at some fixed place unless some special necessity prevents. Some vigorous idiosyncrasies are observable in this Maryland instrument, such perhaps as the headstrong Samuel Chase, a signer of the Declaration of Independence, might have impressed upon the convention. Levying a poll tax, for instance, is declared grievous and oppressive; paupers should not be assessed for support of the government, but every other person should contribute according to his actual worth. [3] The Virginian idea of rotation in public office for executive and legislature [4] is emphasized by a special argument for exempting the judiciary, while plural offices and presents from foreign potentates are condemned besides.

---

[1] The same idea of "compact" is suggested in New Jersey's Revolutionary constitution of July 2, 1776.

[2] Most of our later State constitutions appear, upon experience, less disposed to implicit confidence in this branch of government.

[3] The disposition thus early to dogmatize upon taxation has characterized Maryland constitutions to this day; and some of our later States show an imitative tendency on this subject.

[4] See Virginia Declaration of Rights, No. 5; also Pennsylvania ditto, No. 6.

Among rights not enumerated in either the Virginia or Pennsylvania Declaration are several which Maryland must have led accordingly in proclaiming; such, more especially, as freedom of speech in the Legislature,[1] frequent sessions of that body, the prohibition of *ex post facto* laws, of bills of attainder, and of forfeiture for crime,[2] the exemption of civilians from martial law, and a prohibition of all monopolies and titles of nobility.[3]

Three contiguous States — Virginia, Pennsylvania, and Maryland — are thus seen setting for the American Union the first example of concrete expression in axioms vital to civil liberty. Not perhaps that they originated, but that at least they first formulated in convention truths which these colonists held certainly dear when the struggle for independence began, and yet had never before reduced to written fundamental law in the name of the people. Proceeding southward, we next find North Carolina adopting a " Declaration of Rights " together with its own framework of government, on the 18th of December, 1776, — a Declaration which, though tersely and tastefully composed, drew its inspiration plainly from these earlier conventions, adding nothing original. As for South Carolina, impetuous and hasty, three constitutions were instituted, one after another, between 1776 and 1790, of which the two earliest (in 1776 and 1778) were simply framed and put forth by the Legislature, regardless of convention methods, and hence must have been void in any sense of fundamental obligation, as the judiciary of that State presently decided. In neither of those two enactments do we

---

[1] Originating in English Bill of Rights (1689), No. 9.
[2] Vaguely stated as to forfeitures.
[3] See Maryland constitution of 1776; Poore's Constitutions.

find a regular Declaration of Rights attempted, though that of 1778 embodied at haphazard a few appropriate maxims.[1]   Georgia, in 1777, prepared its own whirlwind constitution in convention; and this was superseded in 1789, after the Federal constitution had been ratified by the requisite number of States, though before it went into operation.   In both of Georgia's constitutions are to be found a few salutary provisions from the early Declarations we have described, but no distinctive "Bill of Rights."[2]

As for States to the northward, the fundamental law of New York contained no express "Bill of Rights," — a fact which Hamilton is seen to adduce in defending the corresponding omission from our Federal instrument.[3]   New York's Revolutionary constitution, framed by convention in 1776, but not adopted until April, 1777, embodied, however, the Declaration of Independence, and denounced "the many tyrannical and oppressive usurpations of the King and Parliament of Great Britain;" and mingled with the framework of that fiery instrument we find some of the recitals suitable to a Bill of Rights.   No attainder, it was proclaimed, should work corruption of blood; and yet bills of attainder for that State were prohibited only after the present war should end.[4]   New Jersey's constitution of 1776, secretly framed and hurriedly put forth almost simultaneously with our Declaration of Independence, uses the word "Colony," for which the New Jersey Legislature in 1777 substituted "State." Such "Bill of Rights" expressions as that instrument

[1] Poore's Constitutions, South Carolina.
[2] Ib., Georgia.
[3] See Federalist, No. 84.
[4] Under an attainder act of 1779, the New York Legislature banished fifty-eight persons (three of whom were women) for adhering to the enemy.   Poore's Constitutions, New York, 1777, notes.

contained originated in Penn's old charter of 1701, which probably had diffused its influence in colonial times.[1] What Bill of Rights Delaware may have adopted when assuming this full and formal title under her constitution of September, 1776, is uncertain; but an impressive article of that constitution forbade all importation of African slaves into the State.[2] For while the pulse of Revolution beat highest, freedom had strong headway.

The New England colonies did not readily accept Southern lead in formulating individual rights; yet the popular sentiment favorable to such announcements seems to have compelled the popular leaders in most quarters to defer to their wishes. Connecticut and Rhode Island sanctioned their several charters from Charles II. as good and sufficient organic law for a sovereign State; and the General Court of Connecticut, while legislating in 1776 to that effect, promised expressly not to deprive the citizen of sundry *Magna Charta* rights "unless clearly warranted by the laws of this State." In Massachusetts and New Hampshire the people wrought out their will much more effectually. Massachusetts, during this Revolutionary period, was for a while governed under its colonial charter, adapted as might be to the emergency; but the people of the State clamored for a constitution, and the General Court accordingly submitted one in 1778, which was voted down at the polls, chiefly because it contained no Declaration of Rights. The sense of the voters having been taken

---

[1] See Poore's Constitutions, New Jersey.

[2] The constitution, inclusive of this clause, was superseded later. See Poore's Constitutions, Delaware. Mr. Poore prints no Delaware "Bill of Rights;" but § 30 of the printed constitution (1776) shows that there must have been one.

once more in 1779, a formal State convention was held, whose labors produced in 1780 a new and complete charter of government; that charter was submitted to the people, and adopted as satisfactory by an immense majority.[1] Of this written constitution, never since superseded though greatly amended in the course of a century or more, we shall speak hereafter concerning its practical distribution of powers; but here let us observe, as to the Declaration of Rights which it embodied, that in more florid and sonorous language popular rights were proclaimed substantially the same that Virginia, Pennsylvania, and Maryland, one or another, are seen to have put forth nearly four years earlier. With greater insistence upon public authority and discipline, the Massachusetts instrument employs largely the word "subject" in preference to "men," "freemen," or the "people." The preamble of this Massachusetts constitution, which was the most perfect and deliberately drawn of all State constitutions during our Revolutionary period, asserts that the end of all government is the benefit of the body politic; and that the body politic is the voluntary association of individuals, — a "social compact by which the whole people covenants with each citizen, and each citizen with the whole people, that all shall be governed by certain laws for the common good."[2] With an enlightened

---

[1] It is said that the Massachusetts constitution was largely the product and inspiration of John Adams. However this may be, as to an informal draft, Adams was abroad on the diplomatic service most of the time that this Massachusetts convention was in actual session.

[2] Poore's Constitutions, Massachusetts. See Maryland Declaration (§ 1) here amplified. The "Mayflower charter" of the Pilgrims may recur to memory in such a connection.

One important, and apparently the most important, maxim of a "Bill of Rights" character which Massachusetts originated in this constitution, consists in enlarging the Virginia Declaration (§ 6) that one cannot be deprived of property for public uses without his consent

regard for public beneficence, this State constitution, abounding as it does in homily as well as sound doctrine, commends the encouragement of literature and the sciences, public schools and education, agriculture, trade, commerce, manufactures, together with the promotion of humanity and general benevolence, industry and frugality, sincerity and good humor, "and all social affections and general sentiments, among the people."[1]

New Hampshire pursued a similar experience in this Revolutionary era; its chosen convention submitting in 1778 a fundamental constitution which the people at their town meetings the next year rejected. Here, as under the Revolutionary constitution of 1776 (which was a brief business-like instrument), all Declaration of Rights was ignored, and the people grew greatly dissatisfied.   Finally, by 1783 a State constitution, modelled closely upon that of Massachusetts, was framed in convention, and in 1784 (just after the end of the Revolutionary War) adopted by town meetings.   With less redundancy perhaps of expression, the Massachusetts general truths appear formulated in this later State instrument.   But as to jury trials, New Hampshire adds the cautious expression that none but qualified persons should serve, and that they should be properly paid.   Next theorizing, in imitation of Pennsylvania upon the evil of sanguinary laws, this State suggests further that the true design of all punishments is "to reform, not to exterminate, mankind."   And, once more, while discouraging pensions, the New Hampshire instrument quaintly suggests that economy is "a

or that of the Legislature.   To this idea the Massachusetts Declaration adds (§ 10), that private property applied to public uses shall always be upon "reasonable compensation."   Cf. Constitution of United States, 5th amendment.

[1] Poore's Constitutions, Massachusetts.

most essential virtue in all States, especially in a young one." [1]

Religious liberty under these Revolutionary Bills of Rights may claim a passing mention. Virginia set forth a rule of toleration broad enough for all time: "Religion, or the duty which we owe to our Creator, and the manner of discharging it, can be directed only by reason and conviction, not by force or violence; and therefore all men are equally entitled to the free exercise of religion, according to the dictates of conscience; and it is the mutual duty of all to practise Christian forbearance, love, and charity towards each other." [2] Pennsylvania's fundamental precept concerning religion was worthy of a State whose colonial history breathed the best spirit of philanthropy. North Carolina, too, clearly pronounced for the "unalienable right" to worship God according to the dictates of conscience. But the Maryland Declaration of Rights used compromising language on this subject, and while conceding the right of any and all inhabitants to worship without molesting others, favored religious taxation, with a disposition to keep the Church of England foremost. The Bible and the Christian religion continued, there and generally elsewhere, a test for civil office; while Delaware, though fairly tolerating religious worship, required a clear profession of belief in the Trinity for the civil service. In general, there was no religious test for mere voters.

---

[1] Poore's Constitutions, New Hampshire.

[2] Virginia Bill of Rights (No. 16). Broad and generous as this expression undoubtedly was, Virginia still taxed dissenters for the support of an English church establishment; nor was it until after the general peace of 1783 that Jefferson's bill for religious freedom passed the Virginia Legislature against a powerful and highly intelligent opposition, and disestablishment became practical.

In a long and diffuse exposition of religious charity, South Carolina's constitution of 1778 held fast to Christian Protestantism for an established religion, and defined the limits of public toleration. Both of Georgia's constitutions (1777 and 1789) are seen to provide for the free exercise of religion, at the same time forbidding clergymen to hold political office. The New York constitution of 1777 was of much the same purport;[1] and Virginia, New York, Delaware, and the Carolinas all manifested thus early that repugnance for clerical politicians which we see to this day exhibited in the fundamental law of so many American States. New Jersey, though avowedly tolerant, confined civil privileges to Protestants. Finally, the Massachusetts constitution, copied in this respect by New Hampshire, while conceding to every one the right to worship without molestation provided he does not disturb or obstruct others (a favorite qualification of religious freedom), enjoined the general right and duty to worship the Supreme Being; and town taxation was further sanctioned to support "Protestant teachers of piety, religion, and morality," at whose stated instructions attendance might be compelled.[2] Parish congregational churches supported by local taxation, and a congregational clergy of great learning and influential in all public affairs, comprised the usual religious establishment of this era in New England; nor, indeed, did the legal equality of sects and a voluntary and self-supporting system of religion become the practice of the United States until this nineteenth century had run the first quarter of its course.

---

[1] Not, however, so that liberty shall become license or justify public disturbance.

[2] See Poore's Constitutions, *passim.*

IV.

EARLY STATE CONSTITUTIONS.

1776–1789.

LET us now consider the main structure of republican government comprised in those separate State
instruments which preceded in date our Federal constitution. First and foremost in the design is seen
that fundamental threefold division of legislature,
executive, and judiciary, as departments which Montesquieu first of the modern sages announced should
be kept distinct and separated.[1] This Montesquieu
theorem appears and reappears in our American State
constitutions, onward from the Revolutionary period:
sometimes concisely stated as in Virginia's Bill of
Rights,[2] and again couched in the stately and resonant
expression of the Massachusetts constitution.[3] But
most political dogmas are of imperfect application;

---

[1] "The celebrated Montesquieu is the oracle always consulted and
cited on this subject." Federalist, No. 47. Yet Aristotle in his "Politics," centuries earlier, distinctly defined the three appropriate departments of a Republic as the deliberative, executive, and judicial, — a
description imperfect only because legislation in a representative instead of collective assembly (which is a modern contrivance) had not
then been invented.

[2] Virginia Declaration, 1776 (No. 5); somewhat amplified, however,
in the Virginia constitution.

[3] "The legislative department shall never exercise the executive
and judicial powers, or either of them; the executive shall never exercise the legislative and judicial powers, or either of them; the judicial
shall never exercise the legislative and executive powers, or either of
them; to the end it may be a government of laws and not of men."
Massachusetts Declaration of 1780 (No. 30).

and the practice of American government has constantly been to so far connect and blend these separate departments of a republic as to enable each to exert a certain constitutional constraint upon the others, so as to unify authority. Nor, as Madison once suggested, does any mere parchment demarcation of constitutional limits warrant against encroachment and tyrannical concentration of power where the governed fail in vigilance.[1] The British constitution, admired by Montesquieu like an Iliad among the epics, was defective in its separation of powers during our colonial period, and so were the constitutions of our original thirteen States, each of whom had nourished colonial traditions which influenced her new and independent condition.

New constitutions during this memorable war for independence transform thirteen dependent colonies into Republics. Virginia and Massachusetts characterize with dignity this new establishment as a " Commonwealth; " Pennsylvania, quite ambiguously, as a " Commonwealth or State; " the other ten as a " State." For times thus early the "convention," composed, like any legislature, of chosen representatives of the people, was the great and sufficient originator and sanction of government and fundamental law. A *de facto* legislature, to be sure, would naturally summon such a convention, and even determine upon the basis for choosing its members; and if that legislative sanction had been wanting at the outset, its subsequent sanction might be given afterwards to the convention product. Indeed, the *de facto* legislature of certain revolted colonies, in 1776, that perilous year of united defiance, had gone much farther. It had in Connecticut (and probably too in Rhode Island) given the colonial charter a prolonged and

[1] Federalist, No. 48.

indefinite survival; in Massachusetts and New Hampshire it had exerted a temporary sway; in South Carolina it had even assumed authority to impose a binding constitution upon the people, — an offence repeated in 1778. But Virginia had set the example, soon universally conceded in these States, of calling a convention, as a fresh and immediate emanation from the people. Each popular constituency chose its own delegates, and such a convention revolutionized political society at its own omnipotent discretion.

At the present day, the United States of America regard a constitution and convention work as a product properly submitted to the voters for their express adoption before it can become fundamental law. But, save for Massachusetts and New Hampshire alone, such was not the implied fundamental requirement of these earlier times. In those two States, where the *referendum* in this respect may be said to have originated for America, the voters in town meetings are seen discussing at the outset the rightful fundaments of constitutional government, and not only sending representatives to a State convention, but rejecting convention results which they deem imperfect, and procuring a new convention; deciding at length by their final suffrage, as a body politic, to ratify the later framework as sufficient and satisfactory to live under. Elsewhere, however, among those thirteen Revolutionary States that wrought out American independence in unison we find no such popular test of adoption or ratification; but under the most favorable conditions for popular expression what the convention once deliberately concludes upon becomes the fundamental scheme of government for that jurisdiction, the fundamental declaration of individual rights. When by 1787 and after a treaty of peace, came further the Philadelphia general convention and its plan of a more perfect Union of these States, no popular sanction of that plan more direct was sought or obtained (next to that of the Continental Congress) than the approval of a State convention. In short, whether for State or Federal fundamental law, the convention, except as above stated, was throughout this Union its own self-sufficient sanction and exponent of that popular will in a community which alters, subverts, and erects anew.

The absence, as a rule, of all *referendum* test at this period is further established when we look into these earliest of our written constitutions to ascertain how they could be superseded or amended. Upon this vital point half of these constitutions, Virginia's included, were silent, and yet every one of them became in time supplanted. This was not because those Revolutionary sires, illustrious in constructive statesmanship, who devoted their best talents to such work, were fatuous enough to suppose that alterations of fundamental law would never be needed; but because they reposed upon their own primary truth, announced repeatedly in Bills of Rights, that the people might amend, repeal, or substitute, at any time later, — namely, in convention. American experience, however, has taught that it is better for a written constitution to be explicit in such matters; and in some of these early constitutions, that course, in fact, was pursued. Thus, Pennsylvania's instrument of 1776 created a "Council of Censors" from the people for every seventh year, who should inquire into constitutional infractions and abuses, and upon a two-thirds vote summon at discretion a new convention, — a fortunate clause, which enabled that immense State to throw off readily in 1790 its badly devised original scheme of self-government, and substitute something more sensible. Georgia, too, in her constitution of 1777, directed the Legislature to call a new convention upon the petition at any time of a majority of voters in each county; and this provision, too, resulted by 1789 in a new and better framework of practical State government.[1] Both Massachusetts and New Hampshire expressly accorded a probationary period to their slowly matured constitutions; and in consequence the latter State, at the end of seven years, framed in convention a new fundamental instrument, while the former continued beyond her experimental term as before. Some of these Revolutionary conventions — those of Pennsylvania, Delaware, and North Carolina, for instance [2] — are seen setting the example of declaring certain fundamental law irrepealable, which practice might suggest a discussion still deeper as to the inherent right of ancestors in general to bind their descendants and successors.[3] Pennsylvania's constitution of 1777 expressly forbade the Legislature to amend or infringe, which doubtless was appropriate enough.

For simple amendment to the constitution a remedy less drastic than calling a new convention is found prescribed (a remedy now universal) in several of these early States. Thus Maryland, in her constitution of 1776, put forward a plan of amendment, by which one legislature might initiate and the next legislature confirm a proposed alteration so as to give

---

[1] Georgia's constitution of 1788 was framed in one convention, and then ratified in 1789 by a new convention chosen quite curiously for the express purpose of accepting or rejecting. Poore's Constitutions, Georgia, note.

[2] And see *supra*, page 13.

[3] Such provisions fortunately relate for the most part to fundamental rights of the individual, which deserve to remain permanent.

it full effect,[1] — a favorite method of these later times, though with the more democratic addition that the amendment shall bear the final test of a submission to the voters.

The elective franchise under our early State constitutions was bestowed with more or less favor, according mainly to colonial practice and sentiment. Colonies such as Rhode Island, Connecticut, Pennsylvania, and Maryland had been treated by British sovereigns with marked liberality in this respect. In general the voter was to be a male inhabitant, twenty-one years of age or more; and "freemen" or "free white men" was a convenient term to employ thus in the written systems of States, nearly all of whom still recognized to some extent, in 1776, the colonial institution of negro slavery. "Freeholders," or real-estate owners, were specially designated for the suffrage in South Carolina, and further in Virginia, New York, and North Carolina, as to certain privileged elections at least; Massachusetts, as under her royal charter, and Maryland, fixed a property qualification in either lands or personalty; while the most liberal of these United States, like Pennsylvania and Georgia, conferred the suffrage upon all tax-payers.[2] Georgia, in her earliest constitution, made a futile effort, as some colonial legislatures had done, to punish a voter's absence from the polls without good excuse by imposing a penalty. Bribery at the polls was punishable under Pennsylvania's constitution, yet rather lightly.[3]

[1] For certain changes, a two-thirds vote was a pre-requisite; otherwise a majority was sufficient. Maryland constitution (1776), § 59.

[2] Sons of freeholders, though not paying taxes, had also the right to vote in Pennsylvania. Georgia favored mechanics.

[3] New Hampshire's constitution (1784) makes conviction of bribery an utter disqualification from office, etc.

Under the Revolutionary constitution of New York, the "elector"

As for the appropriate method of voting, while Massachusetts, New Hampshire, Pennsylvania, and Georgia pronounced thus early for the written ballot, other States (by more or less positive expression) showed some adhesion still to the old English mode of an oral or *viva voce* vote.[1] Indeed, the New York constitution of 1777 indicates a disposition to try the written ballot simply as a novel and experimental substitute for the customary *viva voce* method and subject to the final discretion of the legislature; and that instrument notes as a prevalent opinion "among divers of the good people" that voting by ballot "would tend more to preserve the liberty and equal freedom of the people" than the oral mode.[2]

The image of State government in America, with its threefold distribution of fundamental powers, is visible in the public structure of these thirteen colonies, developing apart for a century or more under the parental supervision of Great Britain. And accordingly, when filial ties were severed, the omnipotence of a local legislature and local representatives was the fact most palpable in continental self-establishment. For the local assembly of the people had long been the bulwark and resource of these various colonies in concerting against parental oppression; and the election of that representative assembly — or, in other words, of the single popular branch of each colonial legislature — had chiefly, and, except for Rhode Island and Connecticut, almost solely occupied the franchise and immediate attention of

at the polls might be required to take an oath of allegiance to the State. Under that of Delaware, soldiers were forbidden to approach the polls on election day.

[1] Connecticut to some extent kept up *viva voce* voting in State elections, — a system which town meetings naturally favor.

[2] Poore's Constitutions, *passim*, 1776–1784.

colonial voters. Thus continued it long after independence had been declared, in most of those
struggling States which have set the pattern for
this new world. But thoughtful statesmen marked
quickly the tendency of republican governments to
aggrandize the Legislature at the expense of all other
departments; and the dangers of legislative abuse
and encroachment were conspicuously manifest in
Pennsylvania before this first stage of experimental
self-government had run its course. The closer to
the people nominally, the more audacious is such
aggression apt to be.

Since, however, a single representative house had
borne in America the symbols of popular confidence
and affection for so many years, we find, not strangely,
that Pennsylvania and Georgia, as free republics,
essayed at once the plan of a legislature which
should consist of a single house. The experiment
was unsatisfactory, producing speedily such public
turbulence, discord, and caprice that by the time
that a Congress of the United States, consisting of
two houses, went into national operation, both
Pennsylvania and Georgia, remodelling completely
their State constitutions, established a corresponding
change. As no other State but the new Vermont
(strong admirer and copyist at the outset of Pennsylvania's first constitution) ever tried again this one-
chambered legislature, and that trial failed, though
with a simple rural people most favorable for such a
system, we may fairly infer that the friction of two
distinct and deliberative houses, is upon the whole
highly salutary to republican government; since,
after all, it is better to continue under defective laws
than to change them on impulse and crude discussion.

The larger and more popular branch of the State
legislature came ready-made to independent America.

As for a smaller branch, the joinder in authority of a provincial or charter council, which, like a lesser House of Lords, had exercised some sort of concurrent authority in passing colonial laws, was readily made over in most of these new States, so as to serve as an upper and more aristocratic House, secret in its proceedings as formerly according to the usual practice, and curbing the mettlesome propensity of the more popular branch. Massachusetts in her matured constitution (followed presently by New Hampshire) pursued a peculiar course in this respect; the old colonial "council," with such executive functions as pertained to it, was transferred to the governor, as an advisory appendage; while a Senate was specially created, so that the Legislature might consist regularly of two co-ordinate branches each with a negative on the other.[1]

The popular branch of the American legislature was made three or four times as numerous as the other, with members to be annually chosen on the representative plan.[2] No such happy adjustment of interests could be contrived in the States for the two separate chambers as the Federal constitution hit upon later for Congress; nobility and life tenure were surely unfit for what freemen disliked to style an upper House; and yet with more strenuous qualifications of age and property in its membership, longer terms, and in some States a remote method of choice, something approximating a conservative or even aristocratic second branch was shaped out. In Massachusetts and New Hampshire, while annual elec-

[1] This State "council," a Massachusetts contrivance in so special a sense, prevails to this day in Massachusetts, New Hampshire, and Maine, but in no other part of the Union. See pages 16, 17.

[2] New York (1777) prescribes clearly a census to be taken every seven years (after the war ends) for reapportioning the popular branch. Cf. Pennsylvania (1776).

tions for either branch were insisted on, the Senate was based upon public taxation or property, and the House upon polls or numbers. New York's original Senate consisted simply of freeholders to be chosen by the body of freeholders. The Maryland plan, a singular one, seems to have foreshadowed the electoral college scheme of 1787 for choosing a President of the United States, so admirable in theory and yet so contemptible in practice; for electors of the Maryland Senate were to be chosen every fifth year by the general voters, with power to meet in mass at a stated time and place, and elect a suitable number of "men of the most wisdom, experience, and virtue," to fill that dignified branch of the Legislature.[1] Classification was an expedient at once applied to the State Senate in Virginia, New York, and Delaware, as a special means of securing for that body stability and experience; whence came that periodical rotation of a certain fraction as each legislature convenes, whose most conspicuous example is furnished in our United States Senate to this day.[2] For in these earliest days of constitutional framework more effort was shown to create a positive basis of difference between the two houses of an American State legislature, aside from larger or smaller representative areas, than political philosophy takes to heart in this nineteenth century.

"General Court," the legacy of colonial times, was the title retained in Massachusetts and New Hampshire for this bicameral legislature;[3] but "Assembly" was the early preference in most States out of New England. New York at once applied to its own department the modern term "Legislature," giving

[1] This Senate electoral plan lasted in Maryland until 1837. Cf. Poore's Constitutions.

[2] Poore, *ib.*

[3] See page 17.

the name "Assembly," as also did New Jersey and
Delaware, to its popular branch. "Assembly" in
Pennsylvania and Georgia meant, however, in these
earlier years, a one-chambered legislative body.
"House of Representatives," as a style of the popular
branch, South Carolina and Massachusetts made fash-
ionable; but "House of Delegates" (no longer
"Burgesses") Virginia called it, seconded by Maryland; "House of Commons" was the name first
given in North Carolina. "Senate" became at once
in leading States the favorite designation for the
smaller and more conservative branch of the legislature; but New Jersey, Delaware, and South
Carolina clung for a few years to the old style of
"Council." [1]

As for the qualifications of a legislator, under
these earliest constitutions, if a State required property or a freehold in order that one might vote at all,
much more was that rule imperative for service in
the Legislature, and most of all to the honorable
incumbent of a State Senate. Freehold or property
qualifications for a legislator were in these years
waived in Pennsylvania alone. Age and length of
residence afforded suitable tests, as they always do;
to which were usually superadded religious qualifications, though ministers of the gospel, as we have
seen, were in various States excluded from politics.
Pennsylvania forbade public service in its single
assembly for more than four years out of seven, and
required each member to swear fidelity to the public
interests, besides taking oath of his belief in God
and the inspiration of the Bible. [2]

---

[1] See Poore, *passim; supra,* page 17.

[2] This legislator's oath (rather an indefinite one, after all) is to the
effect that he will not propose or assent to any bill "which shall appear
to me injurious to the people," nor consent to any act or thing that

The first constitutions of Pennsylvania and New York severally ordained that each House should sit with open doors, except where the public welfare required secrecy. And in various States we see old Parliamentary privileges expressly accorded: there should be freedom of speech in the Legislature; and debates and proceedings could not be questioned elsewhere;[1] no member could be arrested or held to trial while going, attending, or returning.[2] Each branch, moreover, should choose its own officers, determine its own rules, judge of the returns, elections, and qualifications of its members, and at its sole discretion expel any member for misbehavior. Much of this Parliamentary law of England had doubtless been recognized and asserted in the several colonies while owning allegiance to the King. So, too, the power of brief adjournment was free to each branch, but in general the agreement of both Houses was essential for any considerable or final adjournment; and the Executive might convene on an emergency or prorogue when the two Houses were unable to agree. Some of these State constitutions fixed the requisite number for a quorum. Seven States expressly insisted that money bills should originate in the House, — a provision natural enough while that body continued in a State the only really popular one.[3] Virginia's constitution declared that all bills

shall tend to abridge their constitutional privileges; but that he will to the best of his ability conduct himself "as a faithful, honest representative and guardian of the people." New Jersey prescribed an oath somewhat similar, for preventing the repeal of constitutional provisions. See Poore, *passim.*

[1] *Supra*, page 38; and English Bill of Rights, 1689 (No. 9).

[2] See Massachusetts and New Hampshire constitutions.

[3] Thus we find the early constitutions of New Hampshire, Massachusetts, New Jersey, Delaware, Maryland, Virginia, and North Carolina expressed; that of New York being silent. Nor can the Senate amend, but it must assent or reject. Virginia and North Carolina.

must originate in the popular branch. Some State constitutions are seen entering quite minutely into other details of legislative practice which elsewhere reposed, no doubt, upon colonial or Parliamentary usage: as, for instance, the consent of both Houses should be given to a bill; bills should be read three times before final passage; yeas and nays might be entered on request; a journal should be kept and its proceedings periodically printed; and upon disagreement there should be a conference committee. South Carolina ordained that a bill rejected by either House should not be brought up again at the same session without special leave and notice. In New Jersey's constitution is traceable the first clear suggestion of a constraint upon legislation which in one way or another many constitutions of this nineteenth century employ, — that no law shall finally pass except by majorities of all elected to each branch.

No enumeration of legislative powers was needful in these primitive State constitutions, inasmuch as a State legislature might exercise all powers over the domestic, social, and business relations of its inhabitants except such as were expressly delegated to the Union or clearly prohibited otherwise, which at this date of course amounted to very little; yet various

---

The rule of the English House of Commons as to money bills is said to date back nearly to 1400. Colonial practice doubtless fortified this rule for America.

Maryland's constitution made special effort to prevent the abuse of this "money bill" origination in the House. It forbade the House under any pretence to annex to or blend with a money bill other extraneous matter; and it defined as a "money bill" every bill assessing or applying taxes or supplies for the support of government, or the current expenses of the State, or appropriating money in the treasury. No bill, it states, is a money bill which imposes duties or customs for the mere regulation of commerce, or which inflicts fines or enforces the execution of laws, though an incidental revenue might arise. Maryland Constitution, 1776, § 11.

special expressions of legislative authority are found in these early instruments. Constraints, too, were stated, such as a "Bill of Rights" might specify, or upon entails, primogeniture, and the like encumbrances upon political equality. The "wages" of legislators, as of all civil officers, were commonly made payable from the State treasury; but New Hampshire undertook the peculiar experiment (soon abandoned) of making the several towns pay their representatives, while the State appropriated simply for mileage.[1]

The American Executive was an inheritance from colonial subjection; and colonial experience fortified the inclination of State Revolutionary framers to curb and constrain its deputed functions. For more than twenty years previous, executive independence had been nearly synonymous on this American soil with executive tyranny. And yet, excepting the charter governments of Massachusetts,[2] Rhode Island, and Connecticut, the selection of this American chief magistrate, dispenser of public honors and patronage, had been so far removed from the immediate choice of the people, that the leaders of these newly fledged States dreaded a young democracy.

"Governor" became at once the usual style of this chief magistrate, as under the colonial dispensation; but Pennsylvania and Delaware in their constitutions of 1776 called him "President." As for a

[1] The first Pennsylvania constitution, though liberally devised, abounded in loose and precatory language, and badly planned a framework of practical government. Laws "for the encouragement of virtue and prevention of vice" were to be made and kept constantly in force. And, by way of a general check upon hasty legislation, it provided quite ambiguously that bills of a public nature, "*except on occasions of sudden necessity,* shall not be passed into laws until the next session of assembly," after they are read and printed.

[2] Before 1691.

ceremonious title, Massachusetts and New Hampshire dubbed him "His Excellency;" but the other States kept such designations out of their fundamental law, though Georgia appears to have bestowed the title "Honorable" in 1777, dropping it out of her second constitution in 1789. The term of this supreme executive was made annual for the most part. South Carolina, however, set the example of two years, while New York and Delaware promptly fixed a three years' term.

The choice of an American governor, as a comparison of these primitive constitutions will show us, was confided originally to the State Legislature in eight States out of thirteen, — a preponderance of opinion all the more remarkable when one recalls that two out of the other five, in conceding a choice by the people, merely suffered their own favored charters to work on as before. New York took up the singular experiment of a choice by freeholders alone.[1] Wherever the Legislature in the preponderating States consisted of two houses, the ballot of both, separate or concurrent, was made requisite; but Pennsylvania, with her single house, invented an odd method of combining the Assembly with an executive council on a joint ballot for chief magistrate. Here the supreme executive power was lodged not in an individual, but in a sort of Directory, styled "President and Council;" the people in their respective districts chose this "Council" of twelve after a scheme which rotated one-third of that number annually; and both President and Vice-President of the State had to belong to this "Council" in order to be eligible. The last quarter of the eighteenth century and the first quarter of the nineteenth com-

---

[1] The same favored class whose right, as we have seen, was to choose State senators. *Supra,* page 54.

prised the era of strict "majority rule" in a republic. In New York alone among American States was a plurality choice (here by the freeholders) sanctioned thus early; while, on the other hand, both in Massachusetts and New Hampshire,[1] the voters, by failing at the polls on one trial to give some candidate for governor the clear majority, threw the election consequently into the Legislature, which body would then proceed, after a prescribed mode, to elect at discretion from among the highest candidates.[2] The convenience of concluding the choice, once and for all, in favor of the person whose number at the polls was greatest, whether he had received an actual majority of the votes or not, fructified but slowly in State fundamental law, and that, too, after a rigorous experience.

As for qualifications, our American Executive was at the outset required by the majority of States to be a freeholder to a considerable amount.[3] But the earliest instruments of Virginia, Pennsylvania, New Jersey, and Delaware, were silent in this respect. "A wise and discreet freeholder," enjoins the New York constitution; "some fit person within the State," says that of New Jersey; "a person of wisdom, experience, and virtue" is the language of Maryland. Ripeness of age (as, for instance, twenty-

---

[1] *Semble* in Connecticut and Rhode Island, too, under charter rules.

[2] This eventual choice of Chief Executive by the Legislature, on failure of a popular majority, continues a feature of the Federal constitution, though almost obsolete as concerns State practice. See *post*, Part II. As for members of the Legislature at this period (and for Congressmen still later) if no one received a majority of the votes for representative, the contest at the polls was repeated until a majority was reached.

[3] This freehold qualification of £1000 under the Massachusetts constitution of 1780 was abolished but a few years ago, and at the instance of Governor William E. Russell. The requirement had long escaped public notice.

five years) was quite commonly prescribed; so, too, residence within the State for a certain length of time; and finally the Protestant faith in religion. Restrictions upon re-election were a favorite precaution in most States to the southward.[1]

A Lieutenant-Governor (in Pennsylvania a Vice-President) was provided under various constitutions, agreeably to colonial practice, while six States ignored such an office.[2] The incumbent served as executive head of the State for great emergencies. In New York he was designated to preside over the State Senate, giving his casting vote in case of a tie, but otherwise not voting. Georgia, on the other hand, named the President of the Council as next in succession to the Governor; and so too did Delaware. This "Council" (styled sometimes a "Privy Council," or "Council of State") began in 1776 as a great encumbrance upon executive independence, blending in many instances the legislative functions of an upper house. Tacked upon the chief magistracy, this Council would give its "advice and consent" to the most important executive acts; while in Pennsylvania it formed as a pure Directory a constituent part of the Executive itself. In the President and Directors of a private corporation to this day we trace the semblance of a common charter origin. Members of this Council were elected in various ways at State discretion; in Massachusetts and New

---

[1] One was re-ineligible to the office, *e. g.*, for four years after serving three in succession. See constitutions of Delaware, Maryland, Virginia, North Carolina, and South Carolina.

[2] Massachusetts, New York, New Jersey, Pennsylvania, and South Carolina established such an office by fundamental law; the Lieutenant-Governor in the first-named State holding the second official rank with the ceremonious title of "His Honor." No such office was recognized in New Hampshire, Delaware, Maryland, Virginia, North Carolina, or Georgia.

Hampshire, for instance, the people annually chose Senators and Councillors together, and then the Senate thus composed would select the Councillors;[1] but unless Pennsylvania be thought an exception to the early American rule,[2] there was as yet no truly direct choice of Councillors by the people. The idea of an executive "Council" is ere this nearly exploded in the United States; but, considering the regular State practice in 1787, our Federal constitution must have had a narrow, as well as fortunate escape, from a Cabinet capable of tying up our President's hands, unless, as appears most likely, the States themselves had concluded to turn their own councils into senates, with powers more purely legislative than before.[3]

The absorption of executive powers by the legislative department was very great in these times, as we have already seen, and the Governor had little of either personal independence or patronage, save, perhaps, as commander-in-chief in some military emergency. Even the dignity of a council detracted from his authority. Nevertheless, he might convene and adjourn the Legislature, — not arbitrarily, as in 1775, but to much the same extent as defined and copied later in the Federal constitution for a President of the United States. He had no absolute veto,[4] such as provincial governors had exercised, and generally the States were at present indisposed to grant him a veto power at all; but Massachusetts

[1] Here, as already shown, the Council was purely an executive appendage.

[2] *Supra*, page 59.

[3] Massachusetts, Maine, and New Hampshire are seen to furnish to modern America the only real instance of executive "Privy Councils;" and councillors, moreover, are now chosen in these States directly by the people. Pennsylvania and Georgia dropped the "Council" out of their new constitutions of 1789-90.

[4] South Carolina's hasty and temporary instrument of 1776 conferred such power.

by 1780 set the precedent for our Federal constitution and future State practice by conferring a qualified veto which the Legislature by a two-thirds vote might override.[1] The Governor had usually the pardoning power, subject perhaps to the advice of his Council, and with some stated exceptions.[2] He sent messages and recommendations to the Legislature.[3] Usually with consent of his Council he appointed the lesser State officials; but New York, unduly fearful of the one-man power, vested all such public patronage in a "Council of Appointment," or Directory, where the Governor, as a single individual, might be outvoted.[4] Indeed, for such high officers as Secretary or Treasurer (for judges, too, as we shall see presently) and often in military appointments, the Legislature kept sedulously the selection to itself, as the true representative of the people; not unfrequently adding such small county appointments as were not left to the local voters.[5] Massachusetts and New Hampshire, on the other hand, allowed the Governor a considerable patronage, subject, however, to "the advice and consent of the Council," which, if comprising any year a majority of political opponents, might of course obstruct his wishes. As commander-in-chief of the army and

---

[1] The qualified veto was given by the constitution of New York to a special "Council of Revision," or a directory, which consisted of the Governor, the Chancellor, and the judges of the highest court.

[2] Except for impeachments. Massachusetts and New Hampshire. No pardon before conviction. New Hampshire, New York. In treason and murder he may reprieve and then report to Legislature. New York.

[3] New York, 1777.

[4] See New York constitution (1777) as defined in 1801. Pennsylvania's constitution of 1776 vested the public patronage in its directory of President and Council.

[5] In Maryland the Legislature was to choose one Treasurer for the eastern shore and another for the western. No Treasurer can sit in the Legislature until he has settled his accounts. North Carolina.

navy and of all the military forces of the State "by sea or land," the Governor had various powers thus early which were enumerated with much pompous phraseology; he was authorized to embody the militia and direct it when embodied; he might assemble and conduct such forces in martial array, "encounter, repel, and resist" the enemy by sea or land; "kill, slay, or destroy if necessary, and conquer." [1] The forts and garrisons of the State were subject to his supervision, and he might lay temporary embargoes or prohibit exportation; but his power to commence war or conclude peace was kept subordinate to the will of the Legislature. [2] In fine, the Governor was to "take care that the laws were faithfully executed;" [3] and to exercise all other executive powers of government, limited and restrained by the laws of the State. [4]

The Judiciary was recognized in the old thirteen States as an important bulwark of free government; though the scope of its remarkable power in subjecting acts of legislation to the written constitution had yet to be tested. But how to appoint the judges of a free republic was an instant and difficult problem. In general, the local Legislature claimed at once the

[1] This quaint language, still unchanged in the Massachusetts constitution, originates in the expression of the old royal charters, as far back even as that of Virginia in 1609. But under the Pennsylvania constitution (1776) the Governor could not take personal command without approval of the Council.

[2] Much of this authority (especially as to commercial powers and a navy) was practically superseded when our Federal constitution went into operation in 1789.

[3] See New York constitution of 1777. Money (as voted by the Legislature) was to be drawn from the treasury on his warrant. Massachusetts, New Hampshire, North Carolina. But no money could be drawn from the treasury without legislative assent. South Carolina, 1778.

[4] North Carolina, 1776.

right to participate at least in so precious a selection. Six out of thirteen States conceded the choice accordingly without reserve;[1] Georgia set a dubious rule which developed into a peculiar selection by these representatives of the people;[2] Delaware united Executive and Legislature in the choice. Maryland, Massachusetts, and New Hampshire alone permitted the Governor to appoint the judges with consent of Council; a special Directory, or "Council of Appointment," absorbed such functions in New York; and lastly in Pennsylvania (if permitted by the Legislature), that general Directory of "President and Council."[3] The English rule of stable and permanent tenure had usually been in high favor among these colonies; hence good behavior was the judicial term originally adopted by a majority of States.[4] "Ability rather than wealth" being always a maxim of the legal profession, property qualifications for this judicial station were dispensed with.[5] But the less dignified justices of the peace who monopolized more than they do now the petty jurisdiction of local magistrate, were vested usually with a moderate term of office.[6] Courts were left commonly to ap-

[1] New Jersey, Virginia, North Carolina, South Carolina; as also Rhode Island and Connecticut under charter practice.

[2] See constitution of 1789, under which the House chose three candidates, one of whom the Senate finally selected.

[3] Pennsylvania's constitution of 1776, ambiguously drawn, seems to have given the Assembly much latitude in drawing all such patronage to itself.

[4] But New Jersey and Pennsylvania preferred a term fixed at seven years for the highest tribunal, with a right of reappointment. New York already prescribed a limit when the incumbent reached sixty years of age. Georgia, a State which long disfavored a regular judiciary as compared with business referees, or "courts merchant," set a three-years limit.

[5] "Fixed and adequate," "moderate," etc., salaries were sometimes enjoined; as in Virginia, 1776.

[6] Three, five, or seven years was the usual prescribed limit; the

point their own clerks, and in some States the district attorneys, marshals, and sheriffs besides. All such court officials, and even the Attorney-General (where such a State officer was recognized at all), enjoyed a safe and stable tenure in these days.

Colonial usage would determine largely in each free State the scope of the judicial establishment. Outside of New England, separate equity powers as distinct from the common law had considerable range, and sometimes the Governor, though more fitly a Chancellor, conducted that branch of jurisdiction. The sudden stoppage in 1776 of judicial appeals to King and Council caused much perplexity. Maryland's constitution set the prompt example of a specific Court of Appeals by way of substitute, for all cases whether in common law, chancery, or admiralty; but in most other State constitutions of this era we perceive bewilderment, confusion, and a disposition to mix Executive and Judiciary together for a last resort, somewhat as before. New York for both law and equity set up a Court of Errors which (to copy a British House of Lords) consisted of the Senators, the Chancellor, and the Supreme Court Judges; in New Jersey, Delaware, and one or two other States, the Governor and Council constituted a final tribunal; Georgia, with her bald judicial system, comprising a superior but no supreme court, left appellate powers by 1789 to the Legislature. The constitutions of Virginia, Pennsylvania, and North Carolina contained nothing very explicit.[1] Massachusetts and New Hampshire, while trusting the Legislature for

Massachusetts constitution reciting as a reason, "that the people may not suffer" from the long continuance of incumbents who fail in fidelity or ability. In a few States only the tenure of such magistrates was good behavior.

[1] Pennsylvania's constitution gave certain chancery powers to the common-law courts.

a permanent system, left probate appeals and matrimonial matters temporarily with the Governor and
Council. We may further observe here that in
Massachusetts the Governor or Legislature might
require the solemn opinion of the justices of the
Supreme Court, — an expedient for times of perplexity which some other States have since adopted.

Judges in Massachusetts and New Hampshire were
removable by the Governor (with consent of Council)
on address of the two houses, — a summary means
for disposing of men upon the bench personally and
politically obnoxious;[1] but in Maryland, a judge
could be removed only for misbehavior on conviction
in a court of law. All officers of the State, including those of judicial station, might be impeached, as
various constitutions prescribed, and expelled accordingly; the House of Representatives constituting
the body of grand inquest and prosecution, while the
Senate or Council (or some such mixed tribunal as
the New York Court of Errors[2] might afford) tried
and determined the cause, and gave sentence upon
conviction.[3]

As for miscellaneous provisions of these early constitutions worth mentioning, the Legislature was
empowered in some States not only to impeach, as
above, or to expel its own members in either house,
but also to punish persons who were not members for

---

[1] "Shall be removed." South Carolina. Removable by the Legislature for misbehavior. Pennsylvania.

[2] *Supra*, page 66. And see South Carolina, 1778.

[3] In Pennsylvania one might be impeached either while in office or
after his resignation or removal, and the President and Council tried
the case. Persons when out of office might also be impeached in Virginia; and here the trial of impeachments was left undefined, but
"forever disabled" from holding office was made a suitable penalty
Banishment was a permitted penalty in Maryland.

disorderly or contemptuous behavior, by an imprisonment of not more than thirty days.[1] Oaths for members of the Legislature and for officials were plentiful
in several of these instruments, the framers thus
founding a prosecution for perjury as well as more
direct criminal proceedings against the offender.
There was the oath of allegiance to be taken, which
abjured Great Britain and acknowledged the State
as "free, sovereign, and independent;" the oath to
faithfully serve as officer or representative; the oath
of religious belief which conformed to Christian tests;
and the oath of owning the requisite property.[2]

Jealousy of an office-holding class was manifest
beyond the "Bill of Rights" denouncement of inherited
station.[3] Constitutional provisions are seen in a
majority of States against a plurality of public offices,
or the holding of more than one lucrative office at a
time. Judges, sheriffs, and registers were in various
States expressly forbidden to sit in the Legislature;
so also were delegates and others in the Continental
service, military officers, and army or navy contractors;[4] and ministers of the gospel, as already stated,
were placed under a special ban in various States, so
far as political station was concerned, while Massachusetts applied secular exclusion rather to all instructors at Harvard College.[5]

[1] Maryland, Massachusetts, and New Hampshire.

[2] Maryland and Pennsylvania prescribed under penalty various
special oaths; as, for instance (in the former State), not to participate
in the profits of office or of any public contracts; to vote impartially
and for the public welfare, without having promised one's vote, etc.

[3] *Supra*, page 32.

[4] Delaware and North Carolina.

[5] The South Carolina instrument of 1778 forbade the father or
brother of the Governor for the time being to sit in the Council.

Upon office-holding generally, the constitution of Pennsylvania
(1776) observes that, as every freeman, to preserve his independence,
ought to have some profession, calling, trade, or farm for his honest

The Pennsylvania instrument of 1776 — odd and rather fanciful, as we have seen, in its scheme of popular government, though framed by a convention over which the great Franklin presides — was much given to homily and didactic exposition; and so, too, was that of Massachusetts. Greatly as the two commonwealths differed on the question of religious polity at this date, they were alike in announcing a broad scheme of secular instruction such as might place self-government securely upon the sound basis of public intelligence and virtue. Massachusetts, peculiarly proud of her Harvard College as the crown and capstone of a liberal education, confirmed that institution in all its franchises, lands, and endowments, and gave it at once a State association by placing the chief dignitaries of the Commonwealth *ex officio* upon its board of government, — a connection which lasted far into the nineteenth century. Public and grammar schools in the various towns were generously fostered besides by the fundamental law of Massachusetts; and protection was promised to private and public institutions, with rewards and immunities for the arts and sciences.[1] Pennsylvania, too, exhorted her Legislature to encourage one or more universities of useful learning, and to establish schools in each county for the convenient instruction of children, with such public salaries to the masters "as may enable them to instruct youth at low prices."[2]

---

subsistence, "there can be no necessity for, nor use in, establishing offices of profit, the usual effects of which are dependence and servility unbecoming freemen." But whoever is called into public service to the prejudice of his private affairs, "has a right to a reasonable compensation;" and whenever an office becomes so profitable that many compete for it, the Legislature ought to lessen its profits.

[1] Massachusetts, 1780.
[2] Pennsylvania, 1776.

PART II.

THE FEDERAL UNION.

I.

EARLY TENDENCIES TO UNION.

1609–1764.

NEXT to the voyage of Columbus and the disclosure of a New World to civilized Europe, the most pregnant event for the advancement of this western hemisphere, in the North American portion at least, was the planting of thirteen English colonies, adjacent to one another, on our northern Atlantic coast. That grand origination of law-loving liberty occupied most of the seventeenth and eighteenth centuries; and had England, the mother country, ruled her offspring ever so kindly, independence and union must sooner or later have resulted. Most fortunate was it for America that Europe had gained since 1492 more than a hundred years' headway in liberal ideas before this British transplantation commenced; nor can we deem it inauspicious for the coming age that the thirteen settlements, chaotic to some extent in population, yet overwhelmingly British, should, with all their zeal for reformed Christianity and all their inborn love of freedom, have originated apart and developed striking differences of tastes and habits of life in their several colonial confines.

E pluribus unum — the "one from many" — is a clear epitome, forever historical, stated in the most concise phrase possible, of the origin and structure of the present United States of America. The *E pluri-bus* fundamentals have already been discussed; and *unum* now demands our continuous attention. The immense predominance of the Anglo-Saxon element from the very start in these American settlements guaranteed to the soil a people bound by those endur-ing ligaments of a common history, a common lan-guage and literature, common political institutions, and a common jurisprudence. Whatever might have been their differences in colonial origin and affilia-tions, they were unified in loyalty to a common line of sovereigns, whose policy, however differing with individual rulers, embraced essentially one conti-nental scheme for all. There were traits, moreover, in their common isolation from the old world which naturally induced contiguous colonies to enter into mutual leagues and compacts. Arms and succor had to be provided against the Indians, their common foe, where philanthropy could not pacify; reciprocal trade and commerce needed occasional adjustment, as did also the reciprocal right to settle, purchase lands, and inherit, and the extradition of criminals; and the old royal grants were soon seen to have defined colonial boundaries with so little precision that whenever the time should come to push American settlement westward into the Mississippi valley, the conflicting claims of our earlier jurisdictions must needs have merged for the good of the whole people in a common territory with a common pre-emption from the red tribes, and a common and comprehen-sive policy to pursue towards all the frontier foes of American progress. For behind these untamed chil-dren of nature, the aboriginal occupants of the American wilderness, stood France and Spain. Still more instant for adjustment between particular colo-nies were Atlantic problems of coast and harbor jurisdiction, and disputes among adjacent colonies over the use of such navigable waters as the Connecticut, Delaware, and Potomac rivers, and the New York, Delaware, and Chesapeake bays. King and Parliament might arbitrate such disputes for the first century or two of rapid growth and expansion; but the time was sure to come, not many generations distant, when a government remote beyond the seas and monarchical would prove incompetent for a task so immense that Union with home rule could alone achieve it.

That these tendencies to Union existed early in the American colonies, without any clear consciousness of disloyalty or forecast of a coming separation from the mother country, appears from various leagues or compacts of the colonial era, chief and earliest among which should be mentioned that of the "New England Confederacy." Massachusetts, Plymouth, Connecticut, and New Haven, colonies singularly homogeneous in origin and character, formed in May, 1643, what they styled a "perpetual confederation," — "a firm and perpetual league" for themselves and posterity under the name of the "United Colonies of New England." The "sad distractions" of civil war in the mother country, which drove these neighboring colonies to their own resources for mutual succor and advice, furnished the ostensible and perhaps a sufficient motive for so daring an assumption of sovereignty and self-government. This instrument of sectional Union disclosed religious as well as political designs; for which reason it happened, most probably, that Rhode Island, whose free religious tenets found little favor, was refused admission. Mutual offence and defence against native tribes and the Dutch were here sought

most of all; and under the united auspices of this
league the colonies who made the name "New England" lastingly native, fought together unaided the
Pequod and King Philip wars. Mutual reception
of settlers and the mutual extradition of "servants"[1]
and of fugitives from justice were other objects of
the alliance distinctly provided for.

This New England Confederacy, jealously exclusive
and sectional in character, and stipulating expressly
that without a unanimous assent no other colony
should share its benefits, respected scrupulously the
autonomy of each sovereign member of the Union
and all reserved rights. Its management of confederate affairs was in the nature of a joint representative
board, or committee. Eight commissioners comprising the board, with an equality of representation,[2]
and chosen two each from the several colonies, were
to manage the common concerns, meeting once a year
by rotation in Boston, Hartford, New Haven, and
Plymouth, and on extraordinary occasion at convenience. Six out of eight might determine the
common business, "not intermeddling with the government of any of the jurisdictions;" and if six
commissioners could not agree, the subject was to be
referred to the four colonial legislatures for conclusion. No provision was made for amending these
Articles of Confederation; but for any infraction of
the league, commissioners of the other unoffending
jurisdictions should consider and order for the peaceful preservation of this Union inviolate. The charge
of all just wars offensive or defensive was to be
borne by a poll or census enumeration, each colony
rating for itself; and all booty or conquered territory
was to be ratably divided. Any of these confederated

[1] Cf. Constitution of United States, Art. IV. § 2.
[2] Two from each colony, and "all in church fellowship with us."

colonies "invaded by any enemy whatsoever" was to call upon the others for assistance.[1]

Boards of commissioners, mutually chosen on the principle of co-ordinate sovereignty, were found in various other instances a convenient mode of negotiating differences among the colonies or planning concerted action. Thus did the navigation of the Chesapeake and Potomac waters engage Maryland and Virginia from time to time; and disputed boundary rights were elsewhere a cause of irritating collision, demanding a mutual conference for adjustment.

After the New England Confederacy had finally disappeared, various plans were proposed for a more comprehensive union of all the British colonies in North America, which might insure unanimity of action, more especially against the French and Indian allies who menaced their general safety. One such plan was considered at London by the Board of Trade, but the peace of Ryswick caused it to be for-

---

[1] See Bowen's "Documents of the Constitution," 79, for these "Articles of Confederation." This was indeed a daring document for recognized subjects of the British Crown to frame and carry into effect without a submission, so far as appears, to the home government or the procurement of home authority. Some writers have thought that these New England colonists intended a sectional rebellion; but we need not strain the natural purport of the league, which (though styled "perpetual") aimed to provide for immediate needs while Great Britain was absorbed in her own struggle for existence. These New England settlers inclined strongly from the first to resolve all political doubts of authority in their own favor; and there were contingencies certainly, in the English civil war and under Cromwell's usurpation, which might have wrought out a premature colonial independence in America prior to a continental union. To take such contingencies into account was neither rebellion nor disloyalty. This New England Confederation kept its vigor and efficacy for some forty years, and until after the accession of Charles II.; and Hutchinson says that it received English countenance and acknowledgment from its beginning until the Restoration.

gotten. Half a century later, under the new pressure of French and Indian hostilities which threatened to expel British influence from the continent, came two significant tokens of confederate union (1) in the assembling of a Convention (or Congress) of colonial delegates at Albany in 1754, and (2) in the adoption and proposal by that convention of a plan of union which Benjamin Franklin, as a leading delegate, had drafted.[1] Seven colonies north of the Potomac were here represented, the Board of Trade having summoned the convention in view of impending war; and being thus assembled, the delegates, in addition to the Indian treaty business which was the main concern, discussed the weightier subject of union and confederation for the general interests of these North American colonies in peace as well as war. Among other plans accordingly presented, Franklin's was preferred, and after a protracted debate adopted either unanimously, or with the dissent of a single State. But outside of the convention this plan met but little favor. It was rejected presently by all the colonial assemblies which considered it at all, while the Board of Trade declined even to recommend it to the King's notice. As Franklin says, "The assemblies all thought there was too much prerogative in it, and in England it was thought to have too much of the democratic." Indeed, the obvious effort of this instrument to please all parties, and to reconcile dutiful allegiance with home rule, produced its natural result.

In Franklin's plan of 1754, as supplied from his posthumous papers, the various items of proposed government are set forth with annotated reasons and

---

[1] As Postmaster-General of these colonies by appointment of the British Crown, Dr. Franklin had ample opportunity to consider later the advantage of a closer system of continental union.

motives for each of them. Its preamble, in choice
and deferential language, proposed petitioning for an
Act of Parliament which might establish one general
government for these American colonies, under a
reservation that each colony should retain its existing
constitution except in the particulars set forth. The
scheme proper is styled, "Plan of Union of the British
American Colonies;" thus discreetly avoiding any
style savoring of independence, such as the New
England Confederacy had employed, or claiming to
last as perpetual. A Grand Council was created,
after the familiar pattern of a Board of Commissioners, but with this new step in advance, sure to
provoke resistance, that colonies were not to be
coequal in composing it; council representation, in
other words, being based upon a sort of money
apportionment, which proposed taking always into
account the relative contributions of the thirteen
colonies to the general treasury, and under its
preliminary schedule placed Massachusetts, Virginia,
and Pennsylvania distinctly foremost. Such par-
tiality must have provoked the jealousy of smaller
States, while on the other hand compromising theo-
retically the sound democratic doctrine of apportioning by numbers. Then, as if to disconcert the
representative authority of these colonies, a President-General, made after the image of the familiar
provincial governor, was to be appointed by the
Crown to carry into execution with very ample discretionary powers the acts of the Grand Council.
Without his assent their representative decrees were
to be of no avail whatever. Indian peace or war,
and Indian treaties, this President-General might
determine with the advice of the Grand Council;
while as concerned appointments, he was to nominate
all military officers to them, and they were to nomi-

nate all civil officers to him. This common government of the colonies was to raise soldiers, build forts,
and equip vessels to guard the coast and protect
commerce; and for the purposes delegated it was
to levy duties, imports, or taxes at convenience, and
appoint a general Treasurer. One pregnant power
was that of purchasing lands from the Indians and
regulating and governing new settlements in the purchased territory until the Crown should see fit to
form them into particular governments. For, as Dr.
Franklin argued, a single purchaser, in the name
of the Crown or the Union, and a single authority
for developing new colonies, was preferable to many.
No money should issue, however, but by joint
order of the President-General and Grand Council; and (as in most of the individual colonies) all
laws passed by their concurrence were to be trans-
mitted to the King in council, subject to his approval
or disapproval.[1]

On the whole, this Franklin plan of continental
union, though a sagacious emanation for the times,
projected too difficult a political experiment, in
harnessing so closely King and colonies, prerogative
and people, for a general direction of affairs which
each must have felt better competent to undertake alone, — an experiment which, proposing co-
operation, was more likely to end in distraction.
That spirit, too, of self-sacrifice and subordination,
which so many equal jurisdictions would have to invoke when delegating authority for the sake of union,
needed some clearer incentive. The conclusion of
the colonists was wise, therefore, to wait for some
more solemn exigency, when union and home government might more readily coincide. Yet the scheme

---

[1] See Bowen's Documents, 87, for "Franklin's Plan."

proposed by America's most distinguished son and statesman of that early day, and the discussion over its adoption, undoubtedly prepared the minds of American colonists for the genuine continental union which took definite shape a generation later.

II.

INDEPENDENCE AND REVOLUTION.

1765–1780.

DURING the first sixty years of the eighteenth century these transatlantic colonies maintained peaceful relations with the mother country, joining as loyal
sons of Great Britain in the prosecution of the French
and Indian War, and rejoicing over the crowning
conquest of Quebec as their common glory. As
Burke observed in 1775, America owed little to any
care by Great Britain, but had gained "through a
wise and salutary neglect." But there had been early
causes for discontent in particular colonies; and
when Parliament, with arbitrary pride, undertook to
lay the burden of taxation for that war upon the
colonists, — asserting what a minority so aptly styled
"the right to shear the wolf," — colonial resistance
became universal. This French expulsion from the
northwestern frontier had strongly developed both
the martial hardihood and the co-operative inclination
of our colonists; and a dispute, formerly languid,
touching the legal status of their several colonial
assemblies, and the abstract right of Parliament to
levy taxes in America without the assent of local
representatives, blazed at once into a continental
issue vital to colonial liberty itself.

The colonial Stamp Act, which passed the British
Parliament in 1763, gave America the first rude
alarm; the tax itself being slight enough, to be sure,

but the principle of levying it most obnoxious, and the precedent one which might foster other distant impositions. United protest and resistance, almost spontaneous, resulted. As co-ordinate colonies had sent delegates to a convention in 1754 on the King's summons, so now they summoned a convention of their own, which met in New York City in October, 1765. This was the assembly historically known as the "Stamp Act Congress;" and so ominous was the spectacle of such a body that Parliament and the Crown receded a short while from the new endeavor, and early the next year this Stamp Act was repealed.

But Parliament still claimed the unqualified paramount right to legislate for the colonies on all subjects whatsoever; and under the influence of the stubborn George III. the policy of arbitrary taxation for the colonies was resumed in a new mode, and with vexatious accompaniments for humbling Massachusetts, whose rebellious temper, fomented by earlier differences, singled her out for discipline. Our thirteen colonies resolved unitedly that the oppression of one jurisdiction should be deemed the oppression of all; and a Continental Congress was once more convoked; this time, as events compelled, to become the prime agent of unified revolution and of a new unified confederacy. At Philadelphia met the first Continental Congress, September 17, 1774, followed by the second in May, 1775, after bloodshed had begun. Events forced what might have been otherwise a temporary assembly into a permanent one. In this second Congress a commander-in-chief was appointed for all the colonies, continental troops were enrolled, and quotas of men and money were assigned. At the third Congress of 1776, with delegates chosen for the year as before from the several colonies, the war for independence swept like a torrent all scrupulous sense of allegiance, and on the 4th of July of that year the immortal Declaration went forth to the world.

This great body of the American people had taken up arms not to vindicate abstract rights, but to redress practical wrongs; and revolution and independence came to them, in the main, as the logical and unpremeditated result of a hostile domestic resistance. For after a resort to the arbitrament of violence, victory can seldom rest with wiping out the temporary wrong, leaving the opportunity as before to inflict new ones.[1] In reading over this Declaration of Independence, with its earnest indictment of grievances against Great Britain, one perceives that the whole denunciation was concentrated upon the King in person, while Parliament received but an indirect and contemptuous allusion. The "self-evident" truths which this instrument asserted by way of preface are long since familiar to Americans as household words, and doubly cherished as among the fundamental rights of each new State constitution. And one should observe, moreover, that this "Declaration of Independence" recognized thus primarily the composite nature of the political system into which henceforth the old colonies were to be welded; for its solemn announcement to the world is not that these several colonies, but that "these United Colonies" are, and of right ought to be, "free and independent States;" and independence is here published and declared by "the Representatives of the United States of America, in General Congress assembled," and expressed "in the name and by the authority of the good people of these Colonies."[2]

---

[1] Cf. 7 Jefferson's Works, 74.
[2] Cf. Instrument, Bowen's Documents, 102.

In short, the United States of America never consisted of States wholly sovereign and apart from one another, and capable each of independent, separate, and distinct action. As for most of those jurisdictions at present comprising the American Union, their origin, subsequent to the adoption of our present Federal constitution, placed them severally in a filial and subordinate relation; each was nurtured and reared on the national territory, under national regulations, and, when adult, admitted upon fundamental terms prescribed by Congress as a full State and fellow-member of the Supreme Federal Union. Of foreign annexations to the United States, Texas, as a *de facto* republic, but not formally recognized as such by Mexico, adopted the constitutional conditions held out by Congress, while Louisiana and Florida served first a territorial probation. No members whatever of this Federal Union have had the historical right to be considered sovereign and independent in more than a secondary sense, except the old historical thirteen, who together dissolved allegiance with Great Britain, conquered their united independence, and formed for themselves a confederate league, and then, as ordained by the people, a closer union. But even they, until absolved in 1776 from allegiance to the mother country, were all ruled severally as offspring and dependencies of the British Crown; and from that subject condition they each and altogether passed at once into a new subordination to the continental union symbolized by their own Congress. Simultaneously, indeed, with independence, articles of permanent Federal union which should have a delegated operation were contemplated; and during the delay of formulating that new plan, the Continental Congress, without more explicit credentials than necessity and public opinion might have conceded to that body, guarded by the annual choice of delegates in each State through convention or legislature, raised a common army and a navy, contracted common debts, apportioned State quotas of money, men, and supplies, carried on foreign relations as a single sovereign power, and assumed plenary powers of war and peace. From Articles of Confederation, styled perpetual, and so accepted by them, these thirteen States emerged into the better Union devised by our still operative constitution of 1787. Through all such fundamental changes in Anglo-American institutions there was not a moment when any of these Atlantic communities could be deemed sovereign, independent, and free from a supervising political authority in a legal and practical sense, except, perhaps, for Rhode Island and North Carolina, during the year or two following 1788 that they refused to ratify the new Federal constitution, while the other States, choosing Washington for President, and rallying to the united support of his first administration, entered upon the new era of national existence without them.

III.

ARTICLES OF CONFEDERATION.

1781–1789.

THE original United States of the Revolution were, for five years following July, 1776, held together by a sort of *de facto* alliance, and by the practical delegation of common authority to Congress by the old thirteen States without a strictly formal sanction. Some legal writers of unquestioned repute consider that first continental government of this Union as strictly revolutionary in character.[1] Yet the important historical circumstance should not be overlooked that a written and formal plan of permanent confederated union was meant by the Continental Congress to be essentially contemporaneous with the Declaration of Independence itself; that the Declaration by its own language indicates that purpose; and that not only in the Congressional debates which preceded the British separation, but as one of the formal resolves which prefaced that momentous action, a plan of confederated union was, June 11, 1776, to be drawn up for formal adoption. Thus, while one committee prepared the instrument of independence, another was engaged upon that of union, reporting it for debate only eight days after the famous July 4th. Discussed by Congress during the same July in committee of the whole, this plan of union suffered further delay, as such plans are likely to while war

[1] Cooley's Elements of Constitutional Law, 9.

absorbs men's minds; but at length, agreed to in Congress, November 15, 1777, with some unimportant amendments, the scheme of Confederation went out to the States for their formal and separate sanction. A few of the smaller States, however, deferred ratifying, nor was it until 1781 that Maryland, after gaining an important concession to the Confederacy independently of the instrument, made the compact and sanction of continental Union complete.[1] Yet through the whole intervening period Congress had exercised for the emergency its contemplated powers, as though formally clothed with them, while the American people acquiesced because such had been their own fundamental intent. A continental army fought meantime for independence under a continental commander-in-chief, obedient to this unempowered Congress, and in the name and under the flag of the Confederacy; and on behalf, moreover, of the new "United States of America" were sought foreign recognition in Europe, foreign loans, and foreign alliances.

At length, under the ratified and completed Articles of Confederation, and as a fully legitimated parchment government, Congress reassembled, March 2, 1781, for its usual business, making no special recognition of its new status; but rather as though to navigate for the future with a chart where they had been piloting as best they might without one. Examining these Articles of Confederation, we see that the main design, agreeably to their origination,

---

[1] Maryland's delay was not without good purpose; which was to force large States like Virginia, having claims in the unsettled northwest territory beyond the Appalachian range, to cede their individual rights in favor of the common Union. See monograph (1878) of Dr. H. B. Adams. The Articles of Confederation expressly provided that "no State shall be deprived of territory for the benefit of the United States." Articles, IX. 2.

was simply to invest this representative Continental Congress of the thirteen States with such powers as naturally and of necessity pertained to a continental and united exercise of public authority, and as public opinion already upheld.[1]

The general scope, then, of these "Articles of Confederation," as we gather by a study of the adopted instrument, coincides with that of the extemporized and preliminary Revolutionary government of the Union; jealous provision being quickly applied to constrain and limit those formidable powers, by reserving expressly that each State shall retain "its sovereignty, freedom, and independence, and every power, jurisdiction, and right, which is not by this Confederation expressly delegated to the United States in Congress assembled."[2] Except, indeed, for what Maryland is seen to have finally gained in behalf of the common territory, the changes wrought out by time and discussion in Congress after the plan was first reported from committee, seem to have been mostly in the cautious direction of circumscribing this new Federal supremacy; nor was Maryland's happy gain, out of which grew our grand system of public land settlement and the procreation of new States westward, in the nature of an amendment to those Articles, but rather so as to induce

---

[1] The committee appointed, June 11, 1776, to prepare a form of Confederation consisted of one member from each colony. John Dickinson appears to have had the chief hand in drafting the committee's instrument; but the work was most likely a composite one, seeking to formulate a scheme which Congress was already developing into action. Little is really known concerning the details of these "Articles of Confederation" as the composition took its final and historical form.

Dickinson's draft of 1776, as well as one which Franklin had prepared in 1775, proposed ampler powers than the final Articles granted. Story, Constitution, § 284.

[2] Articles, II.

legislation by the old Continental Congress of doubt-ful constitutional warrant, as Articles were expressed, though justified by the terms of Virginia's voluntary cession.

In these Articles, the chief fact that confronts us is that the Montesquieu idea of a distinct separation of powers for well-ordered government is wanting. Such government was thought to answer for States at the outset, but not for the Union. We find, then, no distinct Executive nor distinct Judiciary provided; but all common powers of the Confederacy, as they were first laid off, vested in that general Legislature styled the Continental Congress. Nor was this Congress a fully developed legislative body. It con-sisted of but a single house; its members were chosen in practice not by individual voters, but by a State legislature; [1] members did not vote on questions as representatives chosen upon a poll or property basis, but simply as a State delegation or unit. All States were coequal and alike in that body, no matter what the relative number of soldiers they might supply or the relative sums poured out in the costly struggle for freedom; and it was the noble self-denial of the greater States, not the urgency of the smaller, that first made continental union possible. In fine, the advance of political construction from the old pro-jected Committee, or Grand Council, of colonial times had not been so very great for this first fundamental government of the American Union.

This Continental Congress all the more resembled a colonial Board of Commissioners, or Grand Coun-cil, from its choice to sit constantly as a secret body, publishing no report of its debates, and gaining neither

---

[1] Yet delegates were nominally to be appointed in such manner as each Legislature should direct, and hence might have been popularly chosen. Articles, V.

buoyancy nor direct guidance from public opinion. Delegates, not less than two nor more than seven from each State, made up the quorum that voted as a State unit, thus diminishing still further all sense of individual responsibility to constituents; and it was provided that no person could serve more than three in any term of six years. Each State paid the recompense of its own delegation,[1] and might at any time recall a delegate and send another in his place. And thus did it become matter of familiar remark, after the first impulse of patriotic energy had subsided, that the ablest of Revolutionary civilians gave their talents, in preference, to the service of their respective States, leaving Congress to shift as it might in the continental conduct of affairs, often without a quorum of delegates at all to represent the State on an important issue.

Congress was invested with authority to appoint a "Committee of the States," consisting of one delegate from each State, to sit in the recess; but this expedient did not work well. It had authority, moreover, to appoint a presiding officer; yet the President of Congress was scarcely more than a ceremonial functionary.[2] Seven out of these thirteen States, coequal in voting, might, despite all such obstructions, have proved by their majority competent for conducting affairs, had not these Articles, as though fearful of efficiency, made the affirmative assent of nine States present and voting by a quorum of their respective delegations needful in all the most important public business. For without such affirmative assent of nine out of thirteen States, Congress was forbidden to engage in war, enter into treaties or alliances, coin money and regulate its value, ascertain money quotas, emit bills, borrow or appropriate

[1] Articles, V.   [2] Articles, IX. 5; X.

money on the credit of the United States, agree upon the number of land or naval forces to be raised, or even appoint a commander-in-chief of army or navy.[1]

However fairly one may construe this government with reserved State sovereignty as a confederated league, he should observe that whatever general powers were actually given by this instrument were given as though permanently and forever; for these Articles were styled "Articles of Confederation and Perpetual Union." They expressly invited the further accession of Canada, and provided (with the assent of nine States) for the possible admission of other colonies; and they made solemn stipulation to abide severally by the constitutional determinations of Congress, and that the Articles "shall be inviolably observed by every State, and the Union shall be perpetual."[2] The American people well understood already that in union there was strength, and without it sure disaster. But the practical defect of the whole primitive system of union, and that which finally ruined it was, as history shows us, the want of a practical amending power; for no alteration in these Articles could ever be made, as the instrument prescribed, unless (1) agreed to in Congress, which was proper enough, and (2) confirmed afterwards by the Legislature of every State.[3] But this latter prerequisite proved at the crucial test impossible.

Vast, undoubtedly, were the original powers thus delegated to the Union, had the several States but bestowed them in a manner to permit of their efficient exercise. For the nominal authority of these "United States in Congress assembled," under the sanction of the "firm league," now entered into, was sole and exclusive (with some minor reservations) in determining peace and war; in foreign intercourse and foreign

[1] Articles, IX. 6. [2] Articles, XI., XIII. [3] Articles, XIII.

alliances; in regulating captures and prizes, or granting in times of peace letters of marque and reprisal; in "appointing courts" for the trial of piracies and felonies committed on the high seas, and for determining captures; in regulating the value of coin and the standard of weights and measures; in managing all trade and affairs with the Indians; in establishing and regulating post-offices; in appointing all army and navy officers in the service of the United States, excepting regimental officers of the land service; and generally in regulating and directing all warlike operations.[1] Congress was further empowered to ascertain, appropriate, and apply such sums as might be needful for the public expenditure; to borrow money or emit bills on the credit of the United States, transmitting its accounts half-yearly to the States; to build and equip a navy; to make requisitions on the several States for quotas of troops apportioned on a basis of white population.[2] All charges of war and other expenses "for the common defence and general welfare" were to be defrayed out of a common treasury which the several States were to supply in proportion to the value of lands and improvements in each jurisdiction, as Congress might estimate from time to time. The States themselves, under direction of their several Legislatures, were to levy and collect their several portions of the common tax;[3] and thus, as experiment proved, States became delinquent in supplying their contributions, while the delinquency of one State prompted the delinquency of others. All bills of credit emitted, all money borrowed, and all debts contracted by Congress before these Articles of Confederation went formally into operation were declared solemnly binding upon the United States.

[1] Articles, IX. 1–4.　　[2] Articles, IX. 5.　　[3] Articles, VIII.

Coupled with such grant to Congress of general powers which initiate much of the sovereignty still exercised by our Federal government under a far better sanction, were various prohibitions upon the individual States. They were not to hold independent foreign intercourse nor make independent treaties regardless of Congress; they were not without consent of Congress to enter into alliances or confederations among themselves; they were not to keep up armies and navies of their own in time of peace, but to rely locally upon a well regulated and disciplined militia; they were not at their own instance to engage in war nor to issue letters of marque and reprisal in time of peace unless invaded or in imminent danger.[1] When raising land forces for common defence, each State was still to appoint its own regimental officers.[2]

The interstate advantages of a consociation like this were at once appreciated, as they have been ever since, and as the New England Confederacy had prized them. Articles of Confederation declared the free inhabitants of each State entitled to all privileges and immunities of free citizens in the several States. The free right of ingress and egress was conceded to or from different States, together with reciprocal privileges of trade and commerce, so far as the new and imperfect system might reasonably afford them; the interstate surrender of fugitives from justice was stipulated; and full faith and credit was to be given in each State to the records, acts, and judicial proceedings of every other State.[3]

But restraints upon restriction made the original grant of delegated powers to this Union so parsimonious, after all, in some particulars, that only a minute

---

[1] Articles, VI.   [2] Articles, VII.   [3] Articles, IV.

study of the text itself can enable us to apprehend the true limits. Comparison, therefore, with the broader transfer of Federal powers to our later constitution will be useful when analyzing that more perfect instrument. But it is worthy of final mention here, as showing the league character of our "Articles of Confederation," and the alliance of *quasi*-sovereign States, that the mode of State ratification kept up sedulously the idea of a delegated authority to the new government. Congress, as the single delegated council of these thirteen coequal States, framed the Articles, and then proposed them, not to conventions, but to the several State Legislatures for adoption. These State Legislatures, as representative agents each of the State and its inhabitants, authorized duly their several delegations in Congress to sign the Articles "on the part and behalf of the State." All was done by compact and power of attorney, high above the heads of the common people, and without direct reference in the least for their fundamental approval. Not a word or suggestion of a State convention fresh from the inhabitants, nor of immediate and authoritative sanction derived from them, appears in the whole solemn establishment as if by treaty of this common government of the United States; and yet each State delegation in Congress, while ratifying, as a unit, these Articles of Confederation, "by virtue of the power and authority" given for that purpose, as their signatures recited, solemnly and expressly pledged and engaged the faith of its State constituents to abide by the "perpetual" Union thereby established.[1]

[1] See Articles, ratifying clause at the close.

IV.

THE FEDERAL CONSTITUTION; ITS NATURE AND ESTABLISHMENT.

1787–1789.

It is matter of familiar American history that the Articles of Confederation, feeble enough for their amplest and most essential exercise of supremacy during the long and exhausting struggle for a common independence, failed utterly as the efficient instrument of peace and recuperation. Their radical defect consisted in attempting to operate upon States in a collective capacity, and to exert an authority whose sinews depended upon a co-sovereign supply. Under the unexampled stress and strain of State necessity, the common government of this Union found but a careless heed to its wants, notwithstanding the solemn pledge and obligation to relieve them. Abstractly, to be sure, and as a matter of fundamental right, Congress might have summoned all the military forces of the Union to compel the money quota of a delinquent sovereign; practically, however, any attempted compulsion of the kind could only have hastened anarchy. And thus did the Union, projected nobly in the very sublimity of patriotic passion, sink contemptuously into a government of exhortation, not command; and as one writer said of its Congress, with reference to the delegated supremacy which they sought to exercise, "they may declare everything, but do nothing."

History teaches that the last hope of saving the old Confederacy from irresistible wreck was to gain an amendment to existing Articles which might make Congress potent to collect a modest impost duty for general purposes during a moderate and specific length of time. The positive refusal of a single State bent on self-aggrandizement defeated that amendment, and the doom of the Confederacy was sealed.

How, then, could the American people escape national calamity? Only by resorting to their own final remedies for self-preservation, — their own inherent right, in fact, which the Declaration of Independence had so boldly asserted, to alter or abolish a form of government destructive of its own rightful ends, and to institute a new one. They still wished the United States perpetual, as first proclaimed; and they set in operation a representative engine, new in a national, but old enough in a State, application, that of "Convention." [1] With popular credentials superior to any such partial agency of government as a legislature, men met in convention at Philadelphia in 1787, and prepared a renovated plan of continental union, comprehensive and efficient as never before, and rightly purporting to emanate as an ordinance of the people. Its reference for adoption and a practical establishment was not to State legislatures, but to State conventions. There was this element of revolution — happily a peaceful one — in the new scheme, that so soon as nine conventions should ratify and commit their respective States to it, the new Union would start out on its new career, leaving the old league, misnamed "perpetual," to perish with its obstinate remnant. Revolution was thus far inseparable from the crisis, from "the grind-

[1] See *supra,* page 46.

ing necessity," as John Quincy Adams has styled it, which had compelled an ampler Federal government as the only escape from anarchy. Persuasion accomplished the work of conviction; ten States ratified, and stubborn New York acceded as the eleventh; after which safe alliance the perilous situation of Rhode Island and North Carolina, widely separated as they were, and their own returning sense of national sisterhood, brought them as the last loiterers into the fold, and the new United States of America stood re-created.

But if this dissolution of the old confederate league, or rather its supersedure by a new and more efficient Union, is to be styled revolutionary at all, it was only so in a partial sense. The Articles had expressly forbidden the confederation or alliance of two or more States, "without the consent of the United States in Congress assembled;" and aside from any application here of such a clause, it was impolitic and unfair to ignore the rightful repository of Federal power when promulgating the new Philadelphia plan. Nor did the framers of 1787 propose any such disobedience. No sooner was their finished scheme put forth at Independence Hall than they hastened to procure, first of all, the sanction of the Continental Congress, then in session at New York. That sanction, which permitted the free proposal of this new plan to the several State conventions, was given, and given speedily, before a single State took action upon the instrument.

Any notion that our Federal constitution of 1787 was a spontaneous birth must be a false and fanciful one. Our brief exposition of the facts has shown that it was a gradual conception; in other words, that it ripened as the matured fruit of political experience. Two leading influences are traceable in its composition: (1) the American Confederacy, formulated, defined, and sanctioned by the Articles adopted in 1781, but, in point of fact, originating several years earlier in united Revolutionary resistance to the mother country; (2) the written constitutions, already in full operation, of thirteen individual States. From the former came that mass of delegated Federal powers, which upon experiment were found to need enlargement and addition; from the latter, outlined in bold relief, the main elements essential to a stable and well-ordered government on the Montesquieu plan of a threefold division, inclusive of a bicameral legislature, and also (by the time the plan became modified by the first ten amendments) of a declaration of rights. But the application of existing models to a new and difficult piece of workmanship which excelled them all, was a marvellous creation.

The main change here effected from the former confederate government consisted in replacing the league of co-sovereign States by a national, or, rather, it should be said, a federo-national government, which should operate largely upon the people as individuals, and not upon States collectively; and this made an immense remedial difference. But the several States were still left with great discretionary powers in united concerns; as, for instance, in appointing Presidential electors, and in the voting qualifications needful for choosing Representatives to Congress. When the Federal constitution first went into operation, our States had still the crust of British aristocracy; and the constitution of the United States, as concerned its own structure, permitted of quite an aristocratic operation, had States so willed it; but the contrary happened, and

American institutions, both State and Federal, became gradually democratized through the irresistible genius of popular self-government. Most fortunate was it for the general happiness of America that this instrument of union, so rigid in its textual mould and so difficult to alter, left its political scope so free for circumstances to shape. That the new scheme meant, however, that Federal power should be exerted more independently and effectively than before, and within a wider range of supreme action, whether this or that set of men might happen through State selection to control its exercise, is obvious, not only from a general survey of the constitution itself, but from certain specific expressions compared with those of the superseded Articles. It is no longer the States that "severally enter into a firm league," [1] but "we, the people," who "ordain and establish." Perpetual in intent as before, the new purpose is to establish permanency by suitable means for the people and their posterity. The word "Confederacy" disappears forever from the style of "United States of America." A "more perfect union" is one of the main objects stated in the new preamble; and even when State jealousy pressed an immediate amendment expressive of reserved rights not delegated to the Union, the text of that amendment expressed such reservation not to States alone, as in the Articles of Confederation before, but to "the States respectively or to the people." [2] In the instrument as originally drawn up and formally adopted was no allusion to reserved rights at all.

[1] Articles, III.

[2] Cf. Articles, II., and Constitution, Amendments, X. The letter of the Philadelphia convention, which in 1787 submitted the new instrument for the consideration of the Continental Congress, avowed as the object of the new scheme and the greatest interest of every true American, "the consolidation of our Union."

Not a member of that glorious assembly at Philadelphia approved in all respects our original Federal
constitution when they signed it. By a very close
majority in some of the State conventions did it secure an unqualified ratification at all; and that only
upon the assurance of amendments such as the first
Congress under our new government at once sent
forth, and whose adoption quickly followed.[1] But
here, as always, how best actually to secure the good
and remedy the evil was the problem of the times; for
all good institutions come by accretion; and as Burke
has wisely observed, "Government is a practical
thing made for the security and happiness of mankind and not to please theorists."

---

[1] See Constitution, first ten amendments, proposed in 1789 and
declared adopted in 1791.

V.

FEDERAL CONSTITUTION ANALYZED; STRUCTURE AND DISTRIBUTION OF POWERS; LEGISLATURE.

LET us now examine in detail the constitution of the United States under which we live, and which has preserved American liberties for more than a century; an instrument rather inflexible in form, as any written constitution must be whose change is not readily brought about, and yet within that form capable of giving the nation a splendid development. The exceeding brevity of its expression, its pragmatic, concise language, enumerating powers rather than defining them, and avoiding all "glittering generalities" and the disposition to dogmatize, despite some notable examples among contemporary States of 1787, have elicited the admiration of scholars and statesmen of the old world.[1] It may be that the bitter humiliations which the proud, primitive Union was then undergoing made the present framers indisposed to high-sounding abstractions, since their assembled purpose was to check lawless liberty and teach citizens to obey; and practical, moreover, in pushing their

---

[1] Mr. Bryce, who is fond of impressive comparison, observes that our Federal constitution with its amendments may be read aloud in twenty-three minutes; that it is about half as long as St. Paul's first Epistle to the Corinthians, and only one fortieth part as long as the Irish Land Act of 1881. "History shows few instruments," he adds, "which in so few words lay down equally momentous rules on a vast range of matters of the highest importance and complexity." 1 Bryce, Commonwealth, 363.

plans, they knew it was best to go forth to the States
with an instrument which avoided interpretation and
left something to be imagined. Articles of Confederation had been similarly brief, though often far
more involved and obscure in statement.

The new Federal government, as thus arranged,
was composite; in strictness neither national nor
confederate, but a composition of both. "In its
foundation," explains Madison in the "Federalist,"
"it is federal, not national; in the sources from which
the ordinary powers of the government are drawn, it
is partly federal and partly national; in the operation
of these powers it is national, not federal; in the
extent of them again, it is federal, not national; and
finally, in the authoritative mode of introducing
amendments, it is neither wholly federal nor wholly
national." [1] The justice of this contemporary exposition will appear more fully as our analysis of the
text proceeds. To borrow, again, the demonstration
of a century's experience, the constitution of the
United States is an instrument of government, agreed
upon and established in the several States by the
people through their empowered representatives primarily in convention, to be operative upon the people
individually and collectively, and within the sphere
of its just powers upon the government of the States
also. [2] Furthermore, the Union thus established is
an indissoluble one, in continuance and confirmation
of that which the States had in the nature of a permanent league established previously. If ever there
was ground at all for the interpretation which our
Calhoun school of statesmen once put upon it, —
namely, that States still reserved a sovereign and
paramount right to nullify and to withdraw from the

[1] Federalist, No. 39.
[2] Story's Commentaries, § 311, Judge Cooley's note.

Union, — that theory was quenched in the civil strife and bloodshed of 1861–65, so that the very States which in its advocacy provoked the agonizing test were overwhelmingly defeated. Their State constitutions now repudiate all such dogmas in language unequivocal. Indeed, the ties of common fraternal intercourse, woven with tenfold more complexity than before into the intimate fabric of Union, render this reunited government irresistibly and permanently — short of such unhappy fate as the sword of successful revolt may compel in some remote and unforeseen contingency — "an indestructible Union of indestructible States."[1] Long, in fact, before civil war and the immense sacrifice of blood and treasure which it cost to vindicate this establishment of the whole people as permanent, the whole irresistible tendency of national policy had been to advance the national glory and influence against all rivalry of individual States; and some of the Presidents of the old era, such as Jefferson, Jackson, and Polk, who most protested against encroaching upon State authority, did most, by acquiring foreign territory or otherwise, to consolidate the strength of the Union.

Inexplicit as was our Federal constitution on many points which public policy might historically determine, that policy or national usage, developed from precedents long acquiesced in by the people, tends to efface all constructive doubt and fix permanently the rule of the constitution. But when interpreting any written constitution, we should gather its sense from the general tenor of its language, from the whole scope of the instrument, and

[1] Chief Justice Chase for the Supreme Court of the United States, in 7 Wall. 100.

not from particular terms.[1] We should construe according to the just intendment of the instrument, neither too literally nor too freely; giving to the language used its reasonable and natural sense.[2] We should interpret, furthermore, in the light of the law as existing when the constitution or its particular phrase was adopted, and as reaching out not for new guaranties so much as for guaranties already recognized.[3] And we should so construe as, if possible, to give proper efficiency to powers which are nominally granted.[4]

To enter now upon our analysis of the text, the constitution of the United States is seen to begin with a striking preamble. Preambles in documents of a law-making character are not usually of prime importance, being little more than explanatory of the purpose in changing and of the ills to be overcome; they do not apart confer or take away fundamental powers. But the present preamble is virtually an adaptation from the third of the Articles of Confederation.[5] There it was said that the States "severally enter into a firm league of friendship with each

---

[1] Thus, to take the preamble alone, it has been argued that "we the people . . . do ordain and establish this constitution" sufficiently proves the government national and popular. Yet, when we see among various other provisions that (Article VII.) the ratification of the conventions of nine States shall establish this constitution between the ratifying States, we find that a composite or "federo-national" government is its true character.

[2] 158 U. S. 618.

[3] 156 U. S. 237.

[4] "As men whose intention requires no concealment generally employ the words which most directly and aptly express the ideas they intend to convey, the enlightened patriots who framed our constitution, and the people who adopted it, must be understood to have employed words in their natural sense, and to have intended what they have said." Marshall, C. J., in 9 Wheat. 1, 188.

[5] Articles, III.

other;" but here that "we the people . . . do ordain and establish this constitution," — a profound and highly suggestive difference. Three of the objects stated in that article are here repeated with slight variation: namely, (1) to provide for the common defense; (2) to promote the general welfare;[1] and (3) "to secure the blessings of liberty to ourselves and our posterity."[2] But three new objects are added, hinting at former imperfections now to be remedied: (4) to form a more perfect union; (5) to establish justice;[3] and (6) to insure domestic tranquillity.[4] An ancient philosopher urges that, as in musical composition, every great act of legislation should have its lofty and appropriate prelude; and many a document of Revolutionary origin, many a Revolutionary statute which embodies some grand reform, is prefaced by a high-sounding preamble; that, however, which made this Union efficient, chose only the dignity of a compressed recital.

The first three articles which follow this preamble in the text distribute the powers of government conformably to Montesquieu's maxim, as the States had already done; but without dogmatic announcement, and far more appropriately in some respects than any State had heretofore seen fit to apply the precept. The executive independence here accorded was really remarkable, in view of prevalent State practice, which hampered that department so greatly, though it is possible that the rude experience of some of

---

[1] "Their mutual and general welfare." Articles, III.

[2] "The security of their liberties." Articles, III. In securing "to ourselves and our posterity," the "perpetual" intent of the Union is maintained as before.

[3] A real Federal judiciary had been wanting under the old system.

[4] In special allusion, apparently, to the Shays insurrection and other State disturbances, which induced the convention of 1787.

those young sovereignties had already bred a general discontent with the tyrannous tendencies of the Legislature. "The accumulation of all powers, legislative, executive, and judiciary, in the same hands," says the "Federalist," in that momentous canvass of 1788, "whether of one, a few, or many, and whether hereditary, self-appointed, or elective, may be justly pronounced the very definition of a tyranny."[1] But the accumulation of Federal power under the Confederation had been contemptible enough; and we still find the line of division sometimes indefinitely drawn, so that the Legislature, by formulating action, retains the advantage.[2]

Article I., which defined and set forth the legislative power of the United States, was, however, the foremost and the longest in the whole new compact; and here, with a reforming spirit which by this time pervaded the whole Union, the convention of 1787 transformed the single Congress into a body consisting of two chambers, a Senate and a House of Representatives. By a compromise most admirable the spirited contest between larger and smaller States over a basis of representation was so settled that the new Senate symbolized the equality of States, as in Congress heretofore, while the new House of Representatives was based upon population of the Union as apportioned under a census to be taken every ten years. Senators were to be chosen by the legislatures of the respective States, just as delegates to the Continental Congress had usually been; while members of the House were to be elected "by the people of the several States." Under a further com-

---

[1] Federalist, No. 47. This paper styles Montesquieu "the oracle, if not the author," of the precept of separated powers.

[2] "Legislative power deals mainly with the future; executive with the present; while judicial power is retrospective." Cooley's Elements, 42.

promise — obsolete in effect since the final abolition
of slavery — poll representation under the census was
to be modified by an allowance of three-fifths in each
State for such persons as were held in bondage.[1] As
against existing State and Confederate practice,
which favored annual elections, members of the
House were to be chosen every second year, while
those of the Senate were to serve six years, a considerable term which approached in length the nominal
septenary of the British House of Commons. No
constraint upon re-elections to Congress, as under
the old articles, was imposed for the future.[2]

That peculiar feature of choosing to the House
which left the actual qualification of electors (or
voters) in each State to depend upon the State rule
for electors to its own "most numerous branch" of
the Legislature, has already been noticed.[3] Throughout the Union this rule tends steadily towards full
manhood suffrage regardless of property; though
with reasonable exceptions of crime or pauperism,
and in a very few States of illiteracy besides, — exceptions which our latest Federal amendments declare
shall operate no denial to vote on account of race,
color, or previous condition of servitude.[4] As to
requisite qualifications of those chosen to either
House of Congress, a liberal advance upon State
policy was at once made in our Federal instrument;
for no tests were set up but those of a reasonable

---

[1] This was the real intendment of the expression "all other persons," the word "slave" being judiciously kept out of the text. Constitution, I. §§ 2, 3. Under Amendment XIV. § 2 (1866), the rule of
apportionment is restated so as to meet the new condition of national
freedom; "Indians not taxed" being still excluded from the reckoning
as before. See more fully, *post.*

[2] See Article V., page 88.

[3] *Supra,* page 96.

[4] Amendments XIV., XV. (1866–69).

limit of age beyond majority, a length of citizenship varying slightly for the two branches, and residence when elected as an inhabitant of the State in which one was chosen. Religious and property distinctions cease wholly to apply, and no State has the right to impose them in any national candidacy.[1] Nothing, however, in the text of the constitution forbids the choice of all representatives for any State upon a general ticket; and such really was the earlier method of choice in most States and the long-continued prac- tice in certain of them; but by 1872 Congress required uniformity, and the election of members of the House must now be, as State usage prefers, " in districts of contiguous territory." [2]

The times, places, and manner of holding elections for senators and representatives shall be provided in each State (so the constitution declares) by the Legis- lature thereof; but Congress may by law at any time make or alter such regulations, except as to the places of choosing senators.[3] Hence we find further national enactments by way of judicious regulation: elections (once scattered through the calendar year most inconveniently) are to take place uniformly on the Tuesday next after the first Monday of Novem- ber;[4] all votes for representatives in Congress must be by written or printed ballot;[5] and for the election of United States senators by a State legislature the time and mode of choice are definitely prescribed.[6]

[1] See Story, Commentaries, §§ 624–629, Cooley's ed.

[2] Art. I., § 2; Rev. Stat. U. S. § 23. No Federal provision insists that members of the House shall be residents of their several districts.

[3] Const., Art. I., § 4.

[4] Rev. Stat. U. S. § 25.

[5] *Ib.*, § 27.

[6] On the second Tuesday after the meeting and organization of the Legislature which next precedes the expiration of a senatorial term, such Legislature shall proceed to elect; and at least one ballot shall

Vacancies occurring in either branch are specifically provided for.[1]

No longer dependent upon their several States for a precarious recompense, members of Congress were henceforth to be paid out of the treasury of the United States at a rate of remuneration to be ascertained by law.[2] As under the old articles, and in State fundamental law, they were to be privileged from arrest while in attendance on the Legislature or while going and returning, except for treason, felony, or breach of the peace; and freedom of speech and debate was still assured to them.[3] Office-holding under the United States was, as before, pronounced incompatible with a seat in Congress; and appointment to a Federal office created or with emoluments increased during such service in Congress was further to a stated extent forbidden.[4]

The double-house or bicameral feature has proved in Congress as elsewhere of vast advantage to public stability, introducing delay, afterthought, and the opportunity of correction, all the more salutary wher-

be taken daily during the rest of the session until some one, if possible, is chosen. Rev. Stat. U. S. §§ 14–17.

[1] Const., Art. I., §§ 2, 3.

[2] *Ib.*, § 6. Cf. Articles, V., *supra*, page 88. Congress has by law changed from time to time the method and rate of compensation,—sometimes fixing a *per diem*, but latterly establishing a stated salary. Mileage has also been allowed so as to better equalize the common recompense, since travel from their respective homes to the capital varies with membership so widely. Increase of compensation should be prospective, if possible, for constituents have invariably rebuked a Congress which assumed to raise its own pay. At the outset of Federal government, the Senate undertook to assert a superior dignity, claiming higher pay as an incident; but the House resisted all such pretensions and compelled an equal compensation for both branches.

[3] Const., Art. I., § 6, and cf. Articles, V., *supra*.

[4] *Ib.* As to State example on such points, see *supra*, page 56. The venal and insidious influence upon Parliament of a British ministry served as a warning to Americans in those early times.

ever the two branches combine public influence differently; nor can venality gain its ends so readily under such double adjustment. Public bodies always tend strongly to tyrannize and accumulate force; and while friction ought not to be so great as to block business or dishearten great reforms, deferred legislation is better than crude and unwise enactment. Each branch of our American Congress has a rational and not adventitious basis of its own, — a basis which in a certain sense is popular; and were it not for two faults in our present Federal system, the Senate, despite its exasperating defiance sometimes of national opinion, would prove an excellent bulwark for conservatism. These faults are: (1) the too great facility for creating new States by the concurrence in Congress of bare majorities, so that older States, immense in numbers, wealth, and intelligence, become overborne permanently in the Senate by wild and drifting communities at the remote west who seize upon political power, while yet the elements of statehood are raw and unassimilated; (2) the election of all senators by a legislature, which at least is a method of choice quite out of date with a progressive democracy, and has favored in many States an insidious and underhand manipulation.[1] Designedly, and under favoring conditions in full effect besides, the Senate of the United States — far less even now in numbers than the French Senate or English House of Lords, though more readily, perhaps, commanding an attendant majority — is a deliberative body of

[1] While our Federal constitution continues unchanged in this respect, the best recourse of States and the people is — as Illinois has exemplified on two memorable occasions — to project the candidacy of rivals for Senator into the popular canvass which precedes the choice of legislators, and thus pledge the latter in effect as Presidential electors are pledged.

great dignity and stability, and might command at all times the most talented and virtuous of the whole people, if only the State would summon such men; it is rightfully the forum of national eloquence and the palladium of political wisdom. Our House of Representatives, though a much smaller body than the British House of Commons and the French and Italian chambers which correspond to it abroad, proves less the arena of debate than of action, and under the operation of rules lapses into a huge intellectual machine for the achievement of business; and feeling so quickly, moreover, and so constantly, the passing moods of popular opinion, its members, submissive each under compulsion to his own constituency, allow their own independence to be shackled, or else assert it at the sacrifice of a precarious public agency. In this there are doubtless advantages to the people themselves. But the courtesy, quiet, and freedom of the Senate has been contrasted with the turbulence of the House of Representatives ever since both bodies occupied with open doors the same building. And to make the Senate all the more stable by comparison, with an experienced element in its membership inseparable from deliberation, the classified system of rotation already in vogue in certain States [1] was here applied, so that one-third of this Federal chamber, and no more, should vacate their seats for successors every second year, or as each new House of Representatives came into power.[2] On the other hand, the right of popular district constituencies in the States to choose biennially to the House has kept the whole people alert in public vigilance, and capable of holding one branch, at least, of the Federal Legislature directly amenable to their will.

Congress, as thus constituted, was directed to

---

[1] *Supra,* page 54. [2] Const., Art. I., § 3.

assemble at least once in every year; namely, on the first Monday in December, unless they should appoint by law a different day.[1] The House of Representatives were to choose their own Speaker and other officers; but over the Senate the Vice-President of the United States was designated to preside *ex officio*, while the Senate chose their other officers, including a President *pro tempore* for all contingencies of a vacancy. The fundamental distinction has wrought out great divergence in the practice of the two houses; for the Speaker of the House, invested by consent with the patronage of all committee appointments in that popular branch, has become a national personage of vast consequence, over whose choice a closely divided house has fought many a hard battle at its first gathering; but in the permanent Senate, organization is almost automatic, the subordinate places are quietly filled and committees arranged or rearranged as may seem fit to any existing majority of the members, who thus control their own patronage, while the Vice-President of the United States occupies the chair, unable to vote except in an equal division; and the equilibrium of States, each represented by two members, continues for most of the time unimpaired.[2]

Methods of procedure are defined in the constitution by various rules, some of which State instruments had prescribed already; both State and Congressional usage in America being largely derived, however, from the Parliamentary common law of our colonial era, here set forth in considerable detail. Each house was to judge of the elections, returns, and qualifications of its own members; and a majority of each should constitute a quorum to do business, while a smaller number might compel under penalties

[1] Const., Art. I., § 4.   [2] Art. I., §§ 2, 3.

the attendance of absent members.[1] Each house was to determine the rules of its proceedings, punish its members for disorderly behavior, and with a two-thirds concurrence resort, if so disposed, to expulsion.[2] Each house was to keep its appropriate journal, and publish the record from time to time, entering the yeas and nays of members on any question, at the desire of one-fifth of those present. Neither house could adjourn during the session for more than three days without the consent of the other, nor to any other place.[3] All bills for raising revenue were to originate in the House; but the Senate might propose or concur with amendments as on other bills.[4] The method of passing all bills, orders, resolutions, or votes to which a concurrence of the two houses was needful (except on a question of adjournment) involved submission to the President of the United States for his approval: if approving, he signed, and

[1] See similar State provisions, *supra*, page 56. A majority is the usual quorum for business in a deliberative body; but, regarding the practical difficulty of securing regular attendance, a less number is prescribed as sufficient in many assemblages. Thus, in the English House of Lords three lords constitute a quorum, and in the House of Commons (a body of some six hundred members) forty-five may suffice for the despatch of business. Story, Constitution, § 834. That less than a quorum should be empowered to adjourn or to compel attendance is a salutary rule. Under the Articles of Confederation the want of some such power produced great mischief, for attendance was often very dilatory, at the same time that more than a majority of States was requisite for all important transactions.

We have no external tribunal competent for deciding contested elections, such as England now provides.

[2] Censure or expulsion is the usual punishment. Members of the House have sometimes resigned when censured, and then returned to their seats vindicated by a re-election. As to punishing contempt shown by persons who are not members, see 103 U. S. 168.

[3] See State provisions, *supra*, page 56.

[4] *Ib.* The English rule requires all revenue bills to originate in the House of Commons. May, Const. Hist., c. 7. See also debates in Congress on this subject in 1872. And see pages 56, 57.

thus gave the measure its full validity and effect; but if disapproving, he might interpose his veto, which could only be overcome by a two-thirds recorded vote in each branch of Congress. Silent retention of such bill or resolution by the President for ten days without returning it, unless Congress by adjourning had prevented its return, gave to such measure the same effect as his formal approval.[1] In most of these particulars, the text of the constitution is plainly enough expressed, and wherever doubt may arise, our courts incline to leave the Federal Legislature to its own chosen procedure.[2]

In addition to legislative functions, which work out a distinct routine, while based fundamentally upon common English usage, Congress, like many of our State legislatures, and after much the same fashion,[3] is vested with the Parliamentary powers of a high court of impeachment, to whose jurisdiction all civil officers of the United States, not excepting the President himself nor the Vice-President, are answerable. The House, as grand accuser and prosecutor for the people, is invested with sole power to impeach; while the Senate alone, sitting specially upon oath or affirmation, tries the case, renders judgment, and upon concurrence of not less than two-thirds of the members present, may convict the

---

[1] The executive veto is further considered, *post.* As to State and colonial usage in this respect, see *supra*, page 62.

[2] In 144 U. S. 1, the Supreme Court refused to treat a Speaker's new rule of counting a quorum as an unconstitutional one. Acts of Congress enrolled, officially attested by the Speaker and President of the Senate, and deposited in the State Department with the President's signature, are unimpeachable in the courts for alleged verbal errors. 143 U. S. 649. Nor does our judiciary incline to question the discretion of Congress in passing laws and appropriations. 159 U. S. 590; 163 U. S. 427.

[3] *Supra,* page 67.

person impeached, and award the sentence. At the trial of a President of the United States, the Chief Justice, and not the Vice-President, whose interest in the succession is immediate, shall preside. Treason, bribery, "or other high crimes and misdemeanors," furnish cause of impeachment by the House; and while sentence by the Senate cannot extend beyond removal from office and his further disqualification to hold and enjoy any office of honor, trust, or profit under the United States, the convicted party is nevertheless made further liable to prosecution and punishment in the courts of law like any other criminal.[1]

---

[1] Const., Art. I., §§ 2, 3; Art. II., § 4. These impeachment provisions apply only to "civil officers;" for military and naval officers of the United States are subject to summary trial and sentence by court-martial, whether in time of war or peace. 158 U. S. 109. Members of Congress (to accept the ruling of the Senate in 1799, when Blount, a Senator, was impeached) are not "civil officers" in this constitutional sense; and there are sound political reasons why a legislature in one or the other branch should be confined to such punishment of its own members, including expulsion, as the fundamental law elsewhere prescribes. While some States before 1789 (as seen *supra*, page 67) were clear in declaring that an officer might be impeached while out of office, the text of the Federal constitution is not explicit, and an instance occurred under President Grant where, after a Cabinet officer's resignation had been hastily accepted by the Executive, the House desisted from impeachment upon some such scruple; and yet, with the sentence of prospective disqualification recognized in the text of the constitution, a plenary power might perhaps have been inferred. "High crimes and misdemeanors" is rather a vague offence in common-law interpretation, nor perhaps would Congress consider its own impeachable discretion limited by any common-law barrier.

Impeachment by the Legislature has not been found a satisfactory mode of prosecution and punishment in our American practice. It is a cumbersome process, after all, and political bias is very apt to influence the result. The adverse course of State constitutions in this respect will be traced hereafter (Part III., *post*); and as to our still unaltered Federal mode, it has been found, upon a century's test, best adapted to judicial incumbents whose misconduct provokes no clear issue of political partisanship. A few such persons have been quietly convicted and removed from office; but in the case of a Supreme Court judge, obnoxious to the party majority for his politics, impeachment was once deemed too drastic a remedy to prevail by a two-thirds vote; and so, again, with that of a President of the United States.

VI.

FEDERAL CONSTITUTION ANALYZED; FUNDA-
MENTAL POWERS OF CONGRESS.

THE great fundamental powers of the new Union are seen detailed for the most part in the latter part of Article I. and more especially in its eighth section. True philosophical description would perhaps have stated those powers as belonging to the government of the United States, instead of to Congress, as the text puts it. But Congress had hitherto and for nearly fifteen years personified in fact the whole dignity and authority of the Union, and this, more-over, was the epoch when a representative legislature still stood among American States as the peculiar ægis of a Republican people. The drafting of chief Federal powers, as so much to be detracted henceforth from State sovereignty, was the noblest accomplishment of the whole constitution, as it proved for appli-cation the most delicate and difficult. The discussion to which each important phrase has given rise, in courts and the forum of political debate, the defini-tions and re-definitions as between State and Federal authority which have become needful, are familiar to Americans. And here the brief text of enumeration has been inundated by copious commentary and expo-sition. Contests over the constitutional construction of these powers in and out of court have at times bred political parties and agitated the whole country; giants in intellect and eloquence have been the opposing champions, and sovereignty, State and Federal, have fought for the mastery.

As to fundamental powers, in this complex political establishment of ours, some propositions developed from the long discussion may be stated as well established. Powers are sometimes (1) exclusive in the United States; sometimes (2) concurrent in the United States and the several States; and sometimes (3) exclusive in the States, those several depositories of all residuary public influence. Exclusive powers in the State need no enumeration, for they comprise all undelegated functions of government, such, for instance, as divorce and the probate of wills. Of exclusive powers in the United States, import duties and the regulation of foreign commerce serve for example; while among plainly concurrent powers are those of general taxation and borrowing money. But in connection with enumerated powers in our Federal constitution, and for their better confinement, we find enumerated prohibitions which are positively expressed; and these prohibitions may be (1) to the United States alone,[1] though rarely amounting to more than the qualification of some power expressly given; (2) to the States;[2] (3) to both State and United States governments.[3] Of powers which are expressly vested in the United States, and yet not in terms exclusively so, some are permissively exerted by the several States until Congress legislates and Federal supremacy prevails for the time being.[4]

---

[1] *E. g.* As to slave-trade suppression before 1808, taxation on exports, etc. Const., Art. I., § 9.

[2] Art. I., § 10.

[3] Such as bills of attainder, *ex post facto laws*, and the grant of titles of nobility. Art. I., §§ 9, 10.

[4] As in bankrupt and insolvent systems, which States have regulated thus far in our history more constantly than the United States. "It is not the mere existence of national power but its exercise which

Of express prohibitions to the States some are unqualified in language, while some are simply pronounced subject to the consent of Congress.[1] Sundry powers and prohibitions in this constitution have direct relation not to Congress, but rather to some other department of Federal government.[2] As between States severally and the United States, each government, unless collision occurs, is entitled to complete independence and sovereign exercise within its own legitimate sphere of action; but where such mutual exercise provokes collision, it is the Union that should prevail as supreme.[3] For the present exercise of Federal powers a generous interpretation of the constitution with its amendments may fairly be claimed, to the extent of rendering the Union adequate for great emergencies, and equal at all times to the efficient conduct and preservation of its momentous trust on behalf of the whole people; and yet, on the other hand, the Federal government should not by misconstruction of the language used in the great charter whence national authority is derived, nor by unwarranted enlargement of its manifest expression, destroy or even encroach upon the States and their rightful autonomy; since to each State still belong the intimate concerns of all local inhabitants, save as voluntarily surrendered by fundamental consent given under constitutional forms.

Under the Articles of Confederation we see Congress (then the sole embodiment of Federal authority) vested at once and expressly with "sole and exclusive" rights and powers for various purposes, and express prohibitions correspondingly laid upon the

is incompatible with the exercise of the same power by States." Cooley's Elements, 34.

[1] Cf. different clauses in Art. I., § 10.
[2] See President's power of making treaties, etc., Art. II., § 2.
[3] See 139 U. S. 240; 158 U. S. 98.

States.[1] And in the more perfect Union, as was done under the imperfect one, Federal government should, avoiding "the falsehood of extremes," steer safely between disintegration on the one hand and centralization on the other. To this intent, and not for donating by a sweep powers not elsewhere enumerated, does our constitution of 1787 aid all specific authority by the fit supplementary clause that Congress may make all laws which shall be "necessary and proper" for carrying into execution all the powers vested by that instrument in the government of the United States or in any department or officer thereof.[2]

I. The first power specifically given to Congress is that of taxation, as operating upon the whole Union and its inhabitants, and not, as before, upon sovereign States merely, — that power which, if even stingily bestowed before 1787 by the thirteen States themselves, would probably have postponed indefinitely the convention and its new plan of Union.[3] The power here conferred is "to lay and collect taxes, duties, imposts, and excises, to [*i. e.*, in order to] pay the debts and provide for the common defense and general welfare of the United States."[4] We thus observe (1) that the discretionary choice in Congress is large as between the various kinds of taxes; at the same time that an indirect duty laid upon foreign imports has constantly proved the most popular and indispensable source of national revenue, to which excises (the internal indirect tax), and

[1] See Art. VI. Where constitutionally an act of Congress is passed or a treaty effected, this becomes the supreme law of the land.

[2] Art. I., § 8, final clause.

[3] *Supra*, page 94.

[4] Art. I., § 8, first clause.

direct taxation are but secondary.[1] And (2) that all Federal taxation has its proper enumerated objects, and Congress has no unqualified right to impose it. Taxation by Congress, for some avowedly private or extra-constitutional purpose, would be void.[2] All duties, imposts, and excises must be uniform, or so that the same articles shall bear the same rate of taxation throughout the United States, thereby preventing any Congressional preference of one State over another.[3] Furthermore, for lessening the sacrifice required of our original States in permitting this Federal network to be spread over them and surrendering so many sources of their own revenue, the constitution provides that direct taxes shall be apportioned among the States according to the popular basis of numbers adopted for the choice of Representatives.[4] Finally, no tax or duty can be laid

[1] An income tax may be laid on the principle of a direct tax; and so may a tax upon lands or polls. See 158 U. S. 601. Under the immense war pressure of 1813 and 1862–1865, the greatest variety of taxes were imposed by Congress.

[2] To "pay the debts" of the United States constitutionally contracted must always be a chief object of Federal taxation. As to giving "the common defense and general welfare" a plenary and indefinite interpretation there was great controversy in former times, but opinion seems to have settled upon a moderate and confined interpretation of that clause. See Story, c. 14, and Cooley's notes at length. Those phrases are seen to have been used (in doubtless a limited sense) in Articles of Confederation as well as the present instrument. *Supra,* page 90.

[3] Art. I., § 8, first clause; 102 U. S. 123. Diversity of taxation, either as to the amount or species of property, is perfectly consistent with uniformity and equality. 142 U. S. 339.

[4] Art. I., § 2, third clause; an adaptation from the older method of making requisitions. The meaning of "direct taxes" is now consistently explained by the courts as including any income tax levied upon individuals, as well as taxes on polls or real estate. See 158 U. S. 601, explaining 3 Dall. 171 ("carriage tax") and other former cases. This "apportionment" method of taxation has never been of much practical avail, though the offspring of a very important compromise in the convention of 1787.

upon articles exported from any State,[1] so that our customs revenue system is, after all, one-handed for effectiveness. The power to tax involves when unconstrained the power to destroy; and Federal taxation where rightfully applied is sovereign and paramount.[2]

II. The power to borrow money on the credit of the United States[3] is an obvious and indispensable function of sovereignty, which, as concerns our Union, the Articles of Confederation had already recognized.[4] This Federal power to borrow cannot be controlled by the States; no State taxation of national securities is permissible; but States may still borrow at discretion for their own purposes. The borrowing capacity of the Union should properly be confined to the same just limitations of constitutional purpose as the taxing power. Large public borrowing comes usually in special emergencies, while for ordinary needs money is often borrowed by way of anticipating for convenience the regular revenue. All debts contracted by Congress on behalf of the Revolutionary Confederacy were made obligatory upon the United States by the original Articles, with a solemn pledge of the public faith; and similarly

[1] Art. I., § 9, fifth clause. See 92 U. S. 372. This constraint was procured by jealous staple-raising States for their own immunity.

[2] Thus State bank circulation was wiped out by Federal taxation, so as to be replaced by that of national banks. 8 Wall. 533. But States cannot tax conversely. 4 Wheat. 316.

[3] Articles, IX., clauses 5 and 6, which also expressly granted the right to "emit bills of credit," — a power here omitted, but unfortunately not positively forbidden to the Union. Const., Art. IV., § 8, second clause.

[4] Public debts seem sometimes inseparable from modern government. The constant settled aim of this Union has been to get free from debt; but once only, and for a brief time about 1835, was that happy goal reached. Government may borrow money either by issuing long bonds or by temporary loans.

all debts of the United States under the old Confederation were declared equally binding under the constitution.[1]

III. The power to regulate commerce was a national innovation, and one of the grandest gains for consolidating national influence which the Federal constitution proposed. If the petty commercial warfare of thirteen jurisdictions proved intolerable in 1787, what would now be that of forty or more? The want of some supreme power over navigation conjoined with that of levying uniform customs had most hindered the United States from taking rank in Europe as a nation competent to make a commercial treaty, and degraded the Confederacy fatally in the estimation of its own people. This new power was conceded therefore in the convention of 1787 without opposition or even a division.[2] But the meaning and true extent of this power has occasioned constant controversy and litigation ever since our constitution was adopted, and in no respect is the arbitrament of the Supreme Court more delicate. By "commerce," as it is ruled, the constitution means not traffic alone, but navigation in its amplest sense; hence Congress has passed laws from the beginning, such as favor American enrolled and licensed vessels, command respect for our national flag on the high seas, and employ freely the weapons of reciprocity and favor, on the one hand, and on the other, embargo, nonintercourse, and retaliation, in aid of America's commercial relations with the world. The rights of American seamen, moreover, are thus regulated, lighthouses and buoys are erected, the coast surveyed, and (not exclusive altogether of State policy)

[1] Cf. Articles, XII.; Const., Art. VI.
[2] Art. I., § 8, third clause.

quarantine, pilotage and wrecks provided for. Under an exercise of the same power by Congress the importation of an undesired foreign population may be hindered or suppressed.[1]

All such matters relate especially to American commerce with foreign nations, the first branch specified in the grant of power. The second branch comprises commerce "among the several States," whether by land or water. This second specification blends often with the first, applying the same general doctrine. It has led to the important "interstate commerce act" of 1887, which regulates all transportation over the surface of the United States by railway and other carriers which is not limited strictly to a State's own confines.[2] The third specification embraces commerce with Indian tribes; and here a regulating power in Congress harmonizes with the uniform policy of the Union, which places such of the red aborigines as have not become civilized citizens under the full and immediate control and discipline of the general government, whether as subjects fit for treaty relations or as mere wards.[3]

Much of this Federal exercise of power comes, of course, into conflict with State authority; and as the language of our constitution appears ambiguous on the point of Federal exclusiveness, the supreme tribunal of the Union has been forced to define and apply the rule of constitutional intent in many perplex-

[1] See among other Supreme Court decisions relating to foreign commerce, 13 How. 515; 9 Wheat. 1; 7 How. 238; 91 U. S. 275.

[2] This important enactment by Congress, including the establishment of a Federal commission, followed the decision of the Supreme Court in 118 U. S. 557.

[3] Cf. under our Confederacy the confused though not dissimilar expression of Articles, IX., fourth clause. See also Const., Art. I., § 2, third clause, excluding from representation all "Indians not taxed."

ing instances of State and national collision. Wherever genuine conflict thus arises, it is the State that must yield to the supreme and sufficient potency of the Union.[1] Congress, of course, cannot interfere with the commerce which is confined to one State exclusively; the ordinary trade and traffic of a State pursued among its own inhabitants, local buying, selling and exchange, local contract transactions, for the regulation of local travel and communication, are all at the discretion of the individual State. In short, the commerce of a State which Congress may control must be in some sense and at some essential stage of its progress extra-territorial. As to all extra-territorial, interstate, or foreign trade and commerce, however, a State has no right to legislate at all so as practically to interfere with the United States; and wherever the national sovereignty, dignity, and efficiency would be necessarily impaired in consequence, no matter whether the State so intended it or not, such local legislation is an encroachment upon the powers of the Union.[2] Thus, the regulation of commerce on a stream whose navigable waters are exclusively within the limits of a State belongs properly to that State; but where a river, by itself or by uniting with a lake or other connecting waters, forms a continuous highway over which commerce may be directly carried on with other States or with foreign countries, such commerce becomes properly subjected to the regulation of Congress.[3]

The same distinction holds good of analogous land traffic by railway or canal. Where the State of New

---

[1] 139 U. S. 240; 158 U. S. 98.

[2] 138 U. S. 78.

[3] 14 How. 568; 10 Wall. 557. The test of "navigable waters" in the United States is not, as in England, the ebb and flow of the tide, but their navigable capacity. 10 Wall. 557.

York granted to Robert Fulton and his associates, by way of bounty for the valuable invention of the steamboat, an exclusive right to navigate by steam the waters of that State for a series of years, the act was held void as concerned all highways of foreign and interstate commerce.[1] A State may not safely authorize the construction of a bridge across a navigable harbor or river so as to impede foreign and interstate commerce, without some sort of Congressional sanction;[2] and the power of the Federal government to improve navigable waters is exclusive of States, as well as paramount, whenever called into exercise.[3] A State cannot impose tolls, nor fix a tariff for railways, so far as concerns the traffic which passes into the State from outside or through the State into some other State or country.[4] In general it may be said that no State has the right to lay a tax or imposition on interstate or foreign commerce in any form, whether by way of duties levied on the transportation of the subjects of that commerce, or on the receipts derived from that transportation, or on the occupation or business of carrying it on, for the reason that such taxation is a burden on that commerce, and amounts to a meddlesome regulation of it.[5] Indeed, in all matters of consequence within the

[1] 9 Wheat. 1.

[2] 13 How. 518; 18 How. 421; 123 U. S. 288; 125 U. S. 1; 154 U. S. 204.

[3] Congress may create a corporation for erecting such a bridge. 153 U. S. 525.

[4] 118 U. S. 557.

[5] See Fuller, C. J., in 135 U. S. 161; 136 U. S. 104; 147 U. S. 396. Thus, a State cannot levy a special license tax upon peddlers, "drummers," etc., from other States. 153 U. S. 289. But to require all peddlers, etc., to take a license, not discriminating as to those from other States, is not unconstitutional. 156 U. S. 296. And see 141 U. S. 47. Nor is a State debarred from taxing all traffic from one point to another point within the State. 145 U. S. 192. And see 155 U. S.

present Federal power of Congress, its own inaction does not excuse States from transgressing in order to impose regulations of their own; for the only effect of such inaction must be to leave such extra-territorial commerce free and untrammelled, and subject to the unregulated operation of domestic law.[1]

On the other hand, in applying the extremely delicate limitations of this regulating power, States are readily permitted by our Federal judiciary to impose any tax which is in effect a burden upon local internal commerce alone, or even a tax upon commerce coming in from outside, so long as it is a burden equally shared by local commerce, and in no sense a discrimination upon external commerce.[2] And so, too, the regulation of each State's internal police is left to the State with equal exclusiveness so far as the rule operates only internally, even though foreign and interstate commerce may be indirectly affected by it.[3] Many State enactments which justly amount to no more than equal and just police and inspection regulations, stand thus the test of the constitution;[4] and, in fact, that instrument expressly recognizes the right of any State to levy such impost or duty on imports or exports for the

---

688. It is the State discrimination against what goes to or arrives from without its confines, that the court here condemns as repugnant. A State may levy a tax on its own proportion of railroads, telegraphs, etc., which operate in other States.   141 U. S. 18, 40.

[1] 91 U. S. 275; 120 U. S. 489.

[2] 141 U. S. 18, 40; 163 U. S. 1; 155 U. S. 688.   But taxation upon external traffic alone is void.   *Supra*, page 124, 141 U. S. 47.   There are some very nice distinctions in the later decisions.   See 142 U. S. 217.

[3] A State may require returns to be filed.   153 U. S. 446.   And see 154 U. S. 362; 162 U. S. 565.

[4] 9 Wall. 41; 93 U. S. 99; 136 U. S. 313; 163 U. S. 299; 16 Wall. 36.   But nominal inspection acts (as, *e. g.*, for slaughtered meats) which apply only to such articles as come from without are void as a discrimination against external commerce.   138 U. S. 78.   An oleomargarine State statute is an inspection regulation.   155 U. S. 461.

execution of its own inspection laws as may be absolutely necessary.[1] Competent State regulations have been made concerning liquor traffic, so as to embrace imported merchandise whose bulk has been broken, but not whole packages as they arrive.[2] There are valid State laws of long standing, applicable to pilotage and quarantine in local harbors, which Congress has not, as probably it might, seen fit to supersede; valid State regulations of local fisheries also and the plying of a local carrier trade.[3] In general every State establishes, controls, regulates, and improves its own highways, whether of land or water traffic; besides allowing ferries to be established, railroads constructed, and bridges built after a considerable discretion; and yet, where the interests to be immediately affected are not local, but may prove directly injurious to other States or to a foreign country as a continuous highway beyond the State, the assent of Congress is always desirable if not indispensable, since otherwise the United States might interpose its superior regulation and control.[4]

An important restriction upon the power of Congress to regulate foreign and interstate commerce, as well as upon the power to tax, is found in the express provision that "no preference shall be given by any regulation of commerce or revenue to the ports of one State over those of another; nor shall

[1] Art. I., § 10, second clause. This clause has reference to foreign commerce only. 114 U. S. 622; 8 Wall. 123.

[2] 5 Wall. 462.

[3] 12 How. 299; 2 Wall. 450; 118 U. S. 455. But such statutes must not discriminate against other States. 118 U. S. 90. As to State fisheries, see 152 U. S. 133.

[4] *Supra*, page 122; 102 U. S. 691; 124 U. S. 465; 154 U. S. 204. The line of Supreme Court decisions on this whole important subject, not always distinctly traceable by a layman, need not be here defined more closely. The professional reader may consult at greater length, Story, Comm., ch. 15, with latest notes by Cooley and others.

vessels bound to or from one State be obliged to enter, clear, or pay duties in another."[1] The jealous heed in 1787 that no State should derive substantial advantage over another nor receive special favor under the reformed Federal government explains this clause sufficiently.

IV. National uniformity (1) in naturalization, and (2) on the subject of bankruptcies, is the object proposed by the next power detailed in the present section; and the corresponding discretion vested in Congress is ample.[2] But only in the former respect has that discretion been amply exerted; and in the convention which framed our instrument the latter grant of power appears to have been an after-thought. Under the earlier Confederacy, States retained sole power to naturalize, and complications resulted which obviously needed reform.[3] Seizing at once and occupying this new province of Federal authority, Congress has practically excluded the States from its exercise, ever since the constitution went into effect; while at the same time the law recognizes as still existing on the part of our people a certain citizenship as to the State demanding State allegiance, subordinate, however, to citizenship of the United States and national allegiance, which continue paramount and supreme.[4] The naturalization laws of Congress, with their peculiar bearing upon the admission of foreigners to a full American status, have varied somewhat with the changing policy of the majority in power;[5] but a moderate term of residence within

---

[1] Art. I., § 9, sixth clause. And see 18 How. 421.

[2] Const., Art. I., § 8, fourth clause.

[3] For under Articles, IV. free inhabitants of the Union were accorded many interstate rights. See *supra*, page 91.

[4] See 16 Wall. 36.

[5] The present and usual term of residence is five years; and declara-

the United States and of probation after one's declaration of intent, suffices usually to confer all privileges and immunities of a full status such as the Federal constitution at this day doubly warrants and secures.[1] A citizen, in the full legal acceptation of that term, may be said to be a member of the civil state or community entitled to all its privileges;[2] and there is a clear legal distinction in privilege between citizens and resident aliens. In many American States, to be sure, some of those distinctions are by this date largely abolished, in favor, more especially, of such aliens as have by declaring their intention become prospective citizens of the United States.[3] But an alien is judicially considered, from our national point of view, as resident in the United States by sufferance only, where he takes no steps to become a citizen. Congress has full power to expel or exclude all such persons, or to exclude some and admit others, or even to punish those who attempt to violate its enactments.[4]

---

tion of intent is followed in two years by a full admission. U. S. Rev. Stats., §§ 2165–2174. In 1798 the term was raised to fourteen years, but that illiberal extension did not long prevail.

[1] See Const., Art. IV., § 2. "All persons born or naturalized in the United States and subject to the jurisdiction thereof are citizens of the United States and of the State wherein they reside," and no State can abridge such privileges and immunities. *Ib.*, 14th Amendment, § 1.

[2] Cooley, Elements, 79.

[3] Thus the common-law disqualification to hold real estate is largely removed by State provisions, so that aliens may freely hold, convey, and transmit such property. And see Part III., *post.* American native policy in such respects has always been consistent and enlightened. One of the charges made against George III. in the Declaration of Independence was that of endeavoring "to prevent the population of these States" by obstructing the laws for naturalization of foreigners.

[4] 130 U. S. 581; 142 U. S. 651; 149 U. S. 698; 150 U. S. 476 (applied in the case of imported Chinese laborers). Nor need the courts intervene in such a policy; for Congress may confide enforcement of its will to the Executive. All this (which has been but recently decided) seems to justify, as to constitutional legality, the celebrated "alien act" of John Adams's Presidency.

The treaty power of the United States enlarges Federal control of this whole subject in its diplomatic and international bearings.[1]

As for a uniform bankruptcy system throughout the Union, public opinion appears historically to have thus far considered the aggrandizement of a Federal judiciary at the loss of State local tribunals, a disadvantage outweighing its promised advantage for any permanent establishment. In special instances, however, and chiefly for the temporary advantage of desperate debtors whose creditors were scattered among various States, have bankruptcy laws for national and uniform operation been enacted by Congress; nor have such experiments given clear satisfaction.[2] While, therefore, this constitutional power in the Union remains unexercised, States and State courts continue apart their own insolvent systems, and give local preferences to creditors as State legislatures may determine.

V. Federal power is next given to coin money, regulate the value thereof, and of foreign coin, and fix the standard of weights and measures.[3] The latter power has always remained dormant in the Union, because of the popular indisposition to change old customs of traffic; but for the coinage of money the admirable French decimal standard supplanted

---

[1] Under the former Confederacy the United States was forbidden to make treaties of commerce restraining the respective States from "imposing such imposts on foreigners as their own people are subjected to." What is called "head-money" may now be imposed by the United States alone as a tax upon immigration. 112 U. S. 580.

[2] Cf. United States bankruptcy acts, 1800, 1841, and 1867. Persevering efforts have been latterly made to induce Congress to establish a permanent national bankruptcy system, but hitherto success has not followed.

[3] Const., Art. I., § 8, fifth clause.

British pounds, shillings, and pence, in earlier days of the old Confederacy. Our American "dollar" mode of reckoning, by this time perfected in practice, is the best that ever a nation could invent; and exact science the world over gains gradual familiarity with a like convenient standard for weights and measures. Under Articles of Confederation the United States derived originally the sole and exclusive authority of fixing a standard in both respects; but States were not forbidden to coin money, nor was heed given to regulating foreign coinage.[1] An absolute prohibition of coinage or bills of credit to the States confirmed the Federal power in this new grant of 1787;[2] and States were forbidden moreover by that later instrument to make anything but gold and silver coin a tender in payment of debts.[3]

Here let us add that as a result of the rulings of our supreme tribunal since the Civil War, Congress and the United States are to be deemed under no such constitutional constraint as the States with regard to coinage and a currency. The ills of irredeemable paper money which sovereign fiat invests with the deceptive potency of a legal tender for debts were so widely felt in the old Revolutionary age, both in continental and State currency, that the present constitutional prohibition resulted in 1787, — universal, one would have thought, so far as American experience had supplied an argument. And such appears to have been the prevalent belief down to our Civil War; "bills of credit" having, nevertheless, the restricted sense of a currency intended to

---

[1] Articles, IX., fourth clause. "The sole and exclusive right and power of regulating the alloy and value of coin struck by their own authority, or by that of the respective States; fixing the standard of weights and measures throughout the United States."

[2] Const., Art. I., § 10.

[3] *Ib.*

circulate fully as money, and emanating directly from the sovereign as its responsible source and creator.[1] But under the tremendous stress of conflict, and while the Union was in imminent peril, Congress, by the Act of February, 1862, and later statutes, authorized the issue of notes amounting to four hundred million dollars, as a currency to be issued on the credit of the United States for general circulation, and with the inherent quality of a legal tender for private debts. After the bloody strife had ended, and the Union, vindicated in its national supremacy, sought to recuperate its financial strength, the Supreme Court of the United States sustained, not without a struggle, the full legality of a national paper tender currency for peace or war; concluding at length that the express prohibition of bills of credit and a non-metallic currency to the several States carried no implied prohibition to the United States, and, in short, that Congress was unrestrained in its constitutional discretion upon the whole subject of a national currency standard, whether for making paper money, or gold and silver coin, or coin of either metal alone, a legal tender.[2]

The constitutionality of a national bank, a doctrine which the Supreme Court has constantly maintained

[1] Where a State creates a bank which issues notes on its own credit, there is no such prohibition, though the State should own all the stock. 13 How. 12; 11 Pet. 311; 1 Schoul. Pers. Prop., § 349.

[2] For these decisions, which many sound statesmen must deplore in the sweeping force of their latest judicial utterance, see 110 U. S. 421; also 12 Wall. (1871), overruling 8 Wall. 603 (1870); 1 Schoul. Pers. Prop. § 345, etc. The "greenback" or paper-money craze which made about the time of those decisions an exciting issue in national politics, was succeeded years later by a new agitation in favor of silver mono-metallism as against the world's gold standard. The Presidential election of 1896 seems to have decided the issue unfavorably to those who desire to lower the money standard of the Union by legitimizing a cheaper substitute.

in this and other connections, is another issue over which American parties have contended at different epochs of our national existence.[1]

The next enumerated power, to provide punishment for counterfeiting the securities and current coin of the United States, is an added constitutional grant which flows readily from the preceding one.[2]

VI. The power to establish post-offices and post-roads was novel only in respect to the latter; for the post-office, as conducted on a continental footing, originated under the King in colonial times, and Articles of Confederation had simply sanctioned and continued a "sole and exclusive right and power " in the Union, recognized long before as of great general utility.[3] An establishment dating back to ancient history and ancient nations, as one for sovereign convenience, proves in our modern times an institution conducted equally for popular benefit, though still under sovereign direction. Concerning that power newly added to establish post-roads, the "Federalist," in 1788, described it deprecatingly as "harmless," and "perhaps productive of great conveniency," when judiciously managed.[4] Considering the customs and character of mail transportation when our constitution

---

[1] See 1 Schoul. Pers. Prop., § 350; 4 Wheat. 316. Instead of the single corporate bank with State branches, that odious institution of our government in former days, we now have local banks brought within the scope of a national system and subjected to a prudent national supervision.

[2] Const., Art. I., § 8, sixth clause. States are allowed, in furtherance of the national power over the coinage, to punish such crimes in their own tribunals. See further as to judiciary, *post*, ix.

[3] "Establishing and regulating post-offices from one State to another, throughout the United States, and exacting such postage on the papers passing through the same as may be requisite to defray the expenses of the said office." Articles, IX., fourth clause.

[4] Federalist, No. 42.

was adopted, nothing more was probably meant here than to empower Congress to designate what local roads should be mail routes with an appropriate right of way; but no such narrow construction is in this day favored; and during the present century many have argued from this clause a comprehensive power in Congress to make, establish, and repair independent national highways, and even to buy up and control at discretion all railway and telegraph systems throughout the country on behalf of the Union.[1] The power to establish post-offices doubtless includes everything which may be essential to a complete postal system under Federal control and management, including the power to protect and carry all mails without local hindrance or obstruction.[2]

VII. The power to grant patents and copyrights. " To promote the progress of science and useful arts " is the announced purpose of this next grant to Congress; and the announced method is "by securing for limited times to authors and inventors the exclusive right to their respective rights and discoveries."[3] But an exclusive right to registered trade-marks is not comprehended within this power of Congress to

[1] See 158 U. S. 564. Interstate commerce and other stated powers are cited in furtherance of this authority. Practical difficulties arise, however, under our constitutional and complex system of government when such projects are put in practice. The great "national road" which Congress began constructing with enthusiasm in the era following the War of 1812 cost about $6,670,000; but doubts were presently raised as to whether Federal power existed for collecting tolls or assessing local taxes for keeping the grand highway in repair, and finally the whole stupendous undertaking was abandoned, and the road was donated to the several States in which the various sections lay.

[2] 158 U. S. 564. Lottery or other immoral matter may be excluded from the mails at Congressional discretion. 96 U. S. 727; 143 U. S. 110, 207.

[3] Const., Art. I., § 8, eighth clause.

legislate for individual monopoly.[1] The utility of
some national system of patent and copyright protection is not questioned, and much of the marvellous
development of America in authorship and invention,
adding immensely to the wealth and dignity of the
whole people, is due to its stimulating influence.
The mother country had educated America to such a
system; but the whole subject prior to 1787 was left
when independence was declared to separate State
policy and regulation. Popular institutions, it is
true, do not greatly favor the idea of monopolies to
individuals for their private benefit, nor has public
sentiment in the United States yielded readily our
cheap reprints of foreign books in favor of international copyright protection,[2] such as treaty and
reciprocal legislation now secure. An effort failed in
the Convention of 1787 to enlarge the scope of the
present clause so as to permit of special national
rewards and immunities to persons engaged in agriculture, manufactures, and commerce. But as concerns domestic patents and copyrights throughout the
United States alone, the power here conferred upon
the Union is ample and effectual as well as popular,
nor has Congress hesitated to take and keep control
of the subject. It is wholly discretionary with that
body to make general or special grants or extensions,
to either authors or inventors, in this connection.[3]

[1] 100 U. S. 82. See 111 U. S. 53.

[2] See Act, March 3, 1891, c. 565; 8 Pet. 591.

[3] See at length 1 Schoul. Pers. Prop., §§ 518–541. As a subject of
judicial exposition the law of Patents and Copyrights is interesting
and fruitful. Under our present acts of Congress patents for inventions (based upon novelty and utility) are regularly granted for the
term of seventeen years. U. S. Rev. Stats., §§ 4883–4936. Copyrights
are limited to twenty-eight years, with the further right of extension
in specified instances for fourteen years. States may regulate as an
exercise of police power the use of patented articles, but they cannot
semble restrict the sale of patent rights. See 97 U. S. 501.

VIII. Passing over the Federal power to constitute tribunals inferior to the Supreme Court, — a topic to be considered in a later connection,[1] — we come to that of defining and punishing "piracies and felonies committed on the high seas and offenses against the law of nations."[2] This, too, has its appropriate root in a Federal judicial establishment, vested with full admiralty jurisdiction; but the grant itself is a corollary of those vast powers of war, foreign relations, and ocean commerce and navigation which we at length find fully committed to the Union by the present instrument. Criminal jurisdiction of the United States harmonizes with Federal responsibility on the high seas; and by "high seas" is meant not the ocean only, but all tide-waters along the coast below low-water mark.[3] Piracy is a well-understood offence, by the law of nations, corresponding with robbery on land, which also is forcible and not seldom accompanied by murder or personal violence. By felony is meant at common law a foul crime, more heinous than a misdemeanor; and the power of Congress to define as well as punish piracy, felony, and offences against the law of nations, confers unquestionably a flexible discretion over all infamous crimes whatever, when perpetrated not on land but the high seas.[4]

[1] Const., Art. I., § 8, ninth clause. See Judiciary, *post*, ix.

[2] Const., Art. I., § 8, tenth clause.

[3] 5 Wheat. 76, 184. There is *divisum imperium*, as between the Union and individual States, over the coast between high and low-water mark. As to a guano island, see 137 U. S. 202.

[4] A crime on the high seas committed upon a foreign ship by a foreign subject is not within the jurisdiction of the United States. 3 Wheat. 610.

Articles of Confederation (IX., first clause) gave Congress the power of "appointing courts for the trial of piracies and felonies committed on the high seas;" but as no clear and efficient judiciary for the Union was ordained by those Articles, the grant was of little practical gain.

IX. "To declare war, grant letters of marque and reprisal, and make rules concerning captures on land and water," is the next power enumerated in order.[1] And here in unreserved and unambiguous terms was that vast obligation finally placed upon the Union which it had exercised by common consent on behalf of the States and the whole people from the very first initiation of hostile resistance to Great Britain. This war power is rounded out fully in the five clauses which follow.[2] War with Great Britain, we should remark, was hardly a war in the international sense, but rather the gradual enlargement of rebellion into a revolution. But Articles of Confederation, recognizing the permanent necessity of union for measures offensive or defensive, gave to the United States, as grand representative in all foreign relations, "the sole and exclusive power" in Congress assembled "of determining on peace and war," except so far as States might engage single-handed in war under specific emergencies.[3] So, too, Congress was invested by those Articles with sole and exclusive power of granting letters of marque and reprisal in times of peace,[4] a hostile proceeding nearly tantamount to beginning war, — as also of making, after a feeble fashion, its own general rules concerning captures on

---

[1] Const., Art. I., § 8, eleventh clause.   See corresponding prohibition on States, § 10, third clause, *post*, page 155.

[2] Const., Art. I., § 8, twelfth through sixteenth clauses, to be considered in due order.

[3] Articles, IX., excepting VI.   That exception resembled in the main that of our present Const., Art. I., § 10.

[4] Articles, IX., first clause. Under the Confederation, States might, under Congressional regulation, grant letters of marque and reprisal against the public enemy in time of war (Articles, VI., fifth clause); but that right was wholly taken away by the present constitution. (Const., Art. I., § 10.)   Under the Confederation, a State might, if infested by pirates, fit out vessels of war against them for the occasion, or at least until Congress should determine otherwise. Articles, VI., fifth clause.

land or water.[1] The later constitution allows Congress to declare war or grant letters of marque and reprisal by the simple majority of a quorum or by two-thirds over a Presidential veto, after the usual course of legislation; but under the earlier Confederation no such hostile step could be taken, without the affirmative consent in Congress of nine out of the thirteen State delegations.[2] On the other hand, the power of our Confederate Congress embraced clearly the determination of both war and peace, while that of the Congress of our constitution is in expression confined to war alone, since the full treaty-making power is lodged by the latter instrument (which makes no mention of declaring peace at all) with that new branch of government, the Executive, subject to a two-thirds ratification in the Senate.[3] Such, indeed, is executive discretion, as ordained in 1787 for war and diplomatic dealings, that the initiation or prosecution of foreign war becomes a sort of co-ordinate trust to which the concurrence of President and Congress is essential for preventing public disaster and disgrace. As imposing a salutary check upon precipitate folly and unrighteousness in either branch of government, this is perhaps of real national advantage. For if President and Congress are at issue upon the desirableness of immediate war with any foreign power, each may thwart the other unless public sentiment irresistibly forces a joint decision.

[1] There was no potent Federal judiciary under the Confederation; yet Congress was permitted in express terms, more verbose than in our present constitution, to establish rules for deciding "what captures on land and water shall be legal," and in what manner prizes taken by land or naval forces in the service of the United States should be divided; and had also power for "establishing courts for receiving and determining finally appeals in all cases of captures." Articles, IX., first clause.

[2] *Supra*, page 88.

[3] Const., Art. II., § 2.

In Great Britain, the Crown has the exclusive power to declare war; and usually the earlier practice of nations has regarded the determination of war or peace, like the prosecution of hostile or pacific foreign intercourse, an executive function. Such is not American precedent; though beginning with entire Congressional sovereignty in things national, our people transferred a large share of that sovereignty to the Executive, when other departments of government were added to the Legislature. President Polk in 1846, and President Lincoln in 1861, gave proof that though the power to declare formal hostilities may reside in Congress and the legislative branch, the opportunity to lead up to war is incidental rather to executive policy. President Madison, in 1812, yielded perhaps to the passionate eagerness of young leaders in Congress by sanctioning the declaration of a second war against Great Britain, after having first exhausted all honorable means of adjustment with that country. But in all instances hitherto a President of the United States has initiated war measures, and his message to Congress recommending hostilities has preceded the concurrent action of that body and roused the popular passion. Despatch and secrecy, no less than open energy, are found ingredients in the successful conduct of a war, and only an executive can manage and negotiate in detail, or be clearly cognizant of the real drift of foreign relations. Congress holds the purse-strings, to be sure, and is capable of regulating considerably by favorable or unfavorable legislation. Congress may even by impeachment install the next Executive in succession; but it is the President after all who rightfully expends the money, selects all subordinates, directs military operations, and arranges a settlement. Concurrence of Executive and Congress is therefore indispensable in war measures, sooner or later, to save from disaster.

War is said to be "that state in which a nation prosecutes its right by force;"[1] a definition fair enough if we further allow that one or another of two belligerents is likely to be in the wrong, while the only arbitrament of right is violence with a mutual appeal to God and mankind to witness and aid the vindication. War, or at least a state of hostilities, may practically exist in advance of its declaration and announcement by Congress and legislative provision, through invasion of some foreign power, or because of armed insurrection on a scale which menaces the safety of the Union, whereupon the President as commander-in-chief of the army and navy may at once recognize and repel as befits the emergency.[2] When war exists, this government possesses and may exercise all those vast, extreme, and often despotic powers that any belligerent sovereignty wields under the rules of war currently recognized among civilized nations; among which are powers to acquire territory either by conquest or treaty, to seize and confiscate an enemy's property on sea or land, to create military commissions, and to establish provisional military governments and provisional courts in each conquered jurisdiction.[3] But where the State civil courts are discharging their usual functions, and are capable of enforcing the usual authority, the government of this Union cannot, as

[1] 2 Black. 635, 666.

[2] 2 Black. 635, 668. Congress and the President in declaring the Mexican War in 1846 put it artfully as already existing by the act of Mexico. In 1861 the President pursued his chosen course in dealing with armed rebellion at the south for months before Congress could convene and legalize hostilities. In 1798 Congress authorized partial hostilities against France.

[3] 9 Wall. 129.

to its own civil inhabitants who dwell outside the area of active warlike operations, displace them by courts-martial.[1]

As for making and declaring peace, the power, as already observed, pertains no longer to Congress, but is lodged for negotiation and conclusion in the President. But every treaty with a foreign government requires the concurrence of two-thirds of our Senate;[2] and the House of Representatives has sometimes claimed, not without reason, that if a money appropriation or the relinquishment of public territory should be involved in any treaty to end or prevent war, its own practical concurrence by a majority should not be ignored.[3]

X. The next power stated, "to raise and support armies," is in direct furtherance of the war power conferred in the preceding clause. More than this, the Federal power to raise and support armies is not only indispensable to foreign war or the suppression of domestic insurrection, but a needful precaution for preserving peace at all times. "Join or die" was the motto of the Revolution, not for those times alone; and the league or combination of force under union and united direction has been fundamental in all military operations on this continent from the first era of colonial settlement.[4] But under Articles of Confederation and throughout the conduct of our war for independence, the Union was much hampered by the restrictions which State jealousy had placed. The Continental Congress raised its continental army; not immediately, however, but by making

---

[1] 4 Wall. 2.   [2] Const., Art II., § 2.

[3] Fortunately the United States has waged no war thus far which ended in the relinquishment of public territory or the payment of an indemnity to the adversary.

[4] See New England Confederation, *supra*, page 73.

requisitions on the various States from time to time for their several quotas, and this only by the vote of nine States in that body.[1] For past experience had given these rebellious colonists great dread of a standing army. Under our constitution we have by usage (1) the regular army raised and maintained by and for the Union, but small in numbers when on a peace footing; (2) in great emergencies of war or insurrection, State volunteers, with quotas still assigned by the President, where the States recruit and organize, making State pride a thrilling incentive to patriotism.[2] In either case the troops are sworn into the service of the United States for active duty, and serve accordingly under the terms of their enlistment, though the regimental officers of State volunteers are commissioned by the State, much the same as in the days of the Confederacy.[3] Congress may in times of danger empower a draft upon the able-bodied men of the Union when volunteering fails.[4] But the main reliance of the Union for peace, and the lesser outbreaks of war or rebellion, must be, as hitherto, its own regular army, immediately responsible, kept in constant training and discipline, officered throughout by the Federal Executive, and under direction of the war department stationed in detachments to guard our national frontiers and territories, garrison the forts, and as a military police protect the public property and reservations at all needful points.

Fitly environed for political leadership in North

[1] Articles, VII., IX., fifth clause.

[2] State volunteers with State quotas were much relied upon in 1812 and 1861.

[3] See *supra*, pages 90, 91.

[4] Men were drafted for the Civil War in 1863–1864. A draft was seriously proposed in 1814, but peace came suddenly, and the occasion passed.

America, relieved from all heavy anxieties of the European balance of power, and easily first among nations of the new world, the United States has fortunately required thus far but a small standing army for ordinary times. And to guard against the possible abuses of a permanent establishment, our present constitution expressly limits all army appropriations to the term of two years.[1] In a rare instance or two the House of Representatives has thus exerted its control of the military purse to check dangerous tendencies.[2]

XI. "To provide and maintain a navy" is the next and associated power.[3] Not only for active war, for the defence of ports and harbors and operations on navigable waters conjointly with our land forces, but for the constant protection of the ocean highways and the safeguard of American commerce, and, moreover, as an imposing means of gaining confidence and respect for the American name and flag in distant ports, the navy of the United States was broadly founded. In Revolutionary times some establishment of the sort existed; but Confederate authority was so hemmed in by State emulation in this respect that except for privateering, very little prowess by water redounded to the glory of the Union.[4]

---

[1] Const., Art. I., § 8, twelfth clause.

[2] As in 1856, when military force had been used to coerce the free settlers in Kansas Territory. 5 Schoul. United States, 348. This stoppage of supplies was an old expedient of the British House of Commons.

[3] Const., Art. I. § 8, thirteenth clause.

[4] The Union was authorized "to build and equip a navy," and to appoint "all the officers of the naval forces." Articles, IX., fourth and fifth clauses. The assent of nine States was needful, however, for agreeing upon the naval vessels to be built, or the naval forces to be raised, or for the appointment of a naval commander-in-chief. Articles, IX., sixth clause.

Army and navy were forces recognized together for the Confederate prosecution of war, yet as States might equip their own navies in war times for their own commerce, concentration was not easy; [1] and, furthermore, whether for war or peace, the usefulness of a Federal navy was quite limited. The convention of 1787 readily agreed to enlarge the existing Federal power; but objection was made in some of the State conventions that ratified. Under this constitution, the valor of our infant navy in conflicts with the Barbary Pirate States and during the War of 1812 exalted it to a proud renown which has never since been tarnished. Yet a naval establishment is always costly, and in the long intervals of peace shipbuilding changes its methods, and expensive hulks decay and become worthless. It has been the constant rule of our more perfect Union to maintain simply a regular navy manned and officered for regular service, but in great emergencies volunteer officers have been added to the list of those in regular rank. [2]

Congress may farther "make rules for the government and regulation of the land and naval forces;" [3] a power by way of supplement to the two last enumerated. Though not specified in the original draft of our constitution, the convention of 1787 readily admitted the power as incidental and explanatory. Such rules must not be inconsistent with a President's due authority as commander-in-chief of the army and navy. [4] Congress has by law forbidden such former

[1] The real prohibition of State navies was for times of peace, and then only so as to limit each State to such a number of war vessels as Congress should deem necessary for the State defense or trade. Articles, VI., fourth clause.

[2] Enlistments are thus far voluntary. Probably a fair and impartial draft for the navy might be ordered whenever necessary; but the former English mode of impressments was never permitted.

[3] Const., Art. I., § 8, fourteenth clause.

[4] See Executive, *post.*

cruelties as flogging in the navy; yet for the most part, and subject to occasional enactments of this sort, the discipline and regulation of both army and navy belong to the President, acting through the respective Secretaries of War and the Navy. All crimes committed in strict military jurisdictions by land, or on board naval vessels, are punished exclusively by the United States, and usually as to men in service, by military or naval courts-martial.[1]

XII. "To provide for calling forth the militia to execute the laws of the Union, suppress insurrections, and repel invasions" is the next comprehensive power given for the self-maintenance of the Union by physical force. Reliance mainly upon a trained and well-regulated militia, composed of the mass of civil inhabitants as volunteers primarily and not conscripts, in preference to any standing army of professional soldiers, has been fundamental in the States of free America as with those British-born ancestors who twice dethroned the Stuarts.[2] Articles of Confederation plainly recognize such a principle;[3] nor was the constitution of 1787 deemed satisfactory to the people until made quite explicit in upholding that doctrine.[4] The constitutional object of calling out the militia is seen to be not for offensive war, but for instant

[1] *Supra,* page 113. So far as Union authority might actually extend in such matters, the Articles of Confederation expressly empowered "the United States in Congress assembled" to make rules for the government and regulation of its land and naval forces, and directing their operations. Articles, IX., fourth clause.

[2] See *supra,* page 33.

[3] While the several States are to maintain no body of forces in time of peace except for garrisoning the local forts, "every State shall always keep up a well-regulated and disciplined militia, sufficiently armed and accoutred," besides a good supply of military stores. Articles, VI., fourth clause.

[4] See Amendments II. and III. (1789).

defence against sudden danger from without, and still more readily for putting down internal outbreaks. It is in the latter sense, and when civil authorities and the courts were found powerless or remiss in maintaining order and national obedience within State limits, that both in 1794 and 1861 a President of the Union called out the militia of other States for a few months to enter the disaffected region in arms, assigning to each State its proper quota, and primarily confiding in State executives to put the local troops in motion. And it is noticeable that in each instance a regular United States army was less available for quelling disturbances; also that Congress was not in actual session, and prompt executive action became needful under existing laws in advance of particular legislation for raising and enlisting troops on a long term. Regulars have served alone in some other outbreaks, like that of the Mormons of Utah Territory in 1857; but the power thus inherent in the Union dispenses with a large regular army for ordinary times while enabling the Union to fulfil its fundamental guaranty of orderly Republican government.[1]

Congress may also "provide for organizing, arming, and disciplining the militia, and for governing such part of them as may be employed in the service of the United States, reserving to the States respectively the appointment of the officers, and the authority of training the militia according to the discipline prescribed by Congress."[2] States felt considerable alarm over the power vested in the Federal government by this and the preceding clause. They feared that the Union would weaken each local militia for

[1] See "guaranty clause," Art. IV., § 4. Congress under the Confederation was notoriously deficient in power to summon the State militia, as the Shays Rebellion manifested.

[2] Const., Art. I., § 8, sixteenth clause.

strengthening the regular army; and hence the reservation here asserted, as well as the jealous amendments of 1789.[1]   Congress has not been much disposed thus far to prescribe for the militia of the States a national uniform "discipline," as here permitted, still less to encroach upon the important reserved right of each State to appoint officers and attend to the training.   But by this era it is well settled that when local bodies of militia (though State forces originally) are called into the service of the United States, they are subject not only to the orders of the President as commander-in-chief, but also to those of any officer of superior rank who may under the President's authority be placed over them and their State commissioned officers.   So, too, it is settled that when Congress by statute gives the President discretionary authority to call forth the militia in time of peril, this makes him the exclusive judge as to when or whether the exigency has arisen, so that neither State executives nor militia officers can question it.[2]

XIII.   Exclusive Federal jurisdiction over Federal places is the object of the last specific power here enumerated on behalf of Congress.[3]   Federal jurisdiction is for the most part superposed upon that of States, except for the territorial domain of the Union, where statehood is as yet inchoate.   But Federal government requires for its proper exercise some local reservations over which its own peculiar jurisdiction and authority shall be sole and indisputable.   Hence,

[1] Amendments II. and III. The States have always assurance against centralized despotism in their representation in Congress.

[2] 7 How. 1; 5 Wheat. 1.   During the War of 1812, and again in 1861, some State governors who were unwilling to furnish quotas took issue with the President on this point of an emergency.

[3] Const., Art. I., § 8, seventeenth clause.

first of all, a district (not exceeding ten miles square) was to be set off as "the seat of the Government of the United States." For 1783 had not been forgotten, when a handful of mutineers from the continental army forced Congress from Philadelphia, the State Executive appearing reluctant to interpose his protection.[1] For the first few years of our constitutional government New York and then Philadelphia served as temporary headquarters; but as soon as a district had been chosen and improved for a Federal capital, the permanent abode on the Potomac became a place of exclusive Federal legislation and authority, and as time showed, the essential citadel and rallying-point of loyalty to the Union.[2] A like exclusive authority is vested in Congress "over all places purchased by the consent of the Legislature of the State in which the same shall be, for the erection of forts, magazines, arsenals, dockyards, and other needful buildings."[3]

[1] 1 Schoul. United States, 22. See 146 U. S. 325.

[2] Of the Federal district on both sides of the Potomac, ceded by the respective States of Maryland and Virginia for a seat of government, and first occupied by Congress in 1800, that portion south of the Potomac was retroceded later to Virginia. Washington City now fairly occupies the whole area remaining. Here the jurisdiction of Congress is full and unlimited, both in a political and municipal sense. 147 U. S. 282.

[3] Const., Art. I., § 8, seventeenth clause. To preserve the forts and other property belonging to the whole Union, located on land which had been purchased and paid for by the general government, was the plain issue which first in 1861 united the loyal population under President Lincoln against States in rebellion.

VII.

FEDERAL CONSTITUTION ANALYZED; FEDERAL AND STATE PROHIBITIONS.

BEFORE passing from the Federal Legislature, our constitution enumerates sundry prohibitions which limit or are correlative with the important powers just recited. These prohibitions are either (1) upon Congress and the United States; or (2) upon the individual States.

I. Prohibitions upon Congress and the United States occupy the ninth section of Article I. Next after a constraint long since obsolete, but honored by Congress while it lasted,[1] comes a prohibition against suspending the writ of *habeas corpus*, "unless when in cases of rebellion or invasion the public safety may require it."[2] *Habeas corpus* (recognized but not originating under Charles II. in the celebrated Act of 1679) was a right highly prized by English free-men from the earliest known era of the common law; and under such a writ, issued as of individual right by the common-law courts, a person who had been deprived of liberty was discharged from illegal imprisonment. Maxims denouncing all arbitrary sus-

---

[1] Const., Art. I., § 9, first clause. This constraint upon slave-trade prohibition until 1808 (which Art. V. undertakes to rivet closer) admitted expressly of legislative discouragement in the meantime by a poll tax on the importation of slaves; yet Congress forbore from all such action. When the time (1808) arrived, foreign slave-trade was formally abolished. Here, as elsewhere, our constitution wisely avoids using the word "slave" at all. Cf. page 105.

[2] Const., Art. I., § 9, second clause.

pension of laws are to be found both in the English bill of rights and the Revolutionary declarations of our old thirteen States,[1] suspension by a monarch being chiefly obnoxious. Here we perceive arbitrary suspension equally forbidden in sense to Executive and Congress; though not without qualification, as above expressed, for great exigencies of public danger from within or without, when suspension has always been customary to a certain extent. If one complaining of unlawful arrest and detention sues out this writ, he is brought at once into court for a summary examination of the facts, and the court orders his discharge if the detention was unlawful. Suspension of the writ of *habeas corpus*, it has well been said, is a suspension of Magna Charta, and nothing but a great national emergency can justify or excuse it.[2] The power to suspend in permitted exigencies vests naturally in Congress; but whether the President may not himself suspend at discretion in a constitutional emergency, especially if Congress be not in session and time presses, is open to fair discussion.[3]

"No bill of attainder or *ex post facto* law shall be passed " is a prohibition to the Union borrowed from earlier State constitutions and State declarations of right;[4] and this prohibition is expressly extended to

---

[1] *Supra*, page 32.

[2] May, Const. Hist., ch. 11 ; Cooley, Elements, 300.

[3] During the Civil War, 1861–65, President Lincoln claimed and repeatedly exercised the right to suspend the writ of *habeas corpus;* and this against judicial protest, although the Supreme Court seems never to have passed directly upon that question. Taney, 246. Even after Congress had partially defined the limits of existing suspension he suspended to a greater extent, on the claim of a still greater exigency which the conflict had developed. It would appear that over any jurisdiction which an executive has properly declared subject to martial law, the writ of *habeas corpus* is as a rule properly suspended. 7 How. 1.

[4] Const., Art. I., § 9, third clause. *Supra*, pages 36–38, Maryland.

all States by a later section.[1] The clause has exclusive reference to a sort of criminal legislation justly abhorrent to liberty, at the same time that retrospective civil enactments by a legislature are impolitic and deserve disfavor.[2] Among tax prohibitions upon Congress already mentioned as qualifying the Federal power,[3] we find the rule firmly buttressed that every capitation or other direct tax must be laid proportionately to a census.[4] "No money," proceeds the text, "shall be drawn from the Treasury but in consequence of appropriations made by law; and a regular statement and account of the receipts and expenditures of all public money shall be published from time to time."[5] And finally, to confirm the equal rights of mankind upon which the American government and American society were henceforth to rest, "no title of nobility shall be granted by the United States; and no person holding any office of profit or trust under them shall, without the consent of Congress, accept of any present, emolument, office, or title of any kind whatever, from any king, prince, or foreign State."[6] States are forbidden, besides, to grant any title of nobility.[7]

[1] Const., Art. I., § 10, first clause.

[2] See 107 U. S. 221 ; 152 U. S. 377. Any law is *ex post facto* which is enacted after the offence was committed, and which in relation to the crime or its consequences alters the situation of the accused to his disadvantage.

[3] Const., Art. I., § 10, fourth, fifth, and sixth clauses; *supra,* page 119.

[4] *Ib.,* fourth clause. This reiteration comes in special connection with the first clause. See Article V.

[5] *Ib.,* seventh clause. This admirable and business-like provision explains its own purpose.

[6] Const., Art. I., § 9, eighth clause. States, as Maryland, for instance, are seen to have formulated already for themselves the prohibi-

[7] Const., Art. I., § 10, first clause. And see prohibition to States in Articles of Confederation.

II. The prohibitions upon the States respectively are found in section 10, which follows. Some of these prohibitions we have already incidentally mentioned; as against granting letters of marque and reprisal, coining money, emitting bills of credit, and making anything but gold and silver coin a tender in payment of debts;[1] constraints, which were now laid chiefly for giving the Union its free and untrammelled scope on such national subjects. As for bills of attainder, *ex post facto* laws, or the grant of titles of nobility, always undesirable, express prohibition was enjoined equally upon States and the Federal Union.[2] And to all this was added, that "no State shall enter into any treaty, alliance, or confederation," a prohibition absolute;[3] a similar prohibition having applied to States under the Articles of Confederation, though less concisely and with the soothing qualification that Congress might interpose its consent and give validity.[4] The omission of all such qualification from the new and more peremptory instrument is quite significant.[5]

---

tion of "titles of nobility." *Supra*, page 38. But this clause comes more directly from the broadly expressed Articles of Confederation. "Nor shall any person holding any office of profit or trust under the United States, or any of them, accept of any present, emolument, office, or title of any kind whatever from any king, prince, or foreign State; nor shall the United States in Congress assembled, or any of them, grant any title of nobility." Articles, VI., first clause.

[1] *Supra,* pages 130, 136.

[2] *Supra,* page 149. Const., Art. I., § 10, first clause.

[3] Const., Art. I., § 10, first clause.

[4] "No State, without the consent of the United States, in Congress assembled, shall send any embassy to, or receive any embassy from, or enter into any conference, agreement, alliance, or treaty with any king, prince, or State." Articles, VI., first clause. "No two or more States shall enter into any treaty, confederation, or alliance whatever between them without the consent of the United States, in Congress assembled, specifying accurately the purposes for which the same is to be entered into, and how long it shall continue." Articles, VI., second clause.

[5] The legal bearing of these phrases and their historical alteration,

Another phrase in this tenth section ordains in effect that no State shall pass any law "impairing the obligation of contracts."[1] The underlying principle of such an interdict is salutary, and no good reason can be given for forbidding States alone, and not the Federal government as well, except the possible inadvertence of the Philadelphia convention.[2] Madison, the best-informed member of that body, stigmatizes bills of attainder, *ex post facto* laws, and laws which impair the obligation of contracts as equally "contrary to the first principles of the social compact and to every principle of sound legislation."[3] And he further intimates, that while States had already begun prohibiting the two former in their constitutions, and while all three prohibitions were within the true spirit and scope of State fundaments, a disposition for sudden changes and interference with contracts had become so manifest of late in some State legislatures that it was high time to interpose this new constitutional bulwark on behalf of private rights.[4] A century has justified the wisdom of that action, for few clauses in the present constitution have given rise to more constant and vehement controversy in the courts. To the long array of judicial precedents on this topic the reader must turn for details; a leading case in the Supreme Court on final appeal, that of Dartmouth College, establishing long ago that this prohibition applies to the State Legislature itself, under any unqualified grant or charter by

against the attempted Southern Confederacy of 1861, appears never to have received the attention it deserved for constitutional discussion.

[1] Const., Art. I., § 10, first clause.

[2] So, too, as to "bills of credit," noted *supra*. See 110 U. S. 633.

[3] Federalist, No. 44.

[4] *Ib.* Federalist, No. 7, also alludes to contemporary State laws in violation of private contracts, which amounted to an aggression on the rights of other States whose citizens were injured by them.

the State which amounts in effect to a contract with private individuals.[1] Legal and not moral obligation is here intended; and the obligation of a contract which States must not impair is the legal means of enforcing that contract, and of compelling the parties to fulfil it. Hence, whatever State legislation may lessen the efficacy of these means of enforcement impairs the obligation.[2] But a law which gives validity to what was a void contract does not essentially impair its obligation, unless, at least, other vested rights must suffer in consequence;[3] nor is a State to be thus debarred from forbidding by statute certain kinds of contracts, provided that its enactment be purely prospective in operation.[4]

The two remaining clauses under present consideration leave each constitutional prohibition upon States optional with Congress, as under the old Confederacy. Unless, therefore, Congress consents, no State shall "lay any imposts or duties on imports or exports, except what may be absolutely necessary for executing its inspection laws; and the net produce of all duties and imposts, laid by any State on imports or exports, shall be for the use of the Treasury of the

---

[1] 4 Wheat. 518. Constraints upon local legislation under a State constitution are here material; nor can essential sovereign powers be bargained away by a legislature. For a learned summary of the decisions see Cooley, Elements, 311–327; Story, § 1385, *et seq.* Executory and executed contracts are equally within the protection of this clause of the constitution. But the contract must be a binding one at law and founded upon a legal consideration.

It is State constitutions or legislative acts which this clause constrains, not mere municipal ordinances or judicial decisions. 163 U. S. 273; 146 U. S. 258.

[2] 16 Wall. 314.

[3] Story, § 1385. As to exempting privileged persons from taxation, see 146 U. S. 279.

[4] As, for instance, forbidding private contracts to be hereafter made payable specifically in gold. A State may suitably reserve the right to repeal or alter any charter it grants. 151 U. S. 556.

United States; and all such laws shall be subject to the revision and control of the Congress." Thus the permissive levy of customs duties to a State, henceforth peculiarly a national resource, was, even for an extreme State purpose, closely strained.[1] Nor was a State without-the consent of Congress to lay henceforth "any duty of tonnage."[2]

Again, no State shall without the consent of Congress enter into any agreement or compact with another State.[3] The lesser dread of such compacts (for under this composite government States may still make compacts), in comparison with any confederation or alliance,[4] supplies the permissive assent of the Union through Congress. Compacts and agreements, those of contiguous States, for instance, upon some mutual use of common waters or a spanning bridge, or in disputed boundaries, have frequently been made since, as before, the adoption of this constitution and the consent of Congress removes all national impediment. That consent need not be express unless in some extreme case affecting Federal sovereignty, but is inferable from indirect Federal legislation which imports a sanction.[5] This same qualified prohibition upon the States applies to the less probable contingency of some State agreement or compact with a foreign power, as distinct from a treaty.[6]

Finally, no State shall, without the consent of Congress, "keep troops or ships of war in time of

[1] Const., Art. I., § 10, second clause. Cf. *supra*, page 118.

[2] *Ib.*, third clause. State interference by its own impost system, with the attempted stipulations of Federal treaties negotiated in Europe, was an evil partly guarded against in Articles of Confederation, VI., third clause.

[3] Const., Art. I., § 10, 3.

[4] Cf. *supra*, page 151.

[5] 11 Wall. 39. See also 148 U. S. 503.

[6] Const., Art. I., § 10, 3.

peace; " nor " engage in war unless actually invaded or in such imminent danger as will not admit of delay." [1] The former prohibition favors one regular army and navy establishment for the whole Union, as since maintained; the reason of the latter, with its contingent exception, is obvious. Rarely in these days of land and submarine telegraph and rapid transit would a State find itself so suddenly in the throes of a foreign war as to be compelled to fight before the Federal government could come to its aid; and should such an emergency ever arise, the special consent of Congress would doubtless be found superfluous. The suggestion of all this came from the more primitive Articles of Confederation. [2]

Besides the distinction among express State prohibitions already noticed — prohibitions which of course bear upon all States alike — we should observe that some of them concern delicate functions of public sovereignty, while others affect rather the private rights of the individual. Other prohibitions ingenuity might add which the nature and practical adjustment of our composite government naturally imply; and as for powers, it would have been needless for the constitution to confer any powers expressly on the States, since, as a recent writer [3] reminds us, they or the people retain all powers not actually taken from them.

[1] Const., Art. I., § 10, 3.

[2] See Articles, VI., 5. No State shall engage in any war without the consent of the United States, in Congress assembled, unless such State be actually invaded by enemies, or shall have received certain advice of Indian invasion, and the danger is too imminent to admit of a delay to consult Congress. And see *ib.* as to a State infested by pirates. As to keeping up State war vessels or a State army in time of peace, see Articles, VI., 4.

[3] Mr. James Bryce, American Commonwealth.

VIII.

FEDERAL CONSTITUTION ANALYZED; THE EXECUTIVE.

THE Chief Executive of this Federal constitution was a new creation. His prototype is seen in the State Governor enlarged and adapted to high intercourse with European kings and potentates, by borrowing from the dignified lustre of Holland and Great Britain. For the President of these United States was to be a ruler, supreme in authority before mankind abroad and at home beyond any single State Executive, guardian of the national flag and resources through peace and war, and fit conductor of our common destinies. All the more disposed was the convention of 1787 to give stability and strength to this new chief magistrate, when the Legislature as finally settled was found to have broadened the old Continental Congress so greatly that a powerful balance became needful; and when, too, it was conceded that the first person to occupy this exalted station would be the safest and worthiest of all administrators, and the peer in his republican simplicity of any monarch of the old world.

The powers lodged, therefore, in the President of the United States by our Federal constitution were vast and energetic, and such as befitted a relation where Congressional encroachment might need a strong constraining power. No duality, no directory, was set up for this Federal department, such as some leading States in their dread of a monarch were then attempting. There was not even a cabinet added in the sense of a controlling ministry.[1] The President was himself the sufficient chief magistrate of the Union, empowered to take confidential or public advice at his will, and to summon or change at pleasure his chief department heads like all other high Federal officials, subject to confirmation by the Senate. A wise Executive will doubtless unify his administration and secure efficient action; but his own supreme discretion is, after all, the rule of action, aside from the constitutional direction of Congress; and Presidents have successfully pursued that rule at times, disregarding Congressional clamor, and removing summarily a department secretary who opposed, while rejecting the collective advice of a cabinet.[2]

Our Chief Executive has his own responsibility to the people, independently as to tests from that of either branch of Congress; and Presidents have remained in office with their chosen chief counsellors while both Houses of Congress surged in opposition. This is very different from that Parliamentary direction of affairs by which ministries are displaced when the Legislature votes in opposition. Representative government by the people is here of another sort. The Presidential term itself is limited to four years, and midway comes the opportunity to strengthen, weaken, or secure him in his policy. Hamilton in

[1] No idea of "cabinet" or "council" deliberation is intimated in this constitution; but only a permission given to the President to "require the opinion in writing" of the principal officer in each executive department upon any subject relating to his own official duties. Const., Art. II., § 2. Our present Cabinet meetings with Cabinet voting originated in a chosen usage of President Washington, which most of his successors have for convenience continued.

[2] *E. g.*, Andrew Jackson in 1831 and "the removal of the deposits." But such a course, when public opinion disapproves and both Houses of Congress resist, must be perilous.

1787 would have preferred the tenure of life or good behavior; Jefferson, a seven years' term, once and for all; but the constitution as framed fixed the moderate term of four years, and put no restraint upon re-eligibility. And popular usage for the first half-century made each President the leading party or non-partisan candidate for re-election a second time, with eight years as the final limit,[1] — a usage much modified since 1840.[2]

A Vice-President is designated, corresponding to the Lieutenant-Governor in some of the old thirteen States, to preside over the smaller Senate or upper branch, and thus maintain the equilibrium of State representation in that body; an officer ordinarily without patronage, but in case of the removal of the President from office, or his death, resignation or permanent inability to discharge its duties, successor to the full power and patronage of Chief Executive for the residue of the term of four years, for which they both were chosen.[3] Congress may by law provide for the vacancy by removal, death, resignation, or inability of both President and Vice-President, and it has done so.[4] The double executive

[1] Jefferson, upon this practical construction, finally favored the constitutional tenure as that of eight potential years with an intermediate appeal to the people.

[2] Const., Art. II., § 1, 1. Usage limiting the tenure to eight years still prevails.

[3] Const., Art. II., § 1. Presidents Harrison, Taylor, Lincoln, and Garfield died while in office, and each was succeeded by a Vice-President for the remainder of the term. At least three Vice-Presidents have died in subordinate station while a President survived. The case of a vacancy in both offices has never yet occurred.

[4] Const., Art. II., § 1. Congress by act of 1886 (24 Stats. 1) so changed its former provision as to make the office devolve upon one of the late Presidential advisers (or "cabinet") constitutionally eligible and previously confirmed by the Senate, in a prescribed order, the Secretary of State taking precedence, and the Secretary of the Treasury following next. Such person holds (agreeably to constitutional

candidacy or double ticket is now established in American favor; but in 1787 the case was different; and in Federal usage this nominee for the second highest office, selected carelessly or to conciliate some floating or adverse element in the party, too often while Vice-President attracts counter influences to the administration in power, so that should accident suddenly promote him, the national policy and patronage might take a new and sinister direction.[1] A Vice-President in his normal and inferior station, with no favors to bestow and no responsibility, has little but his casting vote in the Senate to give him a casual importance.[2]

Our constitutional method of choosing President and Vice-President is not felicitous. Wisely intending that the Executive should derive authority from a source external to Congress, yet strongly indisposed to trust the free choice of the people, the framers of 1787 tried the device of an electoral college, such as Maryland's constitution already employed in another connection.[3] No complacency could have been greater than that with which the convention accepted this solution of a perplexing problem. But political subterfuge has rarely given ultimate satisfaction, and in this instance experience has utterly belied the san-

phrase) until the disability be removed, or until a President shall be chosen at the regular election.

[1] In each instance, thus far, except that of Vice-President Arthur's succession, such has been the historical result.

[2] Vice-President Clinton's casting vote (1811) against the recharter of the United States bank, and that of Vice-President Dallas for the Polk tariff of 1846, furnish rare instances where the incumbent of this second office has made his influence felt. More influence, with the people at least, might accrue if a Vice-President asserted more strenuously in these days his constitutional functions as President of the Senate, independent as the law makes him of senatorial favor.

[3] *Supra,* page 54. Europe had pursued some such method in the choice of the Doge at Venice, and of an emperor in Germany.

guine expectation of circumventing the common voters and Congress together. Each State should appoint its proportionate number of electors[1] in such manner as its legislature might determine; and first of all the State legislatures chose electors directly. But public opinion early in this century asserted its strength; this choice of electors reverted to the people of each State, who usually chose by districts, until, for the better concentration of State influence on the elections, the choice by general State ticket became substituted, all selection of modes still depending upon an arbitrary legislative discretion.[2] But whether chosen by one State method or another, the State electors were confessedly, from the very first, agents only of those who choose them for a particular purpose; and while the recreancy of electors to their pledges may in a close Presidential canvass thwart on any constitutional occasion the will of the voters, the inevitable result of this Federal device has been to make each State electoral college in effect a college of proxies. And thus has evolved that choice of President and Vice-President by the common voters which the constitution meant anxiously to avoid, — a choice not unfairly apportioned and guarded, but clumsily arranged for popular ballot, tardily registered, so to speak, and liable always in any State to tyrannous prevention or mischievous perfidy.[3]

The original scheme, indeed, proved in certain details so defective, that by 1803–1804 it was changed by constitutional amendment. Electoral colleges

[1] Equal to the whole number of its Senators and Representatives in Congress.

[2] See 146 U. S. 1, confirming the clear idea that a State legislature may, at any time, by a change in the law, choose electors as formerly, or require the people to choose them by districts instead of on a general ticket. In South Carolina a legislature chose Presidential electors down to the Civil War.

[3] Const., Art. II., § 1, 2.

were not to choose President and Vice-President separately; but two persons were to be voted for and certified together to Congress, and the person proving to have the greatest aggregate number of votes, if a majority upon the Congressional count, was to be President of the United States, while the second highest became *ipso facto* Vice-President. When parties organized, John Adams, one party chief, was chosen President in 1796, while Jefferson, the other party chief, jostled as Vice-President; next in 1800, when the opposition ticket led, Jefferson and Burr, the party candidates for President and Vice-President, proved equal, so that the selection between them was thrown into a house soon to expire and controlled by their common enemies. Anarchy nearly resulted, for the constitution made no express provision for the contingency of no choice by such a house, and intrigue delayed action. Since the twelfth amendment,[1] electors still meet to vote in their respective States, but they vote in distinct ballots for President and Vice-President; and in case of no majority choice by these colleges, whether of President or Vice-President, the House selects a President from the three highest candidates for the one office, while the Senate chooses a Vice- President from the two highest candidates for the other. Voting in either branch is conducted after a peculiar arrangement for the exigency, and in any case where the House fails thus to choose a President by the 4th of March, the Vice-President (sure to be selected) shall act as President. The opening of State certificates and the electoral count take place in

---

[1] See Amendment XII. (1803–1804) superseding Const., Art. II., § 1, 3. And note the specific details of this amendment. No Senator, Representative, or officer of the United States can be an elector; and electors must not vote for a President and Vice-President, both of whom are inhabitants of their own State. Const., Art. II., § 1.

solemn presence of both branches of Congress with the President of the Senate in the chair.[1] Choice of chief magistrate by the legislature, where no candidate has received a majority vote in the first instance, is a remnant of earlier practice, and a compromise between legislative and popular selection. States long ago discarded that principle for the plurality choice of governor at the polls once and for all; but the Federal constitution still remains unchanged in this respect, and that, too, while vesting such eventual choice in a retiring, perhaps a defeated, Congress, rather than a newly chosen one. Nor does even this amended scheme concede that President and Vice-President are rightfully chosen by the people under any circumstances.

State discretion prevails, we have seen, in the method of choosing the electors of President and Vice-President; but Congress may determine the time of choosing electors and the uniform day on which they shall give their votes.[2] Both religious and property qualifications are ignored for President and Vice-President, a great advance for those early times when the constitution was framed; but no person except a natural-born citizen of the United States[3] is eligible to either office, nor one who has not attained to the age of thirty-five, and been four-

---

[1] The President of the Senate is designated to open the certificates thus publicly, "and the votes shall then be counted." This means, as Federal practice has constantly maintained, that the count is under the direction of the two houses.

[2] Const., Art. II., § 1, 4. Not until 1845, and after that depressing experience of 1844, when the Massachusetts popular vote went to a Whig candidate for President after it was known that his opponent had carried the country, did Congress by law fix a uniform day for choosing electors; namely, as at present, the Tuesday following the first Monday in November.

[3] Or a citizen of the United States when the constitution was adopted. Const., Art. II., § 1, 5.

teen years a resident within the United States.[1] One holding foreign intercourse with the world on behalf of our whole people should be swayed by no native prepossessions but those in favor of the United States and this hemisphere.

The President's salary shall be paid him at stated times, and shall neither be increased nor diminished during the period for which he was elected; and he shall receive no other emolument from the United States, or any of them.[2] Before entering on the execution of his office, he must take a simple oath or affirmation to faithfully execute the office of President of the United States, and to the best of his ability preserve, protect, and defend the constitution;[3] whence the further usage of imposing ceremonies at the capital with an inaugural address and procession, none of which are essential preliminaries to his exercise of official power.[4]

The powers and duties of the President, as defined by the constitution, are broad and ample for efficiency and independence. (1) In domestic administration he is sole commander-in-chief of the Federal army and navy, and also of the militia of the several States whenever called into the actual service of the United States, — a responsibility sufficiently exclusive for initiating, conducting, or preventing war, and for sup-

[1] Const., Art. II., § 1, 5; Amendment XII., as to Vice-President. Diplomatic service abroad, like that of Mr. Buchanan shortly before his elevation to the Presidency, does not disqualify for want of a fourteen years' residence.

[2] Const., Art. II., § 1, 7. This salary, fixed originally at $25,000 per annum, was increased to $50,000 in 1873, under President Grant; the increase not taking effect, however, until the second term began for which he was re-elected.

[3] Const., Art. II., § 1, 8, 9.

[4] Historical precedent lessens the ceremonials of a second term, and dispenses with them altogether where the Vice-President succeeds to a legal vacancy.

pressing rebellion, though it must rest discretionally with Congress to declare formal war, and to vote or withhold men and supplies. Purse and sword are here separated. He controls, moreover, his civil subordinates, and, except in cases of impeachment, he has unconstrained power to grant reprieves and pardons for offenses against the United States.[1]

(2) As to foreign affairs, a concern of momentous national dignity and importance, and often involving secret and delicate complications, the President has properly their sole conduct, subject only to an implied right of Congress to press its peculiar views upon specific points of foreign policy, by joint resolution, obstructive legislation, or otherwise;[2] so that co-operation is desirable in all great matters of policy. It is for the President to receive or refuse reception to ambassadors and other public ministers from abroad,[3] fulfilling all diplomatic relations for this government under the established intercourse of nations, which is essentially executive. He commences at pleasure and conducts all foreign negotiations in public affairs, and makes all treaties. But two-thirds of a Senate quorum must concur and give sanction to each treaty, since otherwise it cannot take effect;[4] and, furthermore, any treaty requiring appropriations or new legislation to carry it into effect ought justly to command a majority support in both houses.[5]

[1] Const., Art. II., § 2, 1. He may pardon a person or a class of persons, before conviction or prosecution as well as later, with no constraint except that rights of property vested by the prosecution cannot be disturbed by him.

[2] See "Forum," March, 1897, for the author's views concerning such discordance.

[3] Const., Art. II., § 3. All this, which belonged to Congress alone under the Confederacy, was felt to require executive management.

[4] Const., Art. II., § 2.

[5] In the Jay treaty debates of 1796 the argument was pressed that

(3) In the appointment of all subordinate officers of the United States the permissive patronage of the President is almost that of a monarch. Army and navy officers he posts and details like any other commander-in-chief, issuing and promulgating through his Secretaries of War and the Navy rules and orders which he is competent to change. As for the vast and growing civil list, nothing but civil-service rules, sanctioned and proclaimed by the President himself, can safely operate to curtail his constitutional right, whether immediately or by indirection, of controlling the whole Federal executive patronage from highest to lowest subordinates by appointing to vacancies, and as appears most probable, by creating them at pleasure.[1] Congress exercises fundamentally but a limited constraint over such patronage. An act of Congress creates the office and fixes its term and recompense; periodical appropriations by Congress are essential to the payment of such recompense. But neither House of Congress nor both houses can assume to appoint to civil or military office; there remains only the "advice and consent" of the Senate essential to a full and effectual appointment to the higher offices. In other words, the President nominates to the Senate, and with a majority consent of that body appoints ambassadors, other public ministers and consuls, judges of the Supreme Court, and all other officers of the United States established by

a treaty once ratified by the Senate becomes obligatory upon the House under the constitution, and binds that body to vote appropriations accordingly. But the issue remained open to discussion; and it is now clear that legislation by Congress after the usual course may repudiate any treaty, subject to the President's veto. 11 Wall. 616. As to the international effect of such a breach, that is another question.

[1] The civil-service rules of the present day, for reform of former abuses under each new party President, are aided by legislation in Congress, but it is the President who here, as in the army and navy service, supplies his voluntary enforcement. But see page 170.

law, whose appointments are not otherwise provided for in the constitution.[1] But Congress may (as they have done frequently) vest by law the appointment of such inferior officers as they think proper in the President alone, in the courts of law, or in the heads of departments. The President has power to fill all vacancies that may happen during the recess of the Senate by granting temporary commissions.[2] He shall commission all the officers of the United States.[3]

(4) With regard to Congress and the regular course of legislation, the President has important functions, chief among which is the qualified veto-power already described,[4] — a power so salutary in practice as to have induced most States to adopt it, with here and there an improvement which the Federal instrument might well adopt in return.[5] The President is to inform Congress from time to time of the state of the Union, and recommend such measures as he shall judge necessary and expedient; whence the established custom of a formal message at the opening of each session, which under the two earliest Presidents was made a grand ceremonial occasion.[6] He may on extraordinary occasions con-

---

[1] The Vice-President, like the President, is chosen by electors; members of either branch of Congress are chosen independently of the Executive; and each house controls its own subordinates.

[2] Const., Art. II., § 2.

[3] *Ib.*, § 3.

[4] *Supra*, page 111.

[5] See Part III., *post.* As (1) in giving the President a stated time after final adjournment in which to approve or disapprove the latest bills; (2) in allowing him to veto items of appropriation bills, instead of having to pass upon the bill as a whole.

[6] Under the administration of Washington and John Adams, the President went in state to Congress to deliver the message orally before the assembled houses; after which each house would consider and frame a formal address in reply, bearing it in procession to the executive mansion with corresponding ceremony. President Jefferson

vene both houses or either of them; and where the two houses disagree with respect to the time of adjournment, he may adjourn them to such time as he shall think proper.[1]

(5) Finally the President shall take care that the laws be faithfully executed;[2] and this includes not alone the enforcement of acts of Congress according to their express terms, but all the protection, national or international, which the nature of our constitutional government implies.[3] Nor can the judiciary directly intervene by mandamus, injunction, or otherwise, to control the Chief Executive in the exercise of his high discretionary functions, — not even upon the allegation that he is enforcing an unconstitutional law.[4] But as to Federal subordinates, and in acts purely ministerial, where nothing is left to official discretion, it has been ruled otherwise.[5] Ministerial and executive duties in such a connection should not be confounded; for the exercise of power to enforce the laws is a purely executive political duty, which no remedy short of impeachment by Congress can rightfully restrain. Congress cannot, however, lawfully increase these executive duties by delegating to the President its own legislative authority.[6]

The Executive Department has on the whole been admirably adjusted, and a supreme incumbent of high

in 1801 substituted the simpler and more convenient method of sending to Congress a written message, to which no formal reply was expected, and such has since continued the uniform practice of government.

[1] Const., Art. II., § 3.

[2] *Ib.*

[3] 135 U. S. 1.

[4] 4 Wall. 475; 6 Wall. 57.

[5] 1 Cranch, 137; 9 Wall. 298; 12 Pet. 524.

[6] 143 U. S. 649. But suspension of reciprocity by the President's authorized proclamation is not open to such objection. *Ib.*

character, wisdom, and good sense cannot fail even in times of peace to make a strong and abiding impression. The very fact that Congress has such power for enacting momentous laws unwisely renders it all the more desirable that the President should have a counteracting influence like some tribune of the people. Another strong bulwark against the tyranny of either Congress or the President, another grand popular reliance, will next appear in the Federal Judiciary, and most of all in the Supreme Court; and the tenure of Federal judges, which alone is fixed for life or good behavior by the constitution, places them in the civil service above the reach of arbitrary removal.

IX.

FEDERAL CONSTITUTION ANALYZED; THE JUDICIARY.

THE want of a distinct and efficient Federal judiciary was felt to be so vital a defect of the old Confederacy that the creation of this third department of government under the Federal scheme of 1787 was readily allowed. Here and there in Articles of Confederation we find a permissive establishment of courts for piracies or captures on the high seas, while Congress itself was made the final tribunal for determining disputes between States over such matters as boundaries.[1] Yet in all this there was found no independent Federal establishment, no sanction for Federal judgments, no explicit means of enforcing upon States or their inhabitants a decision rendered. A judiciary aids in the due execution of powers given to a government, by applying compulsion to refractory individuals; its process should be afforded to all invoking the public standards of right for the adjustment of private controversies; it should interpret laws, treaties, and the constitution so as to give a uniform sense to which all good citizens must submit.

The Federal judiciary established by our constitution of 1787 was made accordingly after the Montesquieu formula, as independent and distinct as either Congress or the Executive. One declared

[1] Confed., Art. IX.

object of the preamble to that constitution was to
"establish justice;" and among the enumerated
powers of Congress "to constitute tribunals inferior
to the Supreme Court."[1] The judiciary article itself
declares expressly that "the judicial power of the
United States shall be vested in one Supreme Court,
and in such inferior courts as the Congress may from
time to time ordain and establish."[2] Thus, while
Congress may model and remodel the lower Federal
tribunals from time to time, as may be deemed expedient, the Supreme Court, which is the head and
crown of the whole system and the Federal tribunal
of last appeal, remains as perpetual in functions, as
intact and independent (except for diminishing or
increasing its membership when vacancies occur[3]) as
Congress itself or the Executive. No law can abolish
or supersede it; no Presidential fiat can change the
incumbents. So complete a separation of a judiciary
from the other two departments of government supplied to our Federal system what few States possessed
thus early.[4] In tenure and method of appointment
this Federal system conformed fairly to the spirit of
1787, but unchanging afterwards, as most State
systems have done, it anchors fast to stable conservatism, as so august a judiciary should. All Federal
judges have been regularly appointed by the President, subject to confirmation by the Senate, and those
of the Supreme Court cannot constitutionally be
appointed otherwise.[5] Their tenure is defined unreservedly as "during good behavior;" and their compensation, which they are entitled to receive "at
stated times," shall not be diminished (though Con-

---

[1] Art. I., § 8.
[2] Art. III., § 1.
[3] Vacancies cannot be compelled except by impeachment.
[4] *Supra*, page 66.
[5] *Supra*, page 165.

gress may increase it) during their continuance in office.[1] A Federal judge may be displaced by due process of impeachment, but the Federal constitution gives no power to remove on the simple address or joint resolution of Congress.[2]

Since Congress may change the inferior Federal courts at will, so may it abolish, and thus incidentally deprive judges of their offices. A premature circuit court establishment was thus swept away in 1801 when Jefferson became President, and politics conquered politics. Soon after the Civil War circuit courts with special judges were re-erected by Congress, and in 1891 was interposed a court of appeals to rank next in order to the permanent Supreme Court. District courts in each State were always the Federal tribunals of first resort. Territorial courts, erected as incidental to general sovereignty over national territory, are not within the strict establishment; and judges of such courts may be appointed for definite terms, and are removable by the President.[3] Nor have the President's military provisional courts any permanent civil character.[4]

Our Federal courts have kept to their own domain, performing no functions except those of a judicial nature, and such as the constitution imposes plainly upon them. They refuse to arbitrate political issues or to participate in executive business; they decline to sit as commissioners or determine questions subject to the consideration and supervision of Congress or of some executive officer.[5] The Supreme Court

---

[1] Const., Art. III., § 1. To induce but not compel voluntary retirement at old age after long and faithful service, acts for pensioning such judges have been passed.

[2] Cf. State organic law, page 67.

[3] 1 Pet. 511 ; 141 U. S. 174.

[4] 9 Wall. 129 ; 13 How. 498.

[5] Cooley, 51 ; 13 How. 40 ; 19 Wall. 107, 655.

would not entertain appeals from the Court of Claims until Congress gave a judicial character to that tribunal by making its money judgments competent.[1] Nor does the organic rule of States like Massachusetts obtain for procuring the Supreme Court's advice as a basis for future executive or legislative action; but its opinions are rendered only in the course of regular litigation.[2]

Not to be too technical in describing here the judicial power which United States courts exercise, we may observe that Federal jurisdiction arises under three different conditions: (1) Because of the subject-matter; as where a case, whether in law or equity, civil or criminal, arises under the Federal constitution, the laws or the treaties of the United States and the interpretation thereof is material to the issue; and besides in all cases of admiralty and maritime jurisdiction arising on the high seas or internal navigable waters, or in interstate commerce, subjects vested in the Federal government.[3] And here, both in interpretation and enforcement, the Federal judiciary is supreme. (2) Because of the parties litigating whom local State process cannot fairly conclude. As in civil cases, regardless of the subject-matter, between citizens of different States; so that in consequence our Federal decisions comprehend to-day a great body of commercial and business law, not strictly binding as precedents otherwise

[1] Cf. 2 Wall. 651, and acts of 1863.

[2] During President Washington's administration, and while the Supreme Court had as yet very little judicial business to transact, an opinion upon the legal bearings of certain matters before the Cabinet was refused by Chief Justice Jay on constitutional grounds. This, however, has not prevented judges nor even the Chief Justice from serving in some special capacity for a public emergency.

[3] Federal jurisdiction here is very broad. 12 How. 443.

upon the courts of individual States, but rendered so as to harmonize as far as possible the contemporaneous law and practice of the States where parties litigant resided. (3) Because of subject-matter and parties combined; and with particular reference to the gravity of State or international disputes which might affect the peace and stability of the whole Union. To this head belongs the exclusive Federal jurisdiction of all cases which affect ambassadors, other public ministers and consuls; of all controversies to which the United States shall be a party; of controversies between two or more States,[1] between a State and citizens of another State,[2] or between citizens of different States; between citizens of the same State claiming lands under grants of different States; and between a State or the citizens thereof and foreign States, citizens or subjects.[3]

In this third and gravest class, or rather in all cases which affect ambassadors, other public ministers and consuls, and those in which a State shall be a party, the Supreme Court takes original and uncontrolled jurisdiction under the constitution. But in all such other cases as we have mentioned, the Supreme Court exercises an appellate jurisdiction merely, both as to law and fact; and this, furthermore, subject to such exceptions and regulations as

[1] As in some question of boundaries or division. 11 Wall. 39.

[2] An early decision against the State of Georgia by the Supreme Court (2 Dall. 419), produced such alarm that the constitution was amended (1794–1798) so as to exclude Federal jurisdiction of any suit in law or equity commenced or prosecuted against one of the United States by citizens of another State, or by citizens or subjects of any foreign State. Amendment XI. But a State may expressly waive such defence. 108 U. S. 436. The principle that a sovereign is not amenable, involuntarily, to the suit of an individual, has no application to a suit by one government against another government. 143 U. S. 621.

[3] Const., Art. III., § 2.

Congress shall make.[1] This appellate jurisdiction comprehends the highest State courts as well as inferior Federal tribunals, wherever a cause of jurisdiction affirmatively appears; in considering State constitutions, for instance, or laws, which involve a question of conflict with the Federal "supreme law of the land."[2] But the Supreme Court imposes cautious conditions upon State supervision. A grievance must be affirmatively shown. The appeal must not be upon an agreed statement, but as the result of honest antagonism; nor will it be entertained on any simple issue of facts, nor where the State tribunal might have decided upon some other ground, but only in law and necessarily.[3] Federal courts are indisposed to take a criminal out of State custody by *habeas corpus;*[4] nor can the mere hardship, impolicy, or injustice of any State law or constitutional provision be alleged as an objection to its validity. Aside from all such appellate jurisdiction, cases are removed from State to Federal inferior courts upon proper jurisdiction shown.[5]

Europeans often wonder that Federal and State courts can work together in upholding so complex and conflicting a jurisdiction; but, as English observers admit, the system of Federal supervision works, and now, after a hundred years of experience, works smoothly.[6] For the fundamental principle in the United States is that the supreme law-making power resides in the people, and that whatever they fundamentally enact binds everywhere; so that, whether

---

[1] Const., Art. III., § 2. The Court of Appeals (1891) now renders final judgment in many cases.

[2] Const., Art. VI.

[3] 143 U. S. 339; 150 U. S. 361; 152 U. S. 355.

[4] 156 U. S. 272.

[5] Cooley, 129; U. S. Rev. Stats. 641, and acts of 1887 and 1888.

[6] 1 Bryce's Commonwealth, 245.

in State or Federal application, that which is unconstitutional transcends the permanently expressed will of the people.[1] Delay and patient deliberation by the highest tribunal over what has been fully argued in a concrete case, not arising until the enactment of disputed validity has been put in force, must go far towards preparing the public mind for accepting an adverse judgment. Public legislation submits thus to our sober second thought, and the Supreme Court is keeper of the national conscience, the guaranty of minority rights, as it ought to be. For, as Burke has so fitly observed, every government ought in some sort to make a balance of its judicial authority, and give security to its justice against its power.[2]

One or two provisions of the Federal constitution concerning judicial procedure may be noted in this connection. The ancient trial by jury, which we have seen our Revolutionary States proclaiming among fundamental rights,[3] is clearly secured in the instrument of 1787, so far as all criminal trials (except in impeachment) are concerned. As to vicinage, always an important incident of this sacred right, lest one might be dragged into distant neighborhoods for arraignment, it is further provided that such trial shall be held in the State where the crime shall have been committed; or if not committed within any State, at such place as Congress may by law have directed.[4] But, this original instrument ignoring the civil trial by jury, one of the earliest

[1] Even the Supreme Court of the United States has in one or more great instances been considered as overruled by the people, acting through political change, and imposing their "higher law."

[2] For more technical details of Federal judicial power, see Cooley's Elements, 111–147 ; Story, § 1577, latest notes.

[3] *Supra*, page 32.

[4] Const., Art. III., § 2, 3.

amendments preserved that right in all common-law suits, where the value in controversy should exceed twenty dollars; forbidding to United States courts the re-examination of any fact tried by a jury otherwise than according to the rules of common law.[1] Other amendments insisted upon the presentment or indictment of a grand jury, defined the vicinage more closely as that of the "State and district," wherein the crime shall have been committed, such district having been previously ascertained by law, and added important safeguards to the accused which will be noticed later.[2]

Treason against the United States is most liberally defined, repudiating the odious doctrines of constructive treason once prevalent in the mother country. Such treason, it is stated, shall consist only in levying war against the United States, or in adhering to their enemies, giving them aid and comfort.[3] Equally liberal as to the proof of such treason, against the mockery of English State trials in the preceding century, our constitution declares that conviction of treason must be on the testimony of at least two witnesses to the same overt act, or on confession in open court. And once more setting an example in punishment for the offence, which England followed long after, it repudiates the old common law which cruelly visited the offence upon children and children's children. Congress may declare the personal punishment, but no attainder of treason shall work corruption of blood or forfeiture beyond the life of the

---

[1] Amendment VII.

[2] Amendments V., VI.

[3] Const., Art. III., § 3. This provision is taken from the old Statute of Treasons, 25 Edw. III., which during the English civil war was plainly violated in Sidney's trial. See 4 Bl. Com. 75. A mere conspiracy by force is held not sufficient, without an actual levying of war. 4 Cr. 75.

person attainted.[1] There is no common-law jurisdiction of crimes in the United States, but Federal
crimes must be defined by Congress, subject to the
further written law of the Federal constitution.[2]

[1] See 9 Wall. 339, as to a case under our own civil war of 1861–65;
also English statute 3 & 4 William IV., c. 106. With hanging, drawing, and quartering, the old English punishment of a traitor's person
was barbarous enough. Hanging has been the appropriate modern
punishment; but under Act July 17, 1862, Congress gives the court
discretion to sentence by fine and imprisonment instead. The criminal
offence of treason, though heinous enough, is one of the most difficult
to calmly adjudicate or discern in any body politic. Under our own
composite system there is allegiance due to the United States, and allegiance due to the State, the former being now acknowledged paramount; and one might render himself liable to State prosecution for
some local traitorous offence to which these Federal clauses would not
per se apply.

[2] 8 Pet. 591; 125 U. S. 555.

X.

FEDERAL CONSTITUTION ANALYZED; INTER-STATE AND TERRITORIAL RELATIONS.

ARTICLE IV. of the constitution is largely devoted to interstate provisions which affect private rights and the States themselves. Much of it is an expansion from the earlier text of the Articles of Confederation.

That full faith and credit shall be given in each State to the public acts, records, and judicial proceedings of every other State is admitted to be an essential rule of comity, and particularly so in a co-ordinate Union like ours. The constitutional phrase is almost literally borrowed from Articles of Confederation,[1] with the fitting supplement that Congress may by general laws prescribe the manner and effect of such proof.[2]

The citizens of each State shall be entitled to all privileges and immunities of citizens in the several States.[3] This, too, is a paraphrase only less literal from the Articles of Confederation, which recognized such a comity under the earlier Union, "the better to secure and perpetuate mutual friendship and inter-

[1] Articles, IV.

[2] Const., Art. IV., § 1. Inquiry into the jurisdiction of another State court over parties and subject-matter is not precluded. 138 U. S. 439; and see 141 U. S. 657.

[3] Const., Art. IV., § 2. See also Amendments XIV., XV., enlarging the constitutional effect of this clause.

course among the people," and for equal "privileges of trade and commerce." A sort of mutual State citizenship, with reciprocal privileges and immunities, as in passing through, residing, pursuing business and enjoying liberty and property, is here under the Federal system of 1787 effectively secured. It is further declared in the same connection — once more paraphrasing Articles of Confederation [1] — that fugitives from justice, charged in any State with treason, felony, or other crime, shall be extradited on executive demand, wherever found, to be removed to the State having jurisdiction of the crime.[2] This and another clause, now happily obsolete since the extinction of American slavery,[3] complete the comity provisions which affect our interstate relations more immediately for the individual.[4]

Next as concerns States immediately in their public relations, provision is first made for extending the original Union by the prospective admission of new States. Under the Confederacy a similar extension had been authorized, embracing Canada, with possibly other British-American colonies;[5] but the Continental Congress went beyond such literal authority when title to the vast region of the Mississippi was

[1] Articles, IV. The original article is drawn out rather loosely, and so as to avoid controversy under a confederated system which left all naturalization to coequal States.

[2] Const., Art. IV., § 2. This is a State executive duty which Federal courts cannot compel. 24 How. 66. Local retaliation generally corrects any mischief.

[3] Const., Art. IV., § 2, 3, known historically as the "fugitive slave clause," though purposely avoiding the word "slave;" and requiring State extradition of persons "held to service or labor in one State" and escaping to another. That clause was in expression borrowed from the early New England Articles of Confederation, page 73.

[4] See for technical details, Cooley, 195–201.

[5] Articles, XI.

clearly quitclaimed by leading States to the Union.[1]
Under our present constitution the discretion to
admit new States is lodged unreservedly in Congress
like ordinary legislation; and ever since the Louisiana
purchase of 1803, that discretion, which had clearly
comprised the original territorial area of the United
States westward to the Mississippi, has been repeatedly extended in practice so as to comprehend without constitutional change whatever adjacent foreign
territory on this continent between the two oceans
may be acquired at any time by war or peaceful
purchase. But both as to policy and constitutional
right, so vast and unreserved a power to Congress,
or to the treaty-making department, without limit of
popular referendum, constitutional amendment, or
unusual constraint whatever, to change the whole
scope and character of this Union by the incorporation of foreign soil and foreign populations or races,
is worth challenging on every new occasion; for it is
a power pregnant with the gravest dangers, such as
debauched and finally destroyed the Roman empire.
This confederated system of ours recognizes no permanent political condition anywhere but that of coequal States. And as for admitting new States
formed within existing and recognized domestic territory, the unconstrained power of Congress which
the framers of 1787 intended to bestow is ample
enough to be dreaded.[2] For no State once admitted
to the Union can ever be deprived of its equal

[1] *Supra,* page 85. In the Ordinance of 1787, which our first Congress of 1789 ratified, it had been agreed that new States not exceeding five might be formed from the northwest territory and received
into the Union. Articles of Confederation were in their final form
assented to by all the States but Maryland, before this territorial cession was made at all; hence the insufficient authority which those
Articles had recited.

[2] Const., Art. V.

suffrage in the Senate without its consent.[1] New
States, therefore, may be constitutionally admitted
by Congress into this Union; but no new State shall
be formed or erected within the jurisdiction of any
other State, nor any State be formed by the junction
of two or more States or parts of States, without the
consent of the legislatures of the States as well as of
Congress itself.[1]

Further power is given Congress in this section
"to dispose of and make all needful rules and regulations respecting the territory or other property of
the United States."[2] By 1787 a vast domain west
of the Appalachian range to the Mississippi became
the undisputed "property" of the whole Union, not
under the Articles of Confederation, but rather as a
virtual concession gained when ratifying them from
the older States. Those sovereign cessions from
Virginia and other States were not without special
conditions regarding the future status of American
slavery, which Congress later recognized.[3] Territories most ample, and stretching from ocean to ocean,
have since come into the Union, as the sole fruit of
national purchase and conquest; yet territorial the-
ories have been occasionally broached since 1787, as
though the Union were incompetent to regulate freely
its own soil for settlement and republican education.[4]

---

[1] Const., Art. IV., § 3. The consent of Congress need not be di-
rectly given if fairly inferable from its course of action. 11 Wall. 39.
As might well be surmised, no States have ever been consolidated by
junction on such terms as above; while in repeated instances — *e. g.*,
Maine from Massachusetts and West Virginia from Virginia — old
States have been constitutionally subdivided by triple consent.

[2] Const., Art. IV., § 3.

[3] "Nothing in this constitution shall be so construed as to prejudice
any claims of the United States or of any particular State." *Ib.*
This mollifying clause appears to have been inserted with express reference to territorial jurisdiction.

[4] "Squatter sovereignty" and other such ingenious doctrines served,

Over this general subject, however, as also in the admission of new States, since territories ripen naturally into statehood, Congress exercises a plenary constitutional discretion, which ought to respect the general welfare and wishes; [1] for the constitution was made for States and not for territories, and the territorial condition is in a proper sense only temporary and preparatory.

Finally, it is imposed on the United States as a duty (1) to guaranty to every State a republican government; (2) to protect it against invasion; and (3) to protect it upon due application against domestic violence. [2] The first or guaranty clause, whose perversion in meaning was attempted during the reconstruction era which followed close upon our civil war, presupposes a State government of a republican form already in existence; and while permitting States to change their local organic law, imposes only the restriction that republican shall never be

however, a temporary political purpose, which vanished with the final disappearance of slavery.

[1] The plenary power of Congress over the territories combines that of a local proprietor of land and of a regulator of local government. Doubtless that power is subject by implication to all fundamental limitations in favor of individual rights which are now formulated in the Federal constitution and its amendments. 136 U. S. 1. Methods of territorial government for the Union date back to 1784 and to the Continental Congress, which laid broadly the foundations of the present public land system, clearly recognizing at once the solemn trust of nurturing and educating the new settlements into loyal, self-governing and orderly States. Two forms of territorial government have been from time to time established by Congress as circumstances required: (1) an executive Federal government, somewhat arbitrary, under the immediate appointment of President and Senate; (2) a Federal government partly popular, which recognizes a territorial legislature and local representation; and this is the usual kind. Congress may and usually does impose certain fundamental conditions upon the admission of each new State.

[2] Const., Art. IV., § 4.

exchanged for anti-republican constitutions.[1] By republican government we should understand a government whose representatives are chosen by the people; and while no czar or hierarch would be thus allowable, legitimate republican government may take a wide variety of forms. Moreover, a State republican government once established may demand the Federal assistance because of the hostile action of some invading foreign power, or by reason of some Revolutionary domestic uprising against the constituted authority; and in either case, the intervention of the Federal government to protect the people in their existing government would be proper.[2] In other extreme instances, as where despotism is installed and organized under forms of law,[3] or there has never been a State government, or that which once existed has been displaced in the course of rebellion and attempted secession and lapses into domestic disorder, some just enabling action by the United States may be advisable or even necessary. As for the protection of an existing State against invasion, such is the natural incident of Federal constitutional government for occasions of emergency, as was State self-protection under the previous Confederation. Protection, however, against domestic violence is so delicate an exercise of Federal power, and so liable to abuse and sensitive collision, that it is expressly guarded by requiring the State Legislature, or (if it cannot be convened) the State Executive, to invoke such protection. This expression, however, does not cover the whole ground, for by the present age the network of interstate commer-

[1] Federalist, Nos. 21 and 43.
[2] 7 How. 1; 7 Wall. 700. The Dorr Rebellion in Rhode Island, 1841–42, furnished an instance in point.
[3] As in the Mormon territorial outbreak of 1857.

cial and other common interests has overspread the area of the United States so completely that where State authorities are themselves remiss in putting down local disorder or in calling for Federal aid, the President, supported by Congress, is justified in marching troops to the scene and intervening for the welfare of the whole people and the public concerns.[1]

[1] As in the Illinois disturbances of 1894. By virtue of interstate commerce and carrying the mails, "the government of the United States has jurisdiction over every foot of soil within its territory and acts directly upon each citizen." Debs, *Re*, 158 U. S. 564.

XI.

FEDERAL CONSTITUTION ANALYZED; ADOPTION, POWER TO AMEND, AND FEDERAL SUPREMACY.

CONSONANT to the spirit of that earlier age, both adoption and future amendment of this Federal constitution were deemed sufficiently sanctioned by representatives of the people without a direct reference to the polls. This, indeed, is the essence of republican government as distinguished from democracy, whose fiat is a plebiscitum.[1] Articles of Confederation had been the product of a general Congress submitted to the thirteen State legislatures for confirmation. The constitution of 1787, on the other hand, framed by the Philadelphia convention, went to conventions of the different States for final sanction after a permissive reference by the Continental Congress; a closer reference than before to the will of the people (since conventions are of spontaneous popular origin), yet an incomplete one. The prevalent disregard of immediate popular expression was more plainly manifest in the provisions made for future constitutional amendment, which left the convention or legislative mode a mere matter of option by Congress, still ignoring all direct vote by the people. No inadvertence gave such shape to these provisions as to make amendment difficult; for that Philadelphia convention would never have met, the scheme of

[1] *Supra,* page 47, for earlier State practice.

Confederation could not have been superseded at all at this period, had one specific amendment passed all thirteen legislatures instead of twelve, — had organic change been possible without a universal State assent. Even now, by a sort of revolutionary process, this new constitution of 1787 was to be sufficiently established by the ratification of nine out of thirteen States,[1] and any still reluctant might remain outside.

Two specific modes of future amendment we find set forth: one, the simpler and the only one in fact which a century's experience has applied, is by specific amendment proposed to the several States by two-thirds of both Houses of Congress; the other, by a convention which Congress shall call on the application of the legislatures of two-thirds of the States. In either case Congress takes the direct initiative, though in the latter case its duty becomes formal and imperative, and a mere majority may suffice. In neither instance, however, is the President's approval needed, as though to legislation, but Congress performs a special function which the constitution executes.[2] For calling a new convention the remote initiative vests in scattered but co-operating State legislatures; but as those several legislatures must apply to Congress, no spontaneous Federal convention like that of 1787 is ever again to be legally called, seeking Federal approval afterwards. For the ratification of a new Federal constitution or of prospective amendments, three-fourths of all the States must give assent either by local legislature or convention, as Congress may propose in advance.[3] If such a thing be organically possible as an irrepeal-

[1] Const., Art. VII.   See page 95.

[2] 3 Dall. 378.

[3] Const., Art. V.   Congress has thus far chosen to propose ratification by State legislature.   The mode is not optional with States, nor is reference made at all to a direct popular expression.

able ordinance of man, which we may well doubt, this constitution has in one important particular ruled out all change.[1]

Students of our American system have criticised that rigid Federal conservatism which compelled so large a fraction as three-fourths of all the States to give any proposed change validity. Yet there are sound reasons for making radical Federal amendment more difficult than in the less spacious area of individual States. In fact, a popular impulse that moves two-thirds or even a large majority not sectional of the States to ratify easily widens its propelling force to the greater fraction; and so was it with the adoption of the instrument of 1787 itself. The greater difficulty is rather in initiating change at all, in overcoming the first inertia, in getting Congress by a two-thirds vote to propose something remedial, where, most of all, one or the other branch must be shorn of privileges should the change take effect. A hundred years and more have produced only fifteen articles of amendment, of which the first ten, proposed by the very first Congress, really rounded out the original instrument under a tacit compromise with ratifying States, while the last three were the exaction of a bloody civil strife. The two intermediate amendments, affecting Congressional privilege in no respect, aimed to rectify minor constitutional defects which Federal procedure had disclosed. When public opinion becomes well aroused, the gates of constitutional amendment fly wide open and entrance gives easy exit; but it is the concrete that arouses, and the public mind, dormant through generations of prophetic foreboding, awakes only when sufferings are actual.

[1] Const., Art. V., close of article; (1) as to slave-trade privileges, obsolete since 1808; (2) as permanently guaranteeing the equality of States in the Senate.

The sixth article contains three clauses. The first proclaims all debts and engagements of the old Confederation equally binding upon the new Union.[1] The second, or Federal supremacy clause, constantly invoked by the Federal judiciary when State constitutions or enactments violate the grand ordinance of Union, declares explicitly that this Federal constitution, and all pursuant laws and treaties of the United States, "shall be the supreme law of the land;" enjoining further their paramount obligation not upon the United States judiciary alone, by implication, but upon the judges in every State, whatever the constitution and laws of any State may recite to the contrary.[2] By "supreme law of the land," or paramount comprehensive law essential to the whole Union, is meant that which Congress and all other departments of government must respect at all times, and to which States and their own departments whenever in conflict must yield subordination. The Federal constitution measures therefore the validity of laws and treaties of the United States, which to be valid must conform to its own ordinance; and as between these, a statute or a treaty is equally obligatory in a national and domestic sense, so that the one may supersede the other if later in point of time.[3]

The third clause of this article, consistently with such a doctrine of Federal supremacy, binds all high officers, executive and judicial, as well as all members of the Legislature, whether of the United States or of the several States, to swear to support this

---

[1] Const., Art. VI., § 1. Since all thirteen States entered finally the new Union, this pledge of public faith well fortified the new national policy of sustaining sacredly the public credit.

[2] Const., Art. VI., § 2.

[3] 11 Wall. 616; 143 U. S. 570. Of course in an international sense the repeal of a treaty may involve a breach of public faith with international consequences, as concerns the other contracting power.

Federal constitution, — the simple and only oath or affirmation that the United States of America imperatively asks from any one. And finally, in a most liberal spirit for that eighteenth century, when State official tests were commonly exacting,[1] it is announced that no religious test shall ever be required as a qualification to any office or public trust under the United States.[2]

[1] *Supra*, page 43.   [2] Const., Art. VI., § 3.

XII.

FEDERAL CONSTITUTION ANALYZED;
SUBSEQUENT AMENDMENTS.

THE amendments to the original Federal constitution of 1787 subsequently adopted to this date are fifteen in number. Of these the first ten collectively are in the nature of a supplemental declaration of rights, embracing a careful selection by the First Congress from an immense mass of proposed amendments, which doubtful States, beginning with Massachusetts, had framed and submitted when ratifying the original instrument. Ratifying unconditionally for the sake of harmony what appeared an imperfect constitution in its original draft, these States in convention gave their needed consent upon an understanding that the new Federal government would at once initiate amendments of this general character to broaden and strengthen the safeguards of liberty; nor in this did the new government disappoint them.[1] Many of these "bill of rights" provisions were transferred from State constitutions already established.[2] The eleventh amendment [3] stifled suits in the Supreme

---

[1] Amendments I.-X., all submitted together to the State legislatures in 1789, and declared adopted in 1791. Congress proposed at the same time two other amendments which failed of State adoption. One of them fixed a permanent rule for apportioning the House of Representatives; the other forbade that a law varying the compensation of members of Congress should take effect until after a new election of representatives.

[2] Cf. Part I., c. 3.

[3] Proposed in 1794 and declared adopted in 1798.

Court of the United States obnoxious to State sovereignty, and prevented such litigation for the future. The twelfth amendment[1] corrected defects in the machinery of Presidential elections made patent in the bitter party contest of 1800, but did not radically change the plan. The thirteenth, fourteenth, and fifteenth amendments, completing the list at the present time, were the cumulative result of that fratricidal conflict whence emerged a Union purged of human slavery and readjusted to the new social condition of equal civil rights, regardless of race or complexion.[2]

Congress has at different epochs entertained a vast variety of amendment propositions, many of them crude and transient, which have failed of a two-thirds passage in both houses and public insistence. One memorable one went to the States in 1861 for adoption, but in the tremendous drift of events became overwhelmed; pledging the Union never to interfere with slavery as locally existing in a State, it preceded by only four years that thirteenth amendment whose actual scope was diametrically opposite, for public opinion in those four years underwent a revolution. No co-operative State application to call a convention such as the constitution recognized has ever yet demanded the action of Congress; nor has Congress ever required an amendment to be ratified by State conventions instead of the Legislature.

I. "Bill of Rights" was the compromise addition purposed to the original instrument of 1787. Several important clauses of the original constitution had

---

[1] Proposed in 1803 and declared adopted in 1804.

[2] The thirteenth amendment was proposed and adopted in 1865. The fourteenth was proposed in 1866 and adopted in 1868. The fifteenth was proposed in 1869 and adopted in 1870.

actually that character,[1] but no parade was made of them, as though of blazing formulas our framers were weary. Of the first eight compromise amendments, which touch the individual and civil rights, it should be said that in general they apply exclusively to Federal jurisdiction and procedure;[2] States themselves cherishing similar maxims for application to issues more peculiarly their own. As to the first amendment (1) Congress must make no establishment of religion nor prohibit its free exercise, — a prohibition which is not transcended by breaking down some despotic hierarchy or polygamy pursued under the guise of religion in the Territories,[3] but inculcates non-interference in private preferences of religious worship. (2) Congress must not abridge by law the freedom of speech or of the press, — a maxim already pronounced in the States, where its application must mostly be confined.[4] (3) Congress must not abridge by law the right of the people peaceably to assemble and to petition the government for a redress of grievances.[5]

II. A well-regulated militia being necessary to the security of a free State, the right of the people to keep and bear arms shall not be infringed.[6]

[1] *E. g.*, the humane limit to penalties for treason, the *habeas corpus*, no title of nobility, no religious test for office, and jury trial in criminal cases.

[2] 147 U. S. 490, as to fifth amendment; 124 U. S. 200; Story, § 1782, notes.

[3] 136 U. S. 1.

[4] The "sedition act" of Congress in 1798 appears to have been founded upon a misconception of Federal jurisdiction in such matters as well as of good policy. But anti-lottery acts are no such abridgment of freedom, for freedom is not immoral license.

[5] This does not sanction a threatening demonstration of violence at the capital. To petition is not to demand, but to ask with loyal deference. This, too, we have seen, was a State maxim. *Supra,* page 35.

[6] For State maxims corresponding, see page 33. In the English

III. Soldiers shall not be quartered in time of peace in any house without the owner's consent, nor in time of war except as the law may prescribe, — an abuse of the colonial age while revolution was impending. A common incident of war while belligerent or rebellious soil is occupied, it should not be arbitrary or injurious to peaceful and loyal citizens.

IV. The people shall be secure against unreasonable searches and seizures, and no warrants shall issue but upon probable cause, supported by oath or affirmation and a particular description.[1]

V.-VIII. The next four amendments chiefly concern procedure in the Federal courts, extending safeguards such as States had expressly recognized for protection of the accused. Presentment or indictment must be made by a grand jury for a capital or otherwise infamous crime, as an added prerequisite to the trial of crimes by a jury;[2] though to cases arising in the land or naval forces, court-martial regularly applies, as well as to State militia while in active Federal service.[3] No person shall be twice put in jeopardy of life and limb for the same offence; nor shall any one in any criminal case be compelled to be a witness against himself.[4] The accused in all

Bill of Rights of 1688 was a similar provision as to Protestants, whom the King had disbanded while treating Roman Catholics with favor.

[1] *Supra*, page 33. "Writs of assistance" or general search-warrants were a cause of complaint against George III. before the Revolution, and the eloquent James Otis denounced them. No sealed letter can be lawfully opened except under a search-warrant. But see 96 U. S. 727 as to lottery circulars; 143 U. S. 110.

[2] *Supra*, page 175.

[3] 158 U. S. 109.

[4] Amendment V.; 142 U. S. 148. It is not "twice in jeopardy" to undergo a second trial where the first jury reached no verdict before its discharge. If a witness has absolute immunity against future prose-

criminal prosecutions shall have a right to a speedy and public trial by an impartial jury of the State and district of the crime.[1] He shall be informed of the nature and cause of the accusation, and be confronted with the witnesses against him; he shall have compulsory process for obtaining witnesses in his favor, and shall have the assistance of counsel for his defence.[2] This final clause at least secures valuable rights to the accused which the old common law curiously ignored, and all the foregoing safeguards were well worth expression.

No person shall be deprived of life, liberty, or property, without due process of law; nor shall private property be taken for public use without just compensation.[3] These are broad maxims constantly invoked. Life, liberty, and property comprise those personal rights which are universally dearest to the individual, and deserve most the law's equal protection. "Due process of law" guards those individual rights from all sovereign interference apart from such correct and orderly proceedings, considerate of private right, as are imposed by what has long been called "the law of the land," — a law sound in policy and operating upon all alike.[4] Constitutional or

cution, he may be compelled to testify, as the latest cases rule.   161 U. S. 691.   Cf. 142 U. S. 547.

[1] Various State statutes are constitutional which allow one charged with crime to waive voluntarily a trial by jury and elect to be tried by the court. 146 U. S. 314.   Territorial trials do not require any ascertained "district," as district relates to States. 138 U. S. 157. And see *supra*, pages 32, 34.

[2] Amendment VI.   See 161 U. S. 29.

Amendment VII. as to jury trials in civil suits at common law has been noticed, *supra*, page 175.   In equity and admiralty suits jury trials are in the main discretionary with a court for special issues of fact only.   Nor in the analogous Court of Claims procedure is a jury trial essential. 102 U. S. 426.

[3] Amendment V. at close.

[4] 153 U. S. 716.

"bill of rights" provisions admirably define those
rights in America; and both statute and case law
must respect such fundamental guaranties in order to
apply "due process of law."[1] The identity in meaning of this familiar expression with "law of the
land" — both Anglo-Saxon phrases time-honored — is
now conceded.[2]

"Taking property for public use without just compensation" was already forbidden in State constitutional law,[3] and States to this day preserve the
organic prohibition under some variations of expression. The right of eminent domain in a government
to appropriate and control individual property for the
public use and welfare, as in laying out highways or
erecting public buildings, is admitted, and that right
is often imparted to municipal and other corporations;
but the exercise of such a right in its many manifes-
tations must respect individual ownership by awarding not an arbitrary but a just recompense, which, if
not otherwise agreed upon, must be awarded by some
fair and impartial tribunal.[4] There may be franchises or other incorporeal property as well as property
corporeal subjected to this taking.[5]

Excessive bail shall not be required, nor cruel and
unusual punishments inflicted.[6] Here we find old

---

[1] See Cooley, 229–235. Hence do we find statutes practically tested
by these more fundamental and enduring precepts, whose early inspiration was drawn from such solemn documents as Magna Charta. Our
Federal constitution well distinguishes in this respect by ordaining
that instrument with statutes "made in pursuance thereof," etc., "the
supreme law of the land." *Supra*, page 188.

[2] 18 How. 272. And see Amendment XIV.

[3] *Supra*, page 41.

[4] Cooley, 344–357; 152 U. S. 132; 160 U. S. 499; 142 U. S. 79.

[5] 148 U. S. 312.

[6] Amendment VIII. Electrocution is not a "cruel and unusual
punishment" within the constitution, but rather in sense a humane
one. Nor can the solitary confinement of a condemned criminal be
deemed unconstitutional. 142 U. S. 155.

barriers renewed against tyranny; for constitutions do not so much create new rights in the people as prevent abuse under the forms of justice.   A prisoner once convicted by a jury may be rightfully committed without bail pending an appeal.

IX., X. The last two amendments of the original compromise concern reserved sovereign and public rights not imparted to this new Federal or Federonational government.   Here it is seen that the reservation made is not so much of State sovereign powers as of that general sovereignty of the whole people in whose name the instrument of 1787 had ordained a new and more perfect Union.[1]   Under Articles of Confederation, it was the States that prepared and entered into the league of Union; and those articles distinctly asserted that the powers not expressly delegated to the United States in Congress assembled were retained by the respective States.[2]   But in adapting that assertion to the new constitution by way of amendment, Congress purposely put forth a phrase less favorable to State sovereignty, by omitting the former word "expressly," as though some of the newly delegated authority might fairly be implied, and by reciting that the powers not delegated to the United States by the constitution, nor prohibited by it to the States, were reserved to the States respectively, "or to the people," a pregnant alternative.[3] So, too, in the preceding article it was declared that the enumeration in this constitution of certain rights should not be constrained to deny or disparage others "retained by the people."[4]

In all strict Confederacies, as history teaches, either the strongest States rule or anarchy prevails.

[1] Const., Preamble. [3] Amendment X.
[2] Articles, II.   [4] Amendment IX.

But in America, under the constitution, the subjects of the present Union are not States, but private citizens, and a peculiar representation tends to equalize State influence. To quote from De Tocqueville, the United States constitute no longer a Federal government, but an incomplete national government, which is neither exactly national nor exactly federal, and two sovereignties exist in each other's presence.[1]

XI., XII. The eleventh amendment, which restrains the judicial power of the Union in suits by non-resident individuals against a State, has already been considered.[2] So also has the twelfth amendment, which cured some defects in the primitive machinery of Presidential elections, without essentially changing its operation.[3]

XIII.–XV. Of the three final amendments, the effect is cumulative towards one general end; namely, to establish in essential citizenship a race once held in bondage. The thirteenth amendment, the direct logical outcome of our Civil War and of President Lincoln's military emancipation, abolished forever, in clear and simple phrase borrowed from the old ordinance of 1787, not negro slavery alone, but all slavery and involuntary servitude, within the United States or any place subject to their jurisdiction, except for crime upon due conviction.[4]

The fourteenth amendment, further extending the scope of social reconstruction which followed this first grand achievement and the close of armed con-

---

[1] De Tocqueville's America, 199.
[2] *Supra,* page 173. See 140 U. S. 1.
[3] *Supra,* page 161.
[4] Amendment XIII. Asiatic slavery cannot lawfully exist in America, more than African, nor can a system of peonage or of compulsory adult apprenticeship.

flict, is partly vindictive or retributive, and yet not
harshly so either in expression or enforcement, considering the provocation. President Lincoln was
now dead. The pursuance of a policy towards van-
quished fellow-citizens passed into other control; and
the States lately resisting were compelled to pass
under the yoke, and sanction new terms of pacifica-
tion, before normal relations with the Union were
fully restored. Hence the adoption in turn of the
fourteenth and fifteenth amendments, by States
Southern as well as Northern, in a co-operative assent
under the forms of the constitution.[1]

Three prime objects are presented by the fourteenth amendment: (1) the better protection of the
emancipated negro as a citizen of the United States,
under the broadening of former definitions;[2] (2) the

[1] Article XIII. had been unconditionally ratified by thirty-two
States out of thirty-six. Article XIV. was ratified by thirty-three
States out of thirty-seven, and Article XV. by thirty States out of
thirty-seven. All this was far in excess of the requisite three-fourths.
The States rejecting amendments, in every such instance, were either
border slave States, not under military control, or those of the free
North, where public sentiment opposed the reconstruction policy of
Congress.

The constitutional effect of State rejection followed by acceptance,
and of State acceptance followed by rejection, might have come up for
discussion had the vote been closer in adopting these three amendments, for historical precedents were here furnished. (1) Conditional
ratification is usually to be considered no ratification in a constitutional
sense; and such being the prevalent belief when the constitution of
1787 came before the conventions of the original States, reluctant
State conventions abstained from such action. (2) State acceptance
is probably constitutional, even though a previous legislature or convention has rejected, provided such ratification follows within a reasonable time. (3) But after a full acceptance, it seems that a State
cannot rightfully rescind ratification and then reject; if, at all events,
some other State has meanwhile ratified upon the faith of that previous
acceptance. These three statements of doctrine find analogies in the
common law of private transactions.

[2] Under the well-known "Dred Scott" decision of 1857 (19 How.
393), the rights of American citizenship were denied by the Supreme
Court to the negro, whether as a slave or a freeman.

punishment of citizens lately rebellious; (3) the integrity of public credit and the public debt of the United States, by upholding the claims of loyalty and repudiating those of disloyalty under the late conflict.[1] A broad and enlightened status of citizenship for the future, based alone upon birth or naturalization in the United States subject to its jurisdiction, without other adventitious distractions, is here set forth for application, both to the United States and to the State wherein the person resides. States are forbidden to abridge the privileges or immunities of citizens of the United States; to deprive any person of life, liberty, or property without "due process of law;" or to deny to any person within local jurisdiction "the equal protection of the laws."[2] This amendment, as since construed in the courts, does not change radically the former relation of State and Federal governments; but leaves still to the several States exclusively the protection of all civil rights and privileges which are not expressly or by clear intendment vested in the Federal government conformably to its nature and attributes.[3] Next a new apportionment basis for representatives in Congress, based upon numbers, fitly supersedes that which in 1787 compromised as between the free and slave

[1] Amendment XIV.

[2] *Ib.* § 1. States subject to the above-expressed constraints still retain the police power as before; and a "civil rights" bill of Congress to compel an equal and indiscriminate intercourse of races at hotels, on railway cars, or in the schools, exceeds its prescribed authority. 109 U. S. 3. Separate race accommodations and facilities may be thus provided. 163 U. S. 537.

[3] 92 U. S. 214; 116 U. S. 252; Cooley, 258. This amendment cannot override public rights of a State in the nature of an easement. 160 U. S. 452. Nor State process which affords to all parties alike a fair hearing. 150 U. S. 380; 160 U. S. 389. But all citizens are now equal before the law; and no racial distinctions, so far as certain political rights are concerned, can be permitted. 162 U. S. 565 (as to drawing jurors).

population.[1] Negro representation is to be by numbers henceforth where before it was merely fractional. States are not thereby compelled in consequence to allow all negroes to vote; but wherever a State abridges male suffrage "except for participation in rebellion, or other crime," its basis of representation in the House shall be reduced proportionally.[2] Besides this granted disfranchisement of "rebel participants" (which the resisting States were never inclined to put in force), all former members of Congress and State or Federal officers who had engaged in rebellion in violation of a previous oath to support the constitution of the United States were temporarily banished from the public service under this fourteenth amendment; but Congress long ago by a vote of two-thirds of each house removed this disability, as permitted.[3] Finally the validity of the authorized public debt of the United States, including pensions and bounties for services in suppressing rebellion, shall not be questioned; while, on the other hand, neither the United States nor any State shall assume or pay any debt or obligation incurred in aid of the rebellion, nor any claim for the loss or emancipation of any slave, but all such debts, obligations, and claims shall be held illegal and void.[4]

The fifteenth amendment, though framed and proposed by Congress in turbulent times, rises once more to unimpassioned dignity of statement. By

[1] *Supra*, page 105, "three fifths of all other persons" (*i. e.*, of slaves).

[2] Amendment XIV., § 2. This reduction has never been really enforced by Congress, and there are practical difficulties to determining the constitutional proportion in figures. There are Northern as well as Southern States which apply an educational test in restraint of general suffrage, and thus come equally within scope of the constitutional threat.

[3] Amendment XIV., § 3.

[4] *Ib.* § 4.

this constitutional change the elective franchise is broadened for the late slave's benefit, and a rule is made mandatory upon States which Congress had previously attempted to establish by policy.[1] All abridgment of the right to vote is forbidden as to citizens of the United States in the present ample sense on any account of race, color, or previous condition of servitude; but otherwise local suffrage is still left to each State's regulation as before, with only a new Federal right to interfere against racial distinctions at the polls.[2] For suffrage here means civic participation in government; it is not a natural but a political right; and all such participation is usually limited by the local government policy.[3]

Such was to be the increased responsibility of the Union under these last three amendments that in each instance Congress was expressly empowered to enforce the article by appropriate legislation,[4] — a provision not to be found in any earlier amendments of this constitution. That power is limited, however, in meaning to the just scope of each separate amend-

[1] Cf. Amendment XIV., § 2; page 200.

[2] Amendment XV. Such a prohibition would apply to State ballot laws which exclude a Chinese citizen of the United States, though negroes are more immediately concerned, whose citizenship is so largely their birthright. A State may still impose property or educational tests for the ballot, or disfranchise for crime, but all such tests must apply equally to whites and blacks, without racial distinction. 92 U. S. 214, 542.

[3] See Part III., *post*, showing State restrictions upon suffrage at the present day. Various political reasons induced the passage of this fifteenth amendment, and among them that the ballot would prove to be educational and a means of enlightened self-protection to the freedmen still dwelling among their late masters. But the apprenticeship of liberty proves always slow and arduous; and the first real results of this experiment were certainly disappointing. The full constitutional purpose of this amendment, however, for permanent effect is just and noble, and in aid of a humanity more generous than nations and kingdoms ever compassed before.

[4] Final section in each amendment.

ment; which, as we have seen, to the disappointment, doubtless, of many who aided these constitutional changes, leaves still, as in 1787, a wide range of State discretionary action. The Federal constitution, here as elsewhere, is self-executing in most of its prohibitions, and requires no legislation from Congress to make them binding.[1] This self-executing power may be inferred in various other instances where the public interest requires it; as in enabling the Executive or Supreme Court to maintain due independence of Congress, or so that the citizen shall stand secure in his sacred individual rights against the government.

---

[1] *E. g.*, in the thirteenth and fifteenth amendments, and in most portions of the fourteenth.

PART III.

STATE CONSTITUTIONS SINCE 1789.

I.

HISTORICAL SEQUENCE.

FROM the day that the new Federal constitution of 1787 went into full effect, that admirable scheme of union gained a conspicuousness in the eyes of mankind, and a paramount influence over the destinies of the American people that no single State instrument could possibly have rivalled. This constitution, as perfected by the "bill of rights" amendments which Congress promptly proposed and the States as promptly adopted, became at once a model for the new State constitutions of Pennsylvania and Georgia already in preparation; and scarcely a State in the whole enlarged Union can be named at the present day whose fundamental law does not pattern after that immortal instrument in one detail or another. But we should bear in mind, notwithstanding, that much of that Federal framework is inapplicable to American statehood; and further that some of the best basic ideas of its architecture were derived from thirteen pre-existing State charters in successful operation. Free government in America received by 1789 a redoubled rather than an original impulse. Later States have imbibed in their fundamental written law much of the spirit and formal expression of those leading commonwealths whose glory forever gilds our earliest annals. Thus Kentucky, Virginia's own offspring, took her institutions from the parent State. Much of the substance of the healthy Massachusetts constitution became the flesh and blood of those thriving new States which New Englanders reared in the free territory northwest of the Ohio River; while Vermont, admitted into the Union in 1791, the first of new-born States with Kentucky, chose to pattern her instrument of government very closely after that of Benjamin Franklin's Pennsylvania, which the latter State in 1790 supplanted.[1]

There are at the present day forty-five full-fledged States in the American Union, as against the thirteen that originally composed it; and of that number very few can be named more than fifty years old, whose constitution has not been repeatedly recast in convention and rewritten. Old Massachusetts is the only State of them all which can show, like the present Federal Union, a primitive constitution still vigorously operating, which, once adopted in the eighteenth century, has never been superseded; and in both instances amendments since added have wrought much practical change.[2] New Hampshire and Vermont furnish the only other examples of an eighteenth-century constitution still in force at all. As time goes on, the national flag of this Union seems beautifully to symbolize the true historical relation of the several States to national development. Those thir-

---

[1] Vermont's constitution of 1786 first made this copy; and her constitution of 1793 after admission retained the image.

[2] A computation made in 1885 by a careful historical scholar showed among other statistics that four States — Georgia, South Carolina, Texas, and Virginia — had each lived under five successive constitutions; while Louisiana adopted her sixth constitution in 1879. These figures did not include changes in those States that might have taken place during the Civil War. Horace Davis's American Constitutions, 16; Johns Hopkins Historical Studies.

teen stripes are emblems of thirteen commonwealths, the creative source of the whole American Union; but the more in number the stars that crowd that azure field as time goes on, the less distinctive becomes the individual light that twinkles from them.

During the remnant of the eighteenth century which succeeded 1789, and while the Federalists as a party retained control of national affairs, conservatism was predominant in the States; and this indeed was the essential reason why Pennsylvania and Georgia reformed at once their turbulent establishments. But the latter State, with a restless population, after amending within six years its second constitution of 1789, adopted in 1798 a third new draft of government. The great gain of Federal example to national harmony and stability had been in persuading each of these two States to supersede that tumultuous assembly of a single house which had exerted much undefined authority, by a truly American legislature of two branches; though Vermont chose to experiment further for herself in that former direction. Pennsylvania, besides, chose henceforth a single executive, after the true American model, in place of a directory, strengthening the independence of that department against the Legislature, as the Federal instrument had done.

The Republican era of Jefferson and Madison which merged into the stormy war of 1812 with European embroilment, after a marvellous season of domestic prosperity, and which happily escaped by 1815 with peace and renewed national honor, was not productive of great fundamental change in the existing States. This, however, was the era of new national growth westward and in the valley of the Mississippi, now rapidly reclaimed from Indian occupation and extended by purchase to the wilderness of the Rocky Mountains; and west of the Alleghanies, as indeed throughout the Union, the impulse towards republican and uniform government was strong and steady. Not one of the eighteenth-century States remodelled its constitution during the first seventeen years of the nineteenth century, though local changes were introduced here and there through the process of amendment. Two new States, however, Ohio and Louisiana, the antipodes of national sisterhood, were admitted to the Union during this era.

From 1816 to 1835 ensues a period of perfect peace, recuperation, and internal development, of a growing native confidence in popular institutions, and a boastful disposition to make proselytes of the old world. Self-government had vindicated its claims by American example, and from European systems America felt detached forever. Six new States, each with its accepted constitution, were admitted into the Union during the earlier portion of this era, at the average rate of one State a year.[1] In a majority of the pre-existing States constitutions were largely overhauled, and rewritten or vitally amended; and Connecticut in 1818 threw aside finally the venerable royal charter which had served hitherto for republican government, and clothed herself with a modern constitution after the prevailing fashion. The tendency of the nineteenth century now became manifest, for one and all of these United States, to abolish all property and religious tests, to enlarge the franchise for the white man, to strengthen each State executive against the Legislature, while putting greater curb upon the discretion of that latter body, to use the judiciary as a political check, and generally to give the reins

---

[1] Indiana, Mississippi, Illinois, Alabama, Maine (by separation from Massachusetts), Missouri, 1816–1821.

more completely into the hands of the people, so
that the governed might become the governing also.
By this time the example of American independence,
with its written proclamation of human rights,
became the solace and inspiration of the feebler
Spanish-American colonies to the south of us.

To this era succeeded 1836–1861, — a period when
a still more pronounced and combative democracy
wrestled with conservatism, and other bitter strifes
went on, until the slavery conflict, forcing its own
dangerous rivalry to the front, precipitated the whole
United States into a civil strife so terrible that it
seemed almost as if the sun of the great republic had
gone down forever in blood and sectional dissolution.   In most States, meanwhile, the old barriers of
caste and property were broken down, and through
the brief and impatient tenure that ensued, office-
holding lost much of its traditional dignity and stability.   Not only governors and the high executive
officials were now subjected to the will of common voters, as expressed at the polls, but judicial
incumbents as well.   Party spoils were proclaimed
the prize of party victors; and with wealth increasing besides, which sought special favors from public
officers and the Legislature, corruption grew, which
honest voters strove to repress by straining tighter
the cords of fundamental restraint.   Splendid abili-
ties, devoted love of Union, struggled in the souls
of great statesmen with the weakness of compromise
and a fatal tendency to palter public interests for
temporary advantage, while the arrogance of material
strength tempted to trample upon the rights of
weaker nations.   The star of manifest destiny for a
while led on to continental empire; but though the
Union triumphed steadily and enlarged its broad area
on the Pacific, territorial aggrandizement was not

honorable, as it had been in the earlier and simpler years of the century. A swarm of new States swelled the catalogue of written constitutions for this portentous era; California, the seventh among them, disturbing in 1849 the former equipoise of free and slave States for admission; and the protracted struggle over Kansas, after the repeal of the Missouri compromise, arousing the most vehement sectional passion. The aggregate number of newly admitted States for this period was ten, two of them furnishing the first fruits of Mexican dismemberment.[1]

By 1861 democratizing influences had nerved our whole people, and taught them a self-reliance which was to become yet stronger. Had it been otherwise, a civil war, which drained the resources of States arrayed in deadly strife, would have ruined this Union. Each adversary fought with courage and determination, but victory crowned the stronger and in sight of Heaven the worthier cause. During those four years of fight little heed was given by the Federal government to State extension; but Virginia being torn asunder in the struggle, a loyal and separate State, known as West Virginia, was organized in 1862, and Congress admitted in 1864 from the Rocky Mountain region the sparse mining State of Nevada. The period of southern State reconstruction lasted for about twelve years from the submission and disarmament of that section in April, 1865. New State constitutions now forced southern inhabitants not only to acquiesce in the legal extinction of slavery throughout the Union, but to repudiate, with

---

[1] Arkansas, Michigan, Florida, Iowa, Texas, Wisconsin, California, Minnesota, Oregon, and Kansas. The numerous proposed constitutions of this last-named State prior to its admission, record the desperate struggle of free and proslavery settlers for the mastery.

the repeal of their several ordinances of secession, the whole doctrine of State sovereignty upon which the theoretical right to secede had been based. Other conditions yet more galling were imposed by amendments of the Federal constitution, whose supremacy was henceforth unquestioned.[1]

From the accession of President Hayes in March, 1877, the rehabilitation of the once insurgent States became complete. Military interference in the southern section now ceased, and the Union rapidly regained its normal condition with a former obstacle to national harmony now fairly removed. A new era of fraternal reconciliation now commenced such as the world has seldom witnessed. Federal amnesty was freely accorded by Congress and the President, while Southern States hastened to blot out as they might the disabilities of their military champions under their own organic law. Meanwhile at the North and in the growing West States always loyal have renovated their local institutions with a stronger confidence than ever in the permanence of the American Union, and with a fuller determination to hold government, State or Federal, as closely amenable as possible to public opinion. The appointing of all high officers of the State has been largely taken from chief magistrates and the Legislature. The Chief Executive, now the sole choice of the voters, is viewed more than ever as the vicegerent of popular authority. Fundamental limitations accumulate upon legislation and the incurring of public debt. Even the State judiciary, though strengthened against rash and tumultuous assault, is made to feel its final dependence upon the voters; and the passionate desire of an American democracy to control and limit public government, at the present day, is

[1] *Supra,* page 198.

14

in strong contrast with the deferential and implicit confidence which the common people reposed in their representatives, those especially of their legislatures, a century ago.[1]　Those brief instruments of State government, in the earlier era, which left a skeleton outline for legislatures to fill up at will, have given place long since to lengthy constitutions, full of local specifications and of details jealously worked out by description, like a huge act of legislation.[2]

---

[1] The new States admitted into the Union from 1865 to 1897 are as follows: Nebraska (1867), Montana (1889), North Dakota (1889), South Dakota (1889), Washington (1889), Idaho (1890), Wyoming (1890), Utah (1894).　Total present number of States in the Union, forty-five.

[2] Some have severely criticised the present distrustful and prolix tendency of expression in our latest State constitutions.　One of the ablest of such critics, the late Governor William E. Russell, of Massachusetts, in an address at Yale University (1894), sets forth earnestly some of the most forcible objections to such full and unphilosophical detail in an organic instrument.　But something may be said on the other side.　The notable simplicity of our Federal constitution, on which such critics dwell, is hardly in contrast; for its framers, after much discussion and practical experience of the particular problem, undertook merely to draw out better and define the organic powers adequate for maintaining an efficient Union with a few supreme concerns committed to it; while in the several State governments remains that great residuary mass of functions and authority, such as changes and develops of necessity with the evolution of society.　State legislation for such vast and diversified concerns must necessarily grow and increase in complexity as society multiplies and concentrates its population; and so, too, must the State fundamental law, which controls that legislation, take on a like incongruous growth of provision.　Massachusetts is praised for keeping to the old and simple landmarks of constitutional government; and yet in that roving discretion still left to the Massachusetts Legislature under an ancient constitution, we see the cause and occasion of those constant and prolonged annual sessions from which most other States are now happily exempt; and the fact, for instance, that mere statute enactment in that State promotes private incorporation under general laws, while State constitutions elsewhere compel it, does not deter the schemers from constantly seeking special privileges and modifications for themselves, and thus at least consuming the public time, if not inducing worse dangers.　The true course for States seems to be to avoid the evils of too close a specification, on the one hand, in a written framework of government, and too lax a discretion to transient representatives of the people on the other.

II.

METHODS OF FUNDAMENTAL ADOPTION AND CHANGE.

How little stress, in framing and putting into public force a State constitution, was laid upon the direct approval of the voters prior to the Federal example of 1787, or indeed, in that Federal instrument itself, we have already remarked.[1] American statesmen in those days thought it a sufficient resort to first principles for the people to choose special representatives to a convention — since a convention derived a deeper sanction than a legislature — and then leave that convention to its own unfettered and final discretion. To that earlier practice of the States Massachusetts and New Hampshire are seen to have constituted the only clear exception; but the more fundamental sanction which those States chose so early to rest upon has gradually become the common condition. In one or two very recent instances, to be sure, where a prime and perplexing object of constitutional reform has been to reduce a voting element,[2] a State convention has assumed to establish as well as shape out the new organic law. But for real homogeneous communities of these United States, where the majority rules, the true sanction of a constitutional convention must consist, henceforth and

---

[1] *Supra*, pages 47, 185.

[2] As recently (1896) in South Carolina, where there is a large negro element of population, and (1897) in Delaware.

forever, while self-government sustains itself, not in the choice of constituent representatives alone to that convention, but in the ultimate approval at the polls of that convention's work as formally submitted.

The change in this popular direction came slowly in America, and long after the nineteenth century had begun.[1] New Hampshire's new constitution of 1792 went to the voters, and was ratified by them, like her earlier one. But this was an exceptional instance. On the other hand, the amendments of a New York convention in 1801, artfully procured, were promulgated as final without any such submission; and so was it with new constitutions somewhat earlier, of South Carolina in 1790, Delaware in 1792, and Georgia in 1798.[2] Pennsylvania's convention of 1789 had framed a radically new instrument of government; and after adjourning in 1790, that the people might examine but not pass upon the work, it reassembled a few months later and formally proclaimed this new constitution in force. With States newly admitted to the Union at the close of the last century, the course pursued was the same. Conventions framed and put in force the Kentucky constitutions of 1792 and 1799; those of Vermont in 1793 and of Tennessee in 1796 were ordained in like manner.

Ohio's first constitution (1802), followed by that of Louisiana (1812), each framed by a territorial convention under an enabling act of Congress, but not submitted to the people, recognized among other provisions the right of a legislature [3] to submit to the people on future occasion whether there should

---

[1] See notes to Poore's Constitutions, which the official text of these early instruments serves to confirm.

[2] As also the Georgia amendments of 1795.

[3] In Ohio by a two-thirds vote; in Louisiana by a majority.

be a constitutional convention; but as to the popular *referendum* of such a convention's work the instrument was silent.[1] It was the era next succeeding the peace of 1814 that saw the first decided advance since 1787 of the popular submission doctrine in the United States. Connecticut, in 1818, when setting aside the old colonial charter, submitted, after the Massachusetts and New Hampshire fashion, her new constitution to the people, and that instrument was ratified at the polls. Next, New York in 1821 invoked the same popular test to the adoption of a new framework of government. Massachusetts, in 1820, held a convention and proposed important changes in the organic law, some of which carried at the polls while others miscarried. Great Southern States, from 1830 to 1835, such as Virginia, North Carolina, and Tennessee,[2] held conventions, each of which framed fresh constitutions, and submitted them to the people of the State, by whose majority vote each and all became ratified and effectual.

Pennsylvania's convention of 1790 had been called at discretion on the seventh year by the "Censors," a popular council revived in Vermont's new constitution, just after Pennsylvania had dispensed with it. Other old States, whose Revolutionary constitutions had made no express provision for change or supersedure, felt an inherent competence to summon a new convention at any time for either purpose. But, following the example set by the Federal constitution and some still earlier State instruments, we see special provisions made at once for the process of simple constitutional amendment without calling a convention at all. Thus Delaware (1792) adopted

[1] Tennessee's first constitution of 1796 was in this respect similar, and so were those of Kentucky and Delaware in 1792.

[2] Also, apparently, Mississippi in 1832.

the Maryland rule of 1776, long favored in the
Union, that one legislature shall propose an amendment by a specified vote exceeding a bare majority,
and the next after an intervening general election
shall pass that amendment similarly, and thereby
give it full force.[1] Such a mode of amendment, by
which Maryland herself made four organic changes in
the eighteenth century, without calling a convention
at all, is seen to eliminate the direct sanction of the
voter. But when Connecticut, New York, and
Massachusetts made united demonstration about 1820
in favor of submitting directly to the people all
constitutions framed in convention, those States initiated likewise by co-operation the popular reference
of specific amendments.[2] Each of these three States
at that time improved upon the old Maryland plan of
1776 (which, like our Federal plan, dispensed with
conventions for mere amendment) by requiring: (1)
proposal of the change by one legislature; (2) renewed proposal by a succeeding legislature; and (3)
final approval of the change by a majority vote of the
people. And this, with occasional slight variations,
may be considered the modern American mode still
in vogue for changing a State constitution in specific
particulars where no convention, no rewritten document of government, is thought desirable.

Thus, then, after the United States had fulfilled a
third of their nineteenth-century orbit, and emerged
into the full splendor of . confident democracy, new
constitutions and even amendments to existing instruments, whether initiated by convention or legislature, drew their vital breath, not from representatives
of the people, but from the final sanction of a popular

[1] *Supra,* page 49.
[2] Cf. Alabama's constitution of 1819 on this point, similar but less
explicit.

majority at the polls. All State constitutions, in fact, since 1835, have been thus established as matter of course, with the rarest of exceptions.[1] A New York convention in 1846 invoked such political approval of its work, though the previous constitution had not literally required any test of the kind. Even in Florida (1838–39) the constitution under which that territory, once Spanish, became by 1845 a State, was submitted by schedule to its voting inhabitants. The people of Wisconsin territory rejected summarily the organic instrument prepared for State admission by a convention in 1846, and accepted a later one in 1848. Rhode Island's constitution of 1842, the date when the last of our primitive United States cast off its colonial charter, was a peculiar one in many respects, having an English flavor of local customs; and a majority vote at the polls gave this new instrument validity, though no amendment was to take effect in the future without a three-fifths popular assent. During the busy decade of constitutional change which preceded Civil War, this fundamental submission, whether in State or territory, in old or new jurisdictions, had become so sacred that while the Free-Soil controversy raged hottest on the territorial soil of Kansas, a fair-minded majority in Congress, sustained by the public opinion of both sections, united in refusing recognition to a constitution which in 1858 a territorial convention had sought arbitrarily to ordain as the price of statehood; and submission to a territorial vote being thus compelled, the instrument was buried in ignominy.

So, too, has it been with State constitutional

---

[1] It appears that Arkansas was admitted as a State in 1836 with a constitution promulgated simply by the convention which framed it, harmonizing in that respect with Missouri's neighboring action in 1820 under a constitution quite similar. Recent exceptions in States where unpopular change is contemplated are noted *supra*, page 211.

amendments wherever this later period has given opportunity for regulating anew the amendment methods. The Arkansas constitution of 1836, by way of solitary exception, embodied the old-fashioned scheme of leaving all changes to be wrought out completely in successive legislatures.[1] Elsewhere each new or remodelled State constitution required all new amendments to be submitted to a popular vote. "Each amendment," says in effect the New Jersey instrument of 1844, "shall be distinctly presented for vote, and no amendment oftener than once in five years." American State practice to this day prefers that amendments shall originate in the Legislature, and pass both houses by some fractional vote greater than a quorum majority. Usually, perhaps, a second legislature must after a similar vote confirm the proposition; but in either case, a *referendum* at the polls settles finally the fate of the proposed organic alteration.

Once more, as a sign of increased deference to the people, we find our modern State constitutions expressly providing that the people shall not only vote upon the organic product of any future convention, but upon the preliminary question whether any convention shall be held in the State at all. New York in 1846, liberally favoring the inherent control of republican government by the people for the people, declares that every twentieth year, as well as at intervening times when the Legislature may provide, the people shall vote whether to hold a convention or not, and the decision of the majority shall prevail on that point. That policy has been followed elsewhere with excellent effect.[2] Other States, however,

---

[1] Here, again, Arkansas stood by the example supplied in 1820 by its neighbor, Missouri.

[2] See, *e. g.*, Ohio's constitution of 1851, that of Kansas, 1859, and

more conservative on that point, still prefer specific amendments, by initiation in the Legislature, to any such radical disturbing influence as a remodelling convention. But conventions themselves choose often to propose amendments rather than draft the whole fundamental law anew. The Illinois convention of 1848 broke up its work into parts for separate submission, as New York and other States have since done, with good effect, in order that the rejection at the polls of some doubtful propositions might not prevent a legal acceptance of the worthy residue.[1]

It would be interesting to consider how far fundamental conditions expressed in any sovereign constitution as irrepealable can have binding force upon posterity. Such conditions as recognize the Union paramount may be thought obligatory enough without any State expression, and all such conditions in a government are understood to be subject to the right of revolution. But other provisions expressly declared unamendable or irrepealable may be found, not in the original Federal instrument alone and those of original States,[2] but regularly upon the admission of new States to the Union formed out of the national territory by way of a compact with Congress.[3] A compact to be legally repealed requires the assent of both parties; but no such compact exists

Maryland's in 1867. To such provision we owe some excellent changes in New York's fundamental law.

[1] During the ten years which preceded our Civil War the political convenience of taking the sense of the people separately upon doubtful propositions became obvious when new States, such as Kansas, Oregon, and Minnesota, were to be admitted.

[2] See *supra*, pages 49, 187.

[3] Such, for example, by way of compact with the Union, as these: never to tax the lands of non-residents higher than those of State residents; and that local and adjacent waters shall be a common highway for the whole Union, etc.

between the present people of a State or nation and their own posterity, and mutual repeal in such a sense is as impossible as mutual establishment. No human ordinance can rightfully claim perpetual fulfilment.

To take American institutions in their latter-day sense and throughout this renovated Union, now happily in normal working order, the State constitution is become practically a law which the people make directly by voting at the polls upon a draft submitted to them;[1] meaning by this, however, an enactment fundamental and obligatory upon all State departments, legislature, executive, and judiciary, save as to possibly transcending the supreme Federal constitution. Hence it becomes to this extent a direct exercise of popular sovereignty, a government by plebiscitum. While our Federal constitution still can only be amended by three-fourths of the States ratifying after the old method of separate convention or legislature (in practice the latter, as Congress has hitherto exercised its option),[2] and there is no plebiscitum, no polling of the whole United States at all, a State constitution may usually be changed by a bare majority vote at the polls, however small, after the two legislatures in succession, or (as in some instruments), a single legislature has put the proposed amendment before the people.[3] The last "Council of Censors," with authority to call conventions or amend, has vanished from the States.[4] And in the lengthy constitutions with inflexible regulation on matters liable to fluctuating opinion, which now so often confront us,[5] conventions show some of the

[1] See Bryce's Commonwealth.

[2] *Supra,* page 186.

[3] The requirement of a minimum number of votes cast seems a fair one for fundamental changes. And see Delaware (1831).

[4] See Vermont's amendment (1870) to constitution of 1793.

[5] Among examples of growing verbosity taken at random from

temporizing, lobbying, and log-rolling propensities which they criticise as follies in a legislature. The people of a State choose the convention, but members of that body are the architects and joiners of the new organic framework. All this points in favor of making concrete submission of a new scheme by separate propositions where there is uncertain sentiment; and in favor of proposing an occasional amendment, as far as possible, in preference to holding conventions at all. For all this makes the people more nearly the originators of their own system. The public mind does not readily grasp the full purport of a complete instrument *de novo*, nor balance the probable evils against the probable advantages; but it seizes readily upon specific corrections of specific evils, illustrated by some actual state of facts which has just aroused the common interest. Instead of being eager to summon conventions and re-enact the whole body of fundamental law, our people have generally proved conservative and slow to act, except in plain emergencies.

State constitutions by no means the latest, we find Pennsylvania's instrument of 1873 occupying twenty-three pages of print against ten in that of 1838; Maryland's, of 1867, with thirty-two against twenty-one in that of 1851; and Missouri's, of 1875, with thirty-three against fifteen in that of 1820. The magnitude of new subjects for public attention, such as railways, manufactures, and municipal government, largely accounts for such a growth. See *supra*, page 210.

III.

STATE FUNDAMENTAL MAXIMS.

OF State fundamental maxims in the nature of a declaration of rights, those first familiar through the Revolutionary instruments of Virginia, Pennsylvania, Maryland, and other members of the original Confederation have left their lasting impression in America. The sacred formulas in the preamble of our Declaration of Independence find like recognition, besides those with dispersed lustre in the original text of the Federal constitution, or blazoned together as its first ten amendments. Political truths, like those in the Revolutionary declarations of rights, gained double circulation and credit in the land when stamped as the new coinage of the Union. These bosom truths need here no repetition.[1] In one form of statement or another, and with variations of expression suggested by time and circumstances, they are to be found in all succeeding constitutions, whether of old or new States; most American commonwealths still choosing to devote in their organic code a special chapter to such recital. But of basic State maxims originating since 1789 it is hard to draw out any catalogue; and the more so because States in recent years have taken so greatly to limiting specifically the range of legislative or judicial authority in prohibitions which themselves might often be thought tantamount to formulas of good government. For

[1] See *supra*, page 30.

whenever a people safeguard their individual rights against public action in one department of sovereignty or another, then in a sense one may say that the "bill of rights" maxim finds expression. With this *caveat*, let us enter upon the task of a brief enumeration, favoring most as fundamental maxims those which constitution builders have set apart in that category.

The Montesquieu separation of threefold powers is still inculcated constantly in American State constitutions; nor has modern civil experience devised any radical departure from that method for carrying on popular government. Among the few formulas first derived from Federal example and the constitution of 1787, we may note with satisfaction the spread among States of that which forbade laws impairing the obligation of contracts. The right of petition, on the other hand, embodied by amendment only in this Federal instrument, spread into continental acceptance through State example.[1] Everything ranged under the head of "great and essential principles of liberty," says the Pennsylvania instrument of 1790 for better assurance, "is excepted out of the general powers of government, and shall remain forever inviolate." Perhaps the earliest grand idea to propagate vigorously in this new era of complete Union was that (already advanced by Pennsylvania[2]) which abolished all imprisonment for debt where the debtor in good faith gave up whatever property he had, — a doctrine which Vermont, Kentucky, and Georgia all announced by constitution in the eighteenth century, and which under statute or fundamental law is since the doctrine of the whole United States.

[1] Pennsylvania and Massachusetts, *supra*, page 35. Pennsylvania's instrument of 1790 once more included Penn's colonial clause as to deodands and suicides. See page 35.

[2] Page 36.

An accused person acquitted shall pay no costs unless the majority of judges certify that there was probable cause for prosecution.[1] Banishment as a State punishment is prohibited; and so is corporal chastisement for civilians.[2] Indiana announced by 1816 that a man's "particular services," as well as his property, should not be taken without " just compensation," — a maxim, by the way, to which Ohio in 1802 had given a novel turn from the stand-point of public advantage.[3] Illinois in 1818 mingled with the familiar recital of other private rights that of reserving commons forever to the people, meaning by commons lands that were once granted in common to any town or community by competent authority.[4] Truth as to the facts shall be an admissible defence in all libel suits.[5]

While the new national tendency was steadily to dispense with special qualifications for civil office or the Legislature, tenure of office for life or for good behavior, even in the case of judges, became gradually obnoxious to public sentiment, as the newer constitutions gave expression; Virginia herself extending to the judiciary by 1850 the "return into that body from which they were originally taken," and the election test "at fixed periods" to which the legisla-

---

[1] Delaware, 1792.

[2] Ohio, 1802. Delaware (1897) alone retains the antiquated pillory and whipping-post. Flogging in the army or navy or the merchant service has been a subject for later repression by Congressional enactment.

[3] Private property shall always be subservient to the public welfare, provided just compensation be given.

[4] See constitution of 1848, permitting a legal division of such commons by suitable procedure in the courts.

[5] Mississippi, 1817 and 1832. New York and other leading States made such a change in the common law of libel by simple legislation early in the century. "Unless published from malicious motives" is the prudent qualification of Rhode Island's constitution (1842) and that of some other States.

tive and executive departments alone were declared subject in her famous declaration of 1776.[1] Mississippi had much earlier proclaimed as the universal tenure of State office some limited period of time, provided good behavior shall continue so long.[2] "No office shall be created of longer tenure than four years," is the rigorous rule which Indiana proclaimed in 1851; and yet while holding to the older American prohibition of more than one lucrative office at a time in the same individual, this Indiana convention made stated exceptions in a few deserving instances. No lieutenant-governor, declares the Michigan constitution of 1851,[3] shall be eligible to any office or appointment from the Legislature, except he be chosen to the United States Senate. Property and religious qualifications, whether for office or the right of suffrage, were now disappearing. Extra compensation for public officers or contractors was sometimes jealously forbidden, and public salaries were ordered paid, without increase or diminution during the incumbent's term of office.[4]

As our nineteenth century nears its meridian, we see stronger safeguards than before insisted on for individual security against judicial process. "The writ of *habeas corpus* shall in no case be suspended," observes that Vermont constitution of 1836, which establishes tardily a legislature of two houses. Writs of error shall never be prohibited by law.[5] Criminal indictments must be framed for prosecution, and no one shall be compelled to criminate himself.[6] For the trial of criminals by peers and a jury, the

---

[1] *Supra*, page 37.
[2] Mississippi, 1832.
[3] With perhaps the fresh recollection of some specific abuse.
[4] Wisconsin, 1848. See VIII., *post.*
[5] Wisconsin, 1848.
[6] Cf. U. S. Const., Amendment V.

common law fairly retained its *magna charta* sanctity; but as to civil litigation some of the former reverence faded. "Jury trials may be waived by agreement in civil cases," is the new maxim of various State constitutions;[1] "in civil suits not over fifty dollars" is another experimental change, the Legislature may authorize trial by a jury of six men.[2] "In all criminal cases," declares Indiana's constitution in 1851 somewhat vaguely, "the jury shall have the right to determine both the law and the facts." Oath or affirmation shall be such as most consists with binding the individual's conscience.[3] No person arrested or confined in jail shall be treated with unnecessary rigor. No court shall be secret. "No person shall be incompetent as a witness by reason of his religious belief" is a maxim of the New York constitution of 1846, soon to be adopted elsewhere, as amplifying religious liberty of conscience, already an accepted rule. Amendments of the Federal constitution for protecting those accused of crime find an increasing State acceptance. "No imprisonment for debt" becomes now an unqualified State assertion;[4] and more than this, a new privilege develops in the legal exemption from seizure and attachment (since nearly universal) of a certain reasonable amount of property for every debtor, "that he may enjoy the necessary comforts of life."[5] California in 1849 specified homestead exemptions for heads of families; and recognizing the new conflict now waging in the Atlantic State legislatures for married women's rights, though not without a Spanish-American pre-

---

[1] New York, 1846; California, 1849. *Contra,* Illinois, 1848.

[2] New Jersey, 1844. North Dakota's constitution (1889) allows of a verdict by nine jurors.

[3] Indiana, 1851.

[4] Wisconsin, 1848; Texas, 1845. Cf. page 221.

[5] Wisconsin, 1848.

disposition to the civil law of matrimonial matters, that earliest of Pacific States sanctioned by its primitive constitution the wife's separate property. In the cause of sound morals, duelling had by this time been fundamentally forbidden in many States; and lotteries, too, once so popular a means of raising money for civil and religious objects.[1]

Among State organic provisions of this middle epoch of the century were several whose object was to break up finally manor and patroon systems of landholding, such as had lingered in New York, to abolish feudal tenures, and further to discountenance all leases longer than a single generation.[2] Methods were now prescribed for assessing damages wherever property might be taken for public uses, and the tender of compensation was to precede the taking.[3] Maryland's early precept enjoining equal and uniform taxation was henceforth seen formulated in one set phrase or another. Existing rights of commons, "fishery and the rights of shore," found also fundamental protection.[4]

By the middle of this century bills of rights had become largely eclectic, whatever the pride of a convention in changing old phraseology; new States copied or selected from other constitutions in force in older States; and in one or two instances of that epoch maxims had been scattered through an organic instrument without any distinct grouping.[5] But now appear new and express proscriptions of race or

---

[1] See various constitutions, 1836–1850.
[2] No lease beyond twelve years. New York, 1846. No lease longer than fifteen years. Wisconsin, 1848. The law of primogeniture or entailments shall never be in force. Texas, 1845.
[3] See Michigan, 1850. Cf. page 36; Indiana, 1851.
[4] Rhode Island, 1842. Cf. page 36.
[5] See Michigan, 1850.

15

nationality, due to the drift of political conflict for the next ten years. Indiana, though always a free commonwealth, declares that no negro or mulatto shall come into the State;[1] while free Oregon, upon being admitted as a State, pronounced with rude dogmatism that no negro, Chinaman, or mulatto should have the right of suffrage, and invited "white foreigners" only as settlers.[2] To the time-honored right of free people to bear arms[3] was now annexed, in States where deadly brawls were common, the qualification that carrying concealed weapons was not to be included.[4]

Women's rights have advanced boldly in the organic favor of American States remote from our old Atlantic slope. Many were the States, from 1850 onward, that protected the separate property of married women by constitutional maxims, as California had done,[5] while in all the other States legislation has come to establish such a policy without constitutional announcement. And since the Civil War woman's emancipation, so styled, from her common-law conditions, has progressed towards active participation in a government controlled originally by man alone, and yet not to positive victory.

"In the words of the Father of his Country," quaintly recites the preamble of Rhode Island's constitution in 1842, "we declare that the basis of our political systems is the right of the people to make

[1] Indiana, 1851.

[2] As to Chinese exclusion, Oregon appears to have gained the start of California in its organic law; and it would appear from this first constitution that mining resources were anticipated in that northerly Pacific State beyond what ever became revealed.

[3] *Supra*, page 192.

[4] Kentucky, 1850.

[5] *E. g.*, Michigan, Indiana, Oregon, Kansas, during 1850–1860. Kansas in 1859 went still farther in declaring the rights of husband and wife equal in the custody of their children.

and alter their constitutions of government," but that
what exists at any time is obligatory on all till
changed by an explicit act of the whole people.[1]
Indeed, the recognized American doctrine, with
racial qualifications, perhaps, in the slaveholding
States, appeared more clearly as time went on that
all power was inherent in the people with the right
fundamentally to make and alter whenever the public
good should require it, — this proviso being however
understood, that the government should continue
republican and popular in form. Soon after the
downfall of human slavery in 1865 we find maxims
in the State instruments of reorganized and border
States, formerly slaveholding, which announce henceforth the common faith of universal brotherhood; and
with a repudiation of all property in man, repudiating also all political distinctions founded in race or
color. Various States in this new era recanted
formally the heresy of secession, and declared allegiance to the Union henceforward as paramount to
all claims of State sovereignty.[2] If in this new
and reunited national era, the latest of all, other
maxims of fundamental right are worth recording as
State constitutional expressions, they are suggested
mostly by the growth of wealthy private corporations
or the difficult adjustment of municipal government
to the great and growing cities. Civil rights of the
negro make an additional element.[3]

Except for the racial obstructions noted, aliens
have been liberally regarded in the United States

[1] Rhode Island had just suppressed the Dorr Rebellion.

[2] See South Carolina, 1868; Virginia, 1870. Nevada, when admitted in 1864 as a new free State, had pronounced fundamentally
against the secession theory while civil war was raging.

[3] Thus the right of all citizens to travel on the public highways has
reference to discriminations of race and color by common carriers.
Mississippi and Louisiana, 1868.

for the most part. But some reaction has set in against foreign ownership of lands and corporate stock, as one or two of the latest constitutions indicate.[1]

The enlightened lead of the old thirteen States, and especially New England, in public schools and a liberal education, was not lost upon the new States of the nineteenth century, whose earliest constitutions, Ohio's, for instance, developed the same policy. Most new States, in fact, formed out of national territory, received in succession from Congress when admitted to the Union generous grants of the public land as an endowment in the cause of learning. Equal participation by the inhabitants in such endowed education, we see expressly enjoined in Ohio's first constitution.[2] These Congressional grants, for common schools and a graded system of education capped by a State university, were usually stated to be in consideration of certain fundamental advantages promised to the whole Union under the compact of State admission; and public library funds from the sale of public lots was another stipulation in early instances.[3] Michigan, of the grand tier of new northwestern States, broadly declares in 1835 by fundamental law that the Legislature "shall encourage, by all suitable means, the promotion of intellectual, scientific, and agricultural improvement," California by 1849 employing a similar expression.[4] While "Native-Americanism" swayed American politics somewhat later, the dread of Roman and foreign influence appeared in State systems of education.

[1] Washington, 1889.

[2] Ohio, 1802.

[3] See Indiana, 1816.

[4] This is after the Massachusetts example, set as early as 1783. *Supra*, page 42.

All money raised by taxation for the support of public schools was directed by a Massachusetts amendment of 1855 to be applied exclusively to schools
under legal and public control, and not to those of
any religious sect;[1] and such continues the American
rule to this day. Equality of the sexes in public
education is enjoined in some late constitutions.
But various States, where the white and colored
races are largely blended in a population now wholly
free, forbid their instruction in the same public
schools, and the policy is to educate the races
separately.[2]

"No person," declares Pennsylvania in her constitution of 1790, "shall be disqualified from office on
account of religious sentiments who acknowledges
God and a future state of rewards and punishments;"
dispensing for the future with belief in the inspiration of the Bible, the former limit of toleration. And
with the dawn of the nineteenth century, the impulse
became resistless to adopt Federal example, and get
rid of religious tests for voter, office-holder, or legislator. Maryland by 1810 abolished all taxation for
the support of religion, remitting all Christian sects
to the voluntary plan of sustenance.[3] Still earlier
had Ohio's constitution, which ushered in the present
century, proclaimed the right of conscience, the right
of free worship to the individual, without religious
preference or religious test; yet inculcating further
in the same connection that religion and morality
were essential to society, and hence that schools and

---

[1] See also Kansas, 1859. [2] 1 Bryce, 423.

[3] Much of the American written law by which this voluntary system became finally established in the different States depended upon
simple legislation where the State constitution itself had fixed no definite standard. Virginia's religious freedom act, for instance, antedated
our Federal constitution, and was perhaps the earliest legislation of
the kind.

common instruction, not inconsistent with rights of conscience, should forever be encouraged.[1] Such precedents were not lost upon Congregational New England. Connecticut's bill of rights in 1818 announced freedom henceforward for religious profession and worship, and forbade preference to any Christian sect or mode of worship. And, finally, Massachusetts, by constitutional amendment, abolished in 1833 her time-honored levy of parish taxes, and renouncing the former championship of "public Protestant teachers of piety," remitted all religious sects in the commonwealth to their own private devices for raising money.[2] "Free interchange of thought" (a right which should not be abused) is commended in some later American instruments.[3] It was not, however, until 1877 that New Hampshire, by modernizing amendment, struck out her ancient test of "Protestant religion," which discriminated against Roman Catholics for office. And atheists are still, or at least were recently, disqualified from holding office under the fundamental law of a few States.[4] Vermont's old constitution, moreover, still enjoins fundamentally upon Christians the duty of regular public worship of some sort, and the observance of the Sabbath, or Lord's day.[5]

[1] Ohio, 1802.

[2] See also Alabama's 1819 constitution forbidding religious tests for office.

[3] Indiana, 1851.

[4] In four States (Arkansas, Maryland, North Carolina, and Texas) a man is ineligible to office who denies the existence of God; in Pennsylvania he is ineligible if he does not believe in God and the existence of future rewards and punishments. In Maryland and Arkansas such a person is also incompetent as a witness. See 1 Bryce, 424.

[5] Vermont, 1793. Cf. Delaware, 1831.

Utah's singular experience as a Territory led to constitutional expressions unusually strong upon her admission as a State (1895); there should be no union of church and State, nor domination of any church; polygamous or plural marriages were forbidden, etc.

IV.

THE ELECTIVE FRANCHISE.

THAT admirable forbearance which the fathers of our Federal instrument displayed in leaving the whole delicate regulation of popular suffrage to the several States deserves repeated mention. The new system of Union could hardly have been adopted otherwise. For the House of Representatives of a Federal Congress it was thought sufficient to require that the choice of a member from any particular State should be by the same suffrage standard which that State applied for election to its own most numerous branch of the Legislature. For membership in a Federal Senate, as well as in the supreme choice of electors of a Federal chief magistrate, deference was paid to the wisdom of each State legislature, — that safe embodiment of representative authority, as the earlier practice of modern republics regarded it, in an aggregation of public men, wiser and more trustworthy, it was thought, than the people whom they represented. All this suited well the temper of confederated States in the eighteenth century, and through the nineteenth results have continued on the whole satisfactory. All discussion, all experiment over the extension of the suffrage, then, has been conducted within separate State confines, except perhaps concerning negro suffrage, which civil war compelled the whole Union to consider as in some sense a national problem. Democracy and manhood suffrage have gradually gained Federal ascendency, through ascendency in the several States where regulation is easier and more elastic. And in the meantime the Federal example since 1787 of dispensing with all religious or property tests for participation in civil government stirred quickly the States to emulation.

To repeat our former statement, this Union, so far as concerned the Federal form of government, might have developed into an aristocracy; but State direction and State institutions have compelled it to become a democracy.

This Federal Union, as we have seen, began its operations in 1789 as a combination of States quite conservative and somewhat aristocratic for the most part, showing the force of English environment in the distrustful qualifications which hedged the individual right to vote.[1] But under the sunbeams of enlightened self-government, those qualifications soon began dispersing like a morning mist. The Federalists, as the earliest national party intrenched in power, relied largely upon voters of property, upon the socially influential in established States. There were property tests and religious tests for electors and candidates already; yet, partly through the efforts of a political opposition, concessions soon appeared in one constitution or another. Pennsylvania, with no religious test for the voter, dispensed in 1790 with her former religious qualification to hold office. South Carolina, the one State where caste and cavalier prepossessions stood the strain of democratic innovation down to the defiant strife of 1861, abolished religious tests both for voter and office-holder by organic change.[2] Kentucky in 1799 pronounced in her constitution against religious tests, whether for

[1] *Supra,* page 50.   [2] *Supra,* page 44.

voters or office-holders, choosing the rule of the
Federal Union. Delaware in 1792 enlarged the
franchise so as to embrace every "white freeman"
of full age and two years' residence who paid a State
or county tax. Tax-paying was by the close of the
eighteenth century the minimum standard which
property qualification had reached under the old
enlightened State example so far as constitutional
expression was concerned; yet among the earliest of
new States, Kentucky dispensed with even this before
the century ended, as did also Vermont. Maryland
in 1810 abolished all former property qualifications,
whether for office-holding or voting, even to the payment of taxes. That the voter should be at least a
tax-payer was, however, much longer insisted upon
by most States. South Carolina's constitution of
1790 adhered to the freehold qualification; "five
hundred acres and ten negroes," or a real estate
valued at £150 sterling clear of debt, was the standard set in her organic law.

Connecticut, in her constitution of 1818, favored
qualifications of property, or of militia duty, or of a
State-tax payment within a year. Massachusetts,
abolishing all freehold or property qualifications for
the voters soon after, clung still by the poll tax for a
long period.[1] Delaware in 1831 abolished religious
and property qualifications, except as to paying taxes.
Virginia in 1830 made a technical enumeration for
property qualification, having earlier left the Legislature largely to itself. The democratic tendency
in new States before 1830 was towards dispensing
with even the tax-paying qualification, thus giving
freely the franchise and popular control of government to numbers and not property.[2] New York in

---

[1] Abolished finally in 1891.
[2] Illinois, 1818; Alabama, 1819; Missouri, 1820.

1821 dispensed with its former freehold privileges in voting, at the same time specifying for the franchise various requisites of taxation, or of service in the State militia or among the firemen. During the years 1836–1860 the final abolition of tax-paying as well as of property-holding requirements became very marked in the changed constitutions of our States. Yet there are States which to this day require the payment of a slight tax in order to vote, while Rhode Island still imposes a property qualification.

A buoyant and increasing confidence in the unregulated popular expression at the polls, for city and country alike, seems to have culminated in America about the middle of this nineteenth century. So far as white male inhabitants were concerned, all constitutional change in the States had hitherto tended to so extend the franchise that the poorest local resident not a criminal nor a dependent pauper might readily take part at the polls with those who paid taxes and had a pecuniary stake in the government; while as for bribery and the criminal disqualification not unfrequently denounced in organic law, convictions had been rare and individual disfranchisement by the Legislature still rarer. But now the native-born began to feel the evils of an unrestrained and incongruous migration from foreign lands, and of that organized machine in the largest cities which too often tampered with the ballot-box, and induced riot and corruption at the polling-booths. Greater purity of the ballot, the elimination of fraudulent opportunities, became henceforth a standing task for all good citizens. Hitherto no educational test had been applied to the common voter; but midway in this present century Native Americanism asserted itself. "No elector shall be qualified," declared Connecticut's amendment of 1855 in substance, "who cannot read the constitution or any statute of the State; " and Massachusetts by 1857 confined the ballot to such as could read the constitution in the English language and write their names. To such constraints upon ignorant suffrage those two commonwealths have ever since adhered, claiming that practical experience commends the rule, and a few States for special reasons have lately joined them. This reading and writing test is not the true one for all cases, since sturdy and honest manual labor makes better citizens than a mental training perverted. Foreigners may know their native language, if not ours, nor are the illiterate necessarily ignorant. Nevertheless, moral fitness, though a most desirable exaction, can only be tested by judicial conviction for crime, and an approximate organic satisfaction is better perhaps than none at all.

Meanwhile various other constitutions of the decade 1850–1860 are seen prescribing to one extent or another a registration system in the growing centres of population, so as to reduce the danger of false and repeated personation at the polls;[1] and such safeguards will increase with time rather than diminish.

The new State of Kentucky ordained that elections should last for three days at the request of any candidate; and new Tennessee followed by prescribing two consecutive days.[2] The eighteenth century was then near its close. Likely enough a similar usage had existed previously in Virginia or North Carolina. But the mischiefs of frequent and prolonged elections have since impressed our people; and by 1861 and the era of the Civil War, elections were almost uni-

---

[1] Virginia, 1850; Louisiana (as to New Orleans), 1852; Rhode Island, 1854.

[2] Kentucky, 1792, 1799; Tennessee, 1796.

versally confined by State organic law to a single day, each newly admitted member of the Union favoring that principle. To separate civic from State elections is held desirable in these later days; so, too, where possible, in alternate years, to separate the great State contests from the national.

That controversy, as between the ballot and *viva voce* modes of voting, whose origin we have already remarked,[1] continued far into the nineteenth century. Georgia in 1789, Pennsylvania and South Carolina in 1790, Kentucky in 1792, Vermont in 1793, Tennessee in 1796, each in turn gave fundamental preference to the modern ballot. But Kentucky, veering in her opinion, changed from the ballot in 1799 to *viva voce*, siding in practice apparently with the mother State, Virginia, whose course had been defined by statute discretion. Georgia's change of mind was somewhat similar.[2] And thus stood the issue at the close of the last century.

Since then the use of the ballot under State fundamental law has advanced steadily towards universal acceptance throughout the Union.[3] Original States, like New York and Maryland, which had once experimented with the *viva voce* method, abandoned it forever.[4] And the fair distinction drawn in 1790 by

---

[1] *Supra*, page 51. In Dr. Cortlandt F. Bishop's History of Elections in the American Colonies (III. Columbia College Historical Studies, No. 1), it is shown that proxy voting prevailed very early in Massachusetts and adjacent colonies, and that traces of this practice remained in Connecticut's early election laws down to 1819, when her charter was superseded. This mode, as in private corporations, suggests a possible origin of the American ballot. See pages 50, 51.

[2] Georgia's constitutions of 1777 and 1789 had favored the ballot; but that of 1798 required the electors to vote *viva voce* in all popular elections until the Legislature *should direct otherwise.*

[3] See Ohio, 1802; Louisiana, 1812; Connecticut, 1818.

[4] Maryland, 1810; New York, 1821.

Pennsylvania's constitution is seen recognized in various other State instruments framed previous to 1850, — that all elections shall be by ballot except those by legislators, who shall vote *viva voce*. For those in public station ought to be held by constituents to their public responsibilities and be judged by the record, while to the voter an honest independence, as among candidates, is the chief essential.

But while the method of voting remained debatable, we see in the various conventions of new States of the Mississippi valley a disposition either to compromise or evade the present issue. Mississippi in 1817, at her admission, ordained that the first State election should be by ballot, and all future elections "regulated by law;" Alabama in 1819 that all elections should be by ballot until the Assembly directed otherwise; and Indiana in 1816, earlier than either, that all popular elections should be by ballot, provided that the Legislature might, if thought expedient, change in 1821 to the *viva voce* plan, after which time the rule should remain unalterable. All such dexterous political expedients seem to have ended, as they ought, in establishing permanently for each State concerned the written or printed ballot. But Illinois, on the contrary, put the burden of proof upon advocates of the ballot, just as Georgia had done in 1798; her new constitution of 1818 ordaining that all votes should be given *viva voce* until the Legislature enacted otherwise. Even such subterfuges could not avoid destiny, for in 1848 Illinois permanently established the ballot under a new State constitution. Georgia made apparently no change before 1861, whatever might have been the legislative action. Missouri's convention in 1820 seems to have evaded the issue altogether; while Arkansas in 1836 gave clear preference to *viva voce*, just as Illinois had done when first entering upon statehood. The tendency of the century had now become unmistakable for taking each popular vote by ballot; and Michigan's concession to the contrary in 1835, that township officers might be elected *viva voce*, marks the extreme limit for suffrage by voice and a show of hands, so far as American practice permanently shaped out elections by the people.

Down to the Civil War, however, while States such as we have mentioned might be thought doubtful in their dissent from the ballot, Virginia and Kentucky stood sturdily together to resist the gathering sentiment of sister States. And in the appeal to unflinching manliness at the polls these two States insisted that every voter should show at the hustings the courage of his personal conviction. Custom and statute law seem to have fixed early the *viva voce* standard for the Old Dominion, though her organic law down to 1830 was silent on the subject. But Virginia's new constitution of that year gave to the filial Kentucky a pronounced support, by the declaration that "in all elections" to any office or place of trust, honor, and profit, the votes "shall be given openly or *viva voce*, and not by ballot." And once again in 1850, the emphatic and somewhat humorous expression of Kentucky's constitution, a few months earlier, was duplicated in the new Virginia document of that year, that "in all elections," whether by the people or the Legislature, "the votes shall be personally and publicly given *viva voce*, provided that dumb persons entitled to suffrage may vote by ballot." All this, however, won no more proselytes, for by this time all new States of the Union favored successively the ballot in their written constitutions; and while the Civil War progressed, a decade or more later, Virginia recanted such views and conformed to American practice.[1]

State reconstruction following the Civil War completed the organic triumph of the ballot-box throughout the United States. But, free from all military coercion in her organic institutions, Kentucky seems to have kept longest to the old method. In 1891, however, her constitution, too, was remodelled; and one clause of that instrument expressly declares that all elections by the people shall be by "secret official ballot." This full phrase sanctions the improved method of voting which our latest generation has adopted. Instead of the manifold private and partisan ballots once pressed upon each voter by rival canvassers at the polls, we now have in nearly every State, and as part of the organic law where new State constitutions or amendments dispose of the subject, an official ballot after what is known as the "Australian plan," publicly printed and prepared, on which appear the names of all party candidates for the voter's own secret mark of preference. A system, in short, which guards better than ever before the individual's choice and his personal freedom from corrupt and insidious temptation is the American suffrage reform which signalizes the last decade of the nineteenth century.

Growing evils of machine politics and demagogism are met by numerous provisions in State constitutions of the past forty years, whose main object is to preserve at all hazards the purity of the ballot-box and the rights of each honest voter. Hence are found many details over ballot methods, registration, and

[1] Virginia and West Virginia, 1863-1864. Every voter shall be free to use an open, sealed, or secret ballot as he may elect. West Virginia, 1872.

the appointment of inspection officers to prepare and revise voting lists, especially in the large cities.[1] Those kept at asylums or prisons at the public expense are forbidden to vote, while bribery or intimidation at the polling places, and all false personation, are crimes severely denounced for punishment, and fit reason, moreover, for depriving one of the rights of elector.[2]

A certain brief period of local residence is usually made indispensable to adult suffrage; such, for instance, as a residence within the State for two years and within the town half that time. One must, at all events, according to our State constitutions, vote only at the place where he resides; and within the first half of this century local residence for both voter and representative candidate became strongly insisted upon, as it has been ever since.[3]

Various organic provisions of a miscellaneous character qualify the right to vote. Thus South Carolina in 1810 expressly excluded non-commissioned officers of the United States from such exercise. Sailors and seminary students neither gain nor lose a voting residence by their casual presence.[4] State suffrage has been usually confined to the native-born and to those naturalized under the laws of the United States, except for residents in the last century during the Revolution, or when the Federal constitution was

[1] See New York, 1894, providing for registration lists and a bipartisan election board.

[2] See for such details the constitutions of Maryland (1867), Missouri (1875), Colorado (1876), and New York (amendments of 1894). A few States have shown a fundamental dislike to registration provisions, as in the Texas, North Carolina, and West Virginia constitutions, 1870–1876.

[3] *Semble*, that under South Carolina's constitution of the last century a freeholder might vote where he held land, even though not a resident. The text appears obscure.

[4] New York, 1894.

adopted;[1] and supported paupers are quite generally excluded together with confined criminals. Each voter must have attained majority. During the Civil War and subsequently, gratitude to the citizen soldier induced in various loyal States some special extension of the franchise for the special benefit of that class of persons.[2] Idiots and insane persons are always implied and often express exceptions to the exercise of local suffrage. While the Native American party influenced our politics, an amendment in 1858 to the ancient constitution of Massachusetts compelled an additional residence of two years within the jurisdiction of the United States subsequent to naturalization, before any person of foreign birth could be entitled to vote or eligible to office; but gratitude to the foreign-born who went forth to battle for the Union caused the repeal of that amendment in 1863. In various States at the northwest, on the contrary, the right to vote is extended to aliens who have declared their intention, even before reaching the full status of naturalized citizens of the United States. Latterly, however, some reaction from this policy has set in, Texas and Minnesota in 1896 pronouncing overwhelmingly for amendments which made suffrage by foreign immigrants more difficult.[3]

[1] Vermont by 1828 abolished a right which had been given in 1793 to denizens who were not naturalized citizens.

[2] Thus Massachusetts in 1881 relieved from pauper disqualification every person who had served in the war and been honorably discharged. During the war, provision was made by some States for taking the votes of citizen soldiers in the field. And see New York, 1874.

[3] So large were the majorities for these respective changes that in Minnesota, with no issue of nationality raised, the constitutional amendment requiring an alien to become fully naturalized before he could vote, must have been supported by many foreign-born voters already secure in their rights.

See also New York (1894) forbidding a naturalized foreigner to vote within ninety days after receiving his naturalization papers.

Negro suffrage in the United States remains a puzzling problem, and the revolution of sentiment favorable to its exercise is yet imperfect. State constitutions, those especially in the slaveholding area of the Union, made strong discriminations concerning race and color prior to 1861. This Federal Republic began its high career as the republic of European immigrants. Negroes, mulattoes, and Indians were specially excepted from the right to vote by the first of new slave States admitted into the Union.[1] Ohio, too, first-born of the Ordinance of 1787, began statehood by confining her elective franchise to "every white male inhabitant."[2] Even Connecticut in 1818 conferred suffrage only upon "white male citizens." But Maine in 1820, like her parent State Massachusetts,[3] conferred the right to vote upon "all male citizens," ignoring from the outset all distinctions of complexion. Massachusetts and New Hampshire had always been nominally liberal on this point, though the property test worked out sufficiently a practical difference. Vermont (following Pennsylvania) and Rhode Island belong to the same category.[4] New England's homogeneous population favored all this generosity to races. Yet "free white men" or "white male" inhabitants or citizens grew to be the favorite organic expression during the first sixty years of this nineteenth century, as the nation expanded, whether in slaveholding or non-slaveholding States; and sometimes, by way of recompense for their exclusion, colored free-

[1] Kentucky, 1792, 1799.
[2] Ohio, 1802.
[3] See Massachusetts, Amendment III. (1821). Cf. Massachusetts constitution, as to "male inhabitants" having a property qualification.
[4] It might have been a legal question how far free negroes in this period were to be deemed "citizens of the United States." The Dred Scott decision (1857) is to be recalled in such a connection.

men were exempted from militia duty and all payment of the poll tax.[1] North Carolina's constitution of 1835 withheld the ballot from those descended from negro ancestors to the fourth generation.[2] New York in 1821 applied specially to all negro voters the requirement of three years' State residence and a freehold property.[3] Even Pennsylvania, by 1838, changed from "all freemen" to "all white freemen" in defining the electoral franchise. At the date of our Civil War, unquestionably, the preponderance of State authority, north as well as south, justified the conclusion that America was in general effect a white man's government.[4]

Bloodshed and the long fraternal strife of arms put an end to such racial announcements. With the violent abolition of slavery throughout the land, and the reasserted supremacy of the Federal Union over all State opponents, came, as a secondary grand result, the mandatory extension of the elective franchise to manhood suffrage by Federal amendment, regardless of complexion, race, or the previous condition of bondage.[5] The lately insurgent and slaveholding States embodied that declared extension in their new fundamental codes, as Congress compelled them to do; and as for the loyal States northward, national duty and consistency demanded like organic changes. But even in States where no servile population was now set free, where slavery had never found strong foothold, and negroes still constituted

---

[1] Vermont, 1793; Pennsylvania, 1790; Rhode Island, 1842.

[2] New York, 1821; Tennessee, 1834.

[3] California in 1849 is liberal to all "white males," including those of Mexico who may elect to become citizens of the United States; and even Indians and their descendants (but not negroes) are generously considered.

[4] See Indiana, 1851; Oregon, 1857; Minnesota, 1857.

[5] *Supra*, page 197.

but a small fraction of the inhabitants, the people showed a decided repugnance to changing the old rule which had confined the ballot to " white male " inhabitants. As late as 1864 the new free State of Nevada had been admitted into the Union while the Civil War was in progress, with its organic law thus worded; and only after a long political struggle would the Empire State of New York conform its own organic expression to the fifteenth Federal amendment.[1] The reconstructed slave States, after suffering meanwhile for a few years from the domination of a corrupt political faction which the new and misguided negro vote had helped into local power, threw off the disgraceful encumbrance; and since 1877 the white natural leaders have generally preserved in their own States a practical home rule, while the degraded negro vote has remained dormant or suppressed. A better and stronger participation of whites and negroes at the polls is hoped for hereafter, as the race so long in bondage gains in education and industrial independence through the civilizing process of freedom. Meantime constitutional changes have been wrought in several of these States, which, without actually transgressing the Federal requirements, bear chiefly against the large negro element in the population, by advancing the general tests of education and property for all electors,[2] and perhaps,

[1] Such a proposition had been in 1846 submitted separately to the voters of that great State for adoption, when it was rejected by a vote of two to one. Again submitted by way of amendment in 1860, unrestrained negro suffrage was rejected by an immense majority. A new constitution for New York was framed in 1868, which renewed the proposal of equal suffrage regardless of race or color; and the people negatived that proposal by a closer vote. But by constitutional amendment in 1874 equal suffrage was proposed once more, and that amendment was finally carried at the polls.

[2] See Mississippi's constitution of 1890, and South Carolina's of 1896.

too, by multiplying the enumerated convictions for crime upon which any individual offender may be wholly disfranchised.[1]

The gradual establishment of a plurality poll in place of the majority, as formerly, was in our older States the fruit of hard experience. For repeatedly, when leading parties were so divided that a third candidate held the balance of power, were the people baffled in their preference, so that a new trial at the polls became necessary, or else the Legislature, after a fundamental rule prevalent in the last century, became the umpire of candidates. Several of the leading historical States abandoned the majority for the plurality doctrine soon after the middle of this century,[2] conforming to a practice established much earlier in other parts of the Union. By that period, too, it became common in all newly admitted States to prefer the same electoral test, and thus decide the candidate chosen, once and for all, according to the obvious wishes of the greater number who had voted.[3]

Minority representation is a new political idea recognized in some of the later constitutions, though scarcely favored, being confined naturally to local groups, such as aldermen, representing a single district or city.[4] Cumulative voting, which is much aided by the Australian official ballot, seeks such an end; and here among more nominations on a ticket

[1] "Petty larceny" is included among the offences thus punishable in Virginia's constitution of 1876. See also North Carolina, 1876.

[2] Massachusetts, 1855; Maine, 1856; Virginia, 1880. Cf. Federal constitution, old-fashioned in this respect, page 162.

[3] Vermont, Rhode Island, and Connecticut are probably the only States in the Union which still require a majority to elect at the polls.

[4] See Illinois constitution, 1870. West Virginia, 1872, permits a *referendum* on this issue. So in South Dakota; but the vote proved adverse.

than there are persons to be voted for, voters can accumulate their strength in the selection.

California in 1879 excluded all natives of China from the suffrage.[1] Hitherto the American rule with trivial exceptions is seen to have been, under its most liberal conditions, that of manhood suffrage; and the admission of woman partially or fully to the same political privilege has now become an agitating issue, of whose final outcome in States long organized upon the historical basis of self-government it is yet too early to judge.[2] That the Legislature may disfranchise those convicted of infamous crime is a constitutional permission, founded upon sound reason, which at this day is largely bestowed.[3]

Under some of the earliest constitutions of the new Federal epoch electors were specially privileged from arrest (except for specified heinous offences) during their attendance at the elections or while going and returning; and this privilege from arrest

---

[1] *Semble*, in conflict with the 15th Federal Amendment, unless regulated by some such test as that of religion.

[2] See Minnesota's partial permit to the Legislature in 1875; Utah's constitution (1895) establishes it. See also permissive clauses, North and South Dakota.

[3] Kentucky in 1799 denounced penalties against those convicted of bribery, forgery, or other high crimes and misdemeanors, one of which was exclusion from the suffrage. Special disqualification from voting, as a penalty for criminal conviction, became a just feature of many of our later constitutions; and to the Legislature was given full power on the subject under one fundamental phrase or another. Ohio, 1802; Louisiana, 1812. Connecticut's organic law of 1818 (amended, 1875) required every elector to "sustain a good moral character," and deprived one without reservation of his right to vote on conviction of bribery, forgery, perjury, duelling, fraudulent bankruptcy, "or other offence for which infamous punishment is inflicted." That the Legislature may disfranchise those convicted of infamous crime is the milder expression of many States. Indiana, 1816; New York, 1821; Delaware, 1831; Virginia, 1830; Tennessee, 1834. "Betting on elections" is an offence. New York, 1846. Bribery, or the attempt to bribe, is a felony; and one who offers a bribe may testify without being prosecuted for doing so. New York, 1894.

has become during the present century a feature of many State constitutions.[1] No elector shall be obliged to perform militia duty on election day except in time of war or public danger.[2] And during our latest era the American disposition has increased to combine elections so as to reduce their number and frequency, and give the local people of a State relief from political turmoil and excitement. State and national elections have in consequence been set for the same day, where formerly they were held in different months of the same year; and biennial State elections for both Legislature and the highest executive officers are now decidedly preferred to those annual pollings once deemed so essential to liberty.[3]

Not only in the extension of voting membership, but through increased opportunities for exercising the power to choose among candidates, has the elective franchise made immense progress during the past century in these United States. The choice of local town and county officers at the polls has been consistently maintained from the colonial age, and more than ever do such incumbents derive authority from the people. Instead of choosing members of a single representative assembly, or of the most numerous branch only of the Legislature, as formerly, the mass of voters in each State have become, through the gradual assimilation in representative character of the two houses of a State legislature, electors on a uniform basis of qualification to both State Senate

---

[1] Pennsylvania, Delaware, Kentucky, and Tennessee, 1790–1799. The phrase is suggested by that clause of our Federal constitution which defines the privilege for members of Congress.

[2] Utah, 1895. And see *supra*, page 33.

[3] *Supra*, page 18.

and House. While for years after American independence was declared, the chief magistrate of many States was chosen by the Legislature, that choice now devolves upon the general body of voters instead, as does also that of most other high executive officers, and, by as nearly a direct process as the Federal constitution will permit, of President and. Vice-President of the United States besides. Finally, and as the full triumph of free suffrage longest opposed by conservative citizens, judges and the chief officials connected with the machinery of the courts are now chosen by the voters in nearly every State, — sometimes at large and sometimes by districts. The march of the American democracy to power has proved irresistible.

V.

THE LEGISLATURE.

THE general pattern of an American State legislature, as shaped out by 1789, has served ever since without essential change. And the practical reconstruction of Congress by that important date gave to the more favored plan of a two-chambered body throughout the United States an immense propulsion. For under all republican governments experience teaches that the law-making power needs a constant check upon headlong activity, like that swift messenger of the fairy tale who had to put clogs upon his feet lest he should run too far. Scarcely had the Federal government started upon its nobler career, when Georgia and Pennsylvania, the only States among the old thirteen that had hitherto since 1776 experimented with the Legislature of a single house, gave up forever that tumultuous representative body, and conformed thenceforth to the bicameral rule.[1] Vermont, however, whose young admiration of Pennsylvania's previous instrument of State government was unquenched, entered the Union in 1793 with a single representative body by way of Legislature. But in that bucolic State of small townships, coequal in comparison, under highly favorable conditions for further experiment, the plan did not work well, and by 1836 a legislature of two branches was substituted. These tests appear to have been conclu-

---

[1] 1789–1790, under new State constitutions.

sive enough for American opinion; and the two-chambered Legislature has since remained the only kind set up in the United States.

But a true basis of difference between the two representative branches of a State legislature has not been easy to formulate. That happy composite of the many and the one which supplies historical distinction between the Senate and House of Representatives of Congress finds no analogy in the population of an individual State. Some of our earlier local statesmen would have drawn out a basis of distinction for the commonwealth by opposing property or social standing in the upper or smaller branch to numbers in the lower or larger; but the deep-set repugnance of the common voters to anything like organic recognition of privileged wealth or aristocracy sweeps us farther and farther from such political arrangements. Nothing has been left in the present era by way of a real difference of deputed authority in the two branches of a State legislature, but such as comes from representing geographical voting districts of larger area and population in the Senate, and of smaller area and population in the House, with perhaps a higher standard of age and a more stable tenure in the one branch than in the other. Nor are even such slight differences tolerated patiently in a crisis of excitement by our jealous democracy, eager that its will shall be promptly and implicitly obeyed by the whole Legislature, and that each member shall bend to his constituency. The result of all this is naturally to invite into power flexible and time-serving legislators, seldom very wise, and frequently dishonest, to the exclusion of the free-spoken with minds of their own. In Massachusetts, as in most parts of New England, it was long the rule of representation to apportion the State

Senate by counties and the House by towns; and since candidates were arranged as much as possible by general tickets in the earlier days of the Union, leading citizens and their constituencies made of legislative service a matter for local pride and distinction. The ablest and most popular in the town and county were re-chosen to the General Court year after year. But in course of time, as republicanism grew less compliant, the argument for separate and subdivided candidacies, for numerical representation by one periodical census or another, and for local rather than general tickets, carried such weight that the old system passed into discredit. Temporary geographical lines now made arbitrary groups by districts, combining towns and subdividing counties for one or another branch of the Legislature; and with little left to interest the foremost citizens in sacrificing personal time for the public, little chance for conspicuous service, representation now came much under the control of intriguers and petty seekers for place; instead of centurions in politics were the leaders of tens and twenties; while towns, cherishing local pride no longer, had to be content with bargaining that the common deputy of the geometrically arranged district for the time being should be put up at one locality for one legislature, and at another for the next. Deterioration of ideals and of personal character comes as a necessary consequence of all this modern nicety in fractional representation, though other causes of political degeneracy may doubtless be sought elsewhere; as, for instance, in the undiscriminating extension of the elective franchise among the shiftless and illiterate, and the growing wealth and complexity of society, affording opportunities and temptation for masters of political chicanery to use organization for base ends. Democracy itself, so admirable in most other phases, yields too much to insidious flattery, and by its capricious and uncertain temper towards public servants and its misplaced gratitude for public services, repels many who were best worth trusting above the commonplace.

Pennsylvania's constitution of 1790 apportioned senators of the State by districts. They were never to be less in number than one-fourth nor greater than one-third of the representatives. Both houses are in 1796 declared by the new State of Tennessee "dependent on the people." Following Federal example, the names "Senate" and "House of Representatives" henceforth became usually distinctive of the two branches.[1] New York in 1801 increased her House and diminished her Senate, in order the better to make a fair contrast of size a prime element of distinction. The same period of service for both houses was selected in some new constitutions of the eighteenth century. But other States preferred something more like the Federal arrangement; and so at least that senators should be chosen for a double, treble, or still longer term than members of the House, with perhaps a corresponding division of classes, for effecting a gradual change of membership, as in the United States Senate.[2] While "annual elections" continued still into the nineteenth century the rule of the States for choosing to the popular branch, at least,[3] Tennessee, upon her admis-

---

[1] Delaware in 1792 substitutes this style for "Council" and "House of Assembly."

[2] Kentucky, 1799; South Carolina and Pennsylvania, 1790; Delaware, 1792. Kentucky, 1792, tried the Maryland plan of an electoral college for choosing senators, and by 1799 abandoned it. *Supra*, page 54.

[3] See Kentucky, Vermont, Pennsylvania, South Carolina, Georgia, New Hampshire, 1789–1800.

sion in 1796, ordained biennial elections for either branch. State elections, long held in the spring of the year, became by national influence transferred gradually to the fall, and then absorbed into the month and Tuesday of November designated for Federal ˉelections. While New England favored towns as the early unit of representation in the House, southern States in the vicinity of Virginia chose rather the county for that purpose. And that census plan of periodical apportionment for representatives, which the Federal constitution was not the earliest to offer, becomes rapidly a permanent feature in State systems.[1] Both houses, says Ohio, as the nineteenth century began, are "to be chosen by the people;" and her simple tax-paying qualification for membership in either branch betokened the dawn of a liberal dispensation of former property requirements.[2] As in earlier State constitutions, eligibility to the Legislature was made incompatible with holding other places of public trust; and priests and ministers of the gospel were in many States pronounced ineligible to the Legislature.[3] Laws enacted were to be published at the end of each session.

Distrust of the Legislature appeared in fundamental State provisions very soon after the new machinery of our Federal Union had been set in full motion. And most of the constraints now gradually

[1] See Pennsylvania, Tennessee, Georgia, during the eighteenth century.

[2] Ohio, 1802. But Louisiana, 1812, imposed a landed test, while some older States were abolishing such standards. New York long retained her freehold requisite for membership in the Senate.

[3] The Massachusetts constitution of 1780 placed no such disqualification upon the clergy; but officers of instruction at Harvard College were made specially ineligible, — a rule which was not repealed until 1877.

imposed by the people of the States were doubtless the offspring of public evils practically felt. Thus, New Hampshire ordained in 1792 that no member of the Legislature should take fees or serve as counsel or advocate in either branch.[1] The appointment during one's legislative term to an office not elective, which had been newly created, or whose emoluments had been increased by the Legislature in which he served, was largely forbidden.[2] Secrecy of procedure, in State, as in the United States Senate, came under speedy condemnation. That the galleries of each House shall be open to all persons who behave decently we find proclaimed in various new constitutions before the close of the last century.[3] Ohio's constitution in 1802 set an example of parsimony in fixing the pay of legislators at a low rate, and there has been much regulation of the matter since, in the various States, with an ingenuity to discover some standard which might induce short sessions. That no increase of compensation to members shall go into effect for the same session in which the bill passes has long been the rule of many States.[4] And as the middle of this century approached, the popular purpose grew persistent to settle by basic and precise provisions the relative number of each branch, rules for apportionment and taking the census, and most other details of representative election. A classified Senate, like that of the United States, was now in the height of American favor ; while as to biennial

---

[1] Vermont in 1793 provided similarly.

[2] Pennsylvania, 1790; Delaware, 1792. Nor for one year after. Kentucky, 1799. The Federal constitution is imitated in such provisions.

[3] New Hampshire and Delaware, 1792; Vermont, 1793; Tennessee, 1796. See also Pennsylvania, 1776; New York, 1777. *Supra*, page 56.

[4] See New York, Virginia, Tennessee, Alabama, and Mississippi about 1820.

legislatures, several States had advanced by 1850 to the next stage of making sessions biennial besides, as well as the Legislature itself.[1] No session, prescribes Louisiana's organic law in 1845, shall last beyond sixty days.[2] And when in extraordinary session, says that of Illinois in 1848, those subjects only shall be considered for which the Legislature was convened.

As in the elective franchise, we now see religious and property qualifications for the Legislature dispensed with, age and a local residence being the only enduring requisites for a seat in either branch.[3] In the latter respect State fundamental law has grown more insistent, if possible, as time goes on; and British observers of our institutions have not failed to comment upon the disadvantage of such a rule, in keeping the best talent of a whole State from competing for the public service, in order that local mediocrity may be exalted beyond its deserts. But whatever may be the force of this objection, the American people appear committed beyond recall to such requirement, since it gives mathematical force to each constituency. And in the more ambitious prize of representative to Congress, where State constituencies are still so much at liberty to go outside their own area for a candidate, it rarely happens that a non-resident district representative is sent to the Federal House at Washington by choice of the district voters. For a certain prepossession towards local objects, such as comes from common residence, is deemed needful for a representative; so, too, local interests must be regarded, both in procuring the

[1] See Georgia, Texas, Alabama, Maryland, 1840–1846. This is an advance upon the Federal plan of a biennial Congress holding annual sessions.

[2] And all legislation beyond that date should be null and void.

[3] Delaware was the latest State which required a property qualification for the Senate. But see constitution (1897).

crumbs, however small, of public patronage, and in guarding and shaping special concerns in the vast miscellaneous business of a legislature. For all enactments of a legislature do not affect alike the welfare of the whole body politic, nor aim at general reforms; nor is all public administration an administration for all. A few constitutions of the eighteenth century in its final decade insisted still upon freehold or property qualifications, especially in the State Senate;[1] and the property test outlasted in the new era that of religion; yet Federal example and the genius of American democracy tended speedily to abolish all such distinctions. While the yeomen or property-holders sat together in a legislature, membership was of a higher grade, like that which we now see in a social club.

Federal example set the fashion for various phrases of special description in a State constitution, relating to officers and methods of organization and due procedure for either house in transacting the public business. And so, too, in the relative functions of the two houses, much the same sort of definition became applied. Thus, "bills for raising revenue" (a style henceforth preferable to the State "money bills," so called before 1787) were likewise to originate in the House, or larger body; yet as this nineteenth century developed, and two branches in most States were found in fact equally representative of the people, unlike the American Congress, the disposition of State conventions increased to dispense with such old distinctions, so that all bills whatever might originate in either house.[2] One idea embodied

---

[1] *E. g.*, South Carolina, Tennessee, Delaware, New York.

[2] See Tennessee, 1796, setting an example in this respect, since widely followed.

in a State constitution or two of the eighteenth century,[1] has found much favor since: that every new bill must be read for three successive days, with free opportunity of discussion before it passes, unless in case of urgency a stated fraction of the whole membership much greater than a majority dispenses with the rule in that branch where the bill is pending. More significant still is the spread of an early New Jersey fundamental, which substitutes for the majority of a quorum, in various instances, the majority of all elected to the body. Thus, while Federal practice, and that perhaps of most States, still conforms to the old Parliamentary standard of a majority of the quorum for passing any bill, with a larger fraction, such as two-thirds, for overcoming vetoes and in other special cases, not less than nineteen of the United States could be counted in 1884 which made instead the majority of all elected the test of original passage in either branch, while some nine States applied that standard for passing bills over an executive veto.[2]

Old State precedent[3] has been much followed in permitting a legislature (where the Federal constitution itself is silent) to punish by brief imprisonment persons not members who are guilty of contempt. By 1844 New Jersey put forth another idea for the first time apparently in our organic law, that each bill passed by the Legislature must have but one subject, the same to be expressed in its title; and New York in 1846 confining the idea rather to private and local bills, that rule more or less compre-

[1] Kentucky, 1799, and prior Virginia and North Carolina provisions; also Illinois and New York, 1816–1835.

[2] See New Jersey (1776); tables in Horace Davis's Constitutions, 67, 68. Kentucky, 1799, first illustrates the latter instance of requiring a majority of all elected in either branch to overcome a veto.

[3] *Supra*, page 67.

17

hensive has since found its way into many other State constitutions, often with the added proviso that no law shall be enacted at all except by a bill.[1] That no public act shall be in force until a stated period after the end of the session corrects some mischiefs of the old common law, peculiarly distressing before steam locomotion and the telegraph were invented. Not even the public contracts of a legislature have escaped the vigilance of constitution framers in the newer States. Those for fuel or for stationery must be given to the lowest bidder; extra compensation on public contracts must never be awarded; nor may any member of the Legislature be lawfully interested in public contracts.[2] In New York State the stringent constitutional rule is now that all money bills and such as appropriate money or other property for local or private purposes shall require for their passage in each branch of the Legislature the two-thirds vote of all members elected.[3]

The era of strong fundamental restraint upon legislative power in America opened with the second quarter of the nineteenth century. The patronage of electing the chief executive and all other high State officials became by this time quite generally taken from legislatures that had once enjoyed it, and vested by State constitution in the suffrage of the people. And, furthermore, the brief constitutional text applicable to legislative action in the earlier instruments, importing great confidence in the discretion of the people's representatives, ceases forever to

[1] California's constitution in 1849 well rounds off the expression, adding that no law shall be revised or amended by reference to its title, but the section amended shall be published at length. Appropriation bills shall contain no other provisions. Illinois, 1848.

[2] Wisconsin and Illinois, 1848.

[3] New York, 1894.

characterize these written fundamental ordinances. Nothing so convincingly manifests the progress of a popular self-confidence and strength among Americans, as contrasted with the old customary repose of constituents in the superior wisdom of the social superiors who represented them, as the nineteenth-century development in this special respect. Instead of leaving such public agents, as in Revolutionary times, to formulate and philosophize over the extent to which it might be safe to admit the commonalty to participate in government, we see communities as the efficient principals binding public agents by their own fundamental rules and cutting down credentials, as though deference to statesmanship were at an end. Instead of looking up to the Legislature as the arcanum of fundamental liberties, we see the people inclining rather to governors and the courts, as a needful corrective upon legislatures tempted to go astray. Instead of hailing each new session of the people's representatives as the advent of salutary reform, we see legislatures shortened and kept adjourned as much as possible, because of their sinister disturbing influence upon the sober pursuits of life; and beyond all delegation of authority is seen the popular determination to bend this and all other departments of government to public opinion, and render each public servant responsible for his stewardship.

These restrictions upon legislative action have become so varied and numerous in our modern State constitutions, and so diffuse, moreover, as scarcely to admit of a clear classification. First and foremost, they show by 1835 a positive disrelish of special legislation, and especially of that for the benefit of business corporations. General laws become henceforth insisted upon as much as possible by way of substitute. Thus, the Legislature shall have no power to suspend a general law for individual benefit, nor to pass laws for individual benefit which are inconsistent with general laws, nor to grant special privileges, immunities, and exceptions.[1] No private law shall be passed unless upon due notice of application.[2] Private and special privileges and appropriations are seen checked in various ways. Some States shortly before the middle of the century tried to hamper the private creation of corporations; others forbade that corporations, excepting municipal ones, should be specially created, but remitted their formation altogether to general laws, with a general reservation that the Legislature might alter or repeal.[3] Laws for loans or for pledging the State credit are expressly limited, both in the amount to be borrowed and the method of legislative enactment.[4] The particulars of taxation, too, under a just assessment, are defined; and those, too, of collection.[5] Before the middle of the century, and following the disastrous crisis of public State improvements about 1837, still more specific and stringent constraint was placed by organic law upon loans of State credit, and the authority to create State debts where no emergency of war or insurrection existed. Municipal borrowing, furthermore, was expressly limited, and municipal authority in other respects; nor should the State, through legislation, aid private individuals or corporations.[6] Banks were the first among chartered

---

[1] Tennessee, 1834.   [2] North Carolina, 1835.

[3] See California, 1849; also various States (1835–1849), such as Rhode Island, New York, Pennsylvania, Michigan, Florida, Texas, Wisconsin.

[4] Mississippi, 1832.

[5] Maine, 1820.

[6] See 1842–1849, Rhode Island, Maine, New York, New Jersey, Illinois, Florida, Wisconsin, Texas, California.

private corporations to encounter such popular dislike;[1] but after the Civil War it was chiefly the railway-carrier.

There shall be no act of incorporation hereafter, says Delaware in 1831, unless two-thirds of each branch concur; a power of revocation shall be reserved, and the term (unless for public improvement) shall not extend beyond twenty years. In divorce and alimony matters, the alteration of names, adoption, and the restoration of voting rights to those convicted of crime, States authorized general legislation, but forbade special enactments on the subject.[2] And so, too, in organizing churches and private societies, and in authorizing the sale of lands, general laws, with a special procedure in the courts, now found fundamental favor.

The impulse thus given by 1850 to legislative regulation and constraint by State fundamental law has since been steadily felt, and extended to every quarter of the Union. Every later reform has been in the same direction of fundamental constraint by the people, so that public servants may not feel above their masters. As for the structure of our American Legislature of two houses, New England States still prefer that each branch shall come wholly fresh from the people at each election; which election in Massachusetts and Rhode Island alone is still annual, after the eighteenth-century fashion.[3] But

---

[1] See Indiana, Illinois, Missouri, Mississippi, 1816–1820. No more than one bank shall ever be chartered by the same act. Pennsylvania, 1838, recalling Governor Snyder and the "litter of banks" which he killed by a veto.

[2] North Carolina, 1835.

[3] An amendment proposing the change from annual to biennial legislatures was submitted to the people of Massachusetts in 1896 and voted down at the polls.

all other States of the Union, old or new, have
adopted biennial terms, — a system which has given
satisfaction wherever tried. And in choosing biennial legislatures the State preference by two to one
is, furthermore, in favor of biennial sessions, unlike
the rule of Congress.[1] Senators hold usually in our
States by the classified plan and with longer tenure
than the House; but a half rotation at each election,
so as to bring the Senate in closer touch with public
sentiment, modifies the Federal example.[2] For either
branch of the Legislature the candidate, local by
district and local in residence, is chosen at the polls.
About half the United States limit the general session of a legislature, even though it be only a biennial
one, to a fixed number of days, averaging less than
ninety.[3] Nor has it been thought ignoble to so regulate the pay of legislators as to spur them up to
organize promptly and push their work to its conclusion; for we find a gross salary fixed for the whole
session,[4] or a *per diem* for so many days, and no
longer;[5] while Indiana's constitution of 1851 made
the humiliating rule that each legislature must organize within five days from assembling a quorum, or
else have all the pay stopped until the organization
is complete.

Other stringent provisions are found. No new
bill shall be introduced after so many days[6] of the

[1] New York, New Jersey, Kansas, and Wisconsin, besides some New
England and various scattered Southern States, prefer annual sessions
for a biennial legislature.

[2] New York, in 1846, took this new departure as the result of long
experience, and Michigan, Ohio, and other States presently joined her.
See Table (1884) Davis's Constitutions, 68.

[3] Davis, *ib*. No session to last longer than the length prescribed by
organic law, unless two-thirds of all elected vote to extend it. Kentucky, 1850; and see Virginia, 1850.

[4] Oregon, 1857.

[5] Michigan, 1850.   [6] Fifty. Michigan, 1860.

session have expired. No law shall pass by either house on the day prescribed for adjournment, but bills may then be enrolled.[1] Acts shall not pass to cure former omissions, but by general statutes the courts may be authorized to apply such remedy. The people shall choose a State printer; stationery contracts shall be awarded by a legislature to the lowest bidder; perquisites of members in public documents, books, newspapers, and postage are cut down or forbidden. No State paper shall be selected or established for publishing the laws.[2] A date is designated when all acts of a session with fixed exceptions shall take effect, having by that time been duly published and circulated. Technical terms must be avoided in legislation; every act shall have its title, and only one subject; all acts are to be presumed public acts, nor shall revision be made by mere reference. Riders shall not be placed upon appropriation acts, but every such act shall appropriate only.[3] Many compulsory provisions of this character originated in States of the Mississippi valley, or west of the Rocky range; but some, the oldest and wealthiest of Atlantic commonwealths, like New York, have since made similar regulation, tired of the long usage in bodies unrestrained like Congress, of deferring enactments both trivial and momentous to the closing days of a session, and then, with shameful haste, much scandal and little scrutiny, pushing the whole mass through together.[4]

Massachusetts, proud of traditions and her old framework of government, not only resists to the last

[1] Minnesota, 1857.   [2] See Michigan, 1850; Ohio, 1851.

[3] Virginia, Ohio, Indiana, Oregon, 1851–1857.

[4] By New York's amendments of 1894, all bills must have been printed and distributed to the legislators at least three days before their passage.

such modern organic changes, but stands for the broadest discretion still possible in legislative procedure and policy. After temporizing for a while in her basis of membership with the modern embarrassment of growing cities and depleted towns, that State conformed before the Civil War to the new necessity of district numerical representation. Virginia, after a somewhat similar effort to temporize, found herself overwhelmed with a solution of the representative problem which in the Civil War cost the State her whole western population. A strict apportionment rule for the two legislative branches under a periodical census became the almost invariable practice of American States before 1861. Limitations were by that time usually fixed or clearly designated in new constitutions concerning the size of each house. Many, however, of the changes which in more modern constitutions of our States have been seen fundamental[1] are by force of mere statute wrought out in Massachusetts and the few other States which still confide in the discretion of representatives, and hug the old theory that legislatures, freely chosen and frequently convening, are the palladium of republican liberty. Biennial legislatures, with biennial sessions, would hardly suit a commonwealth until fundamental checks had been put upon legislation itself.

Scarcely a State in the Union, except Delaware,[2] exists at the present day, outside of New England, whose constitution does not enter into details which prohibit special legislation. During the decade preceding our Civil War the constitutions of Indiana and Oregon enumerated the instances at length where

---

[1] E. g., the preference of systematic organization and procedure under general laws to special enactment.

[2] A new Delaware constitution (1897) is just ordained.

general legislation should be rather applied; for
instance, in duties of justices of the peace and con-
stables; in regulating court practice and the venue
of actions; in divorce, the change of names, and
inheritances; in sales of the real estate of minors and
insane persons; in laying out highways and town
plats; in regulating county and township business;
in taxation, the support of schools, official fees and
salaries; as to interest and usury and the conduct of
elections. Minnesota just before 1860 set an organic
rule relative to lending the credit of the State to
certain railroads; and wearied of recent experience
in mingling State liability with private enterprises,
we see various States prohibiting thenceforward all
debts of that character, while arranging to sell out
the State stock held in existing schemes of improvement. Constraints already prevalent upon
private incorporation, and the incurring of debt,
State or municipal, increase rather than diminish as
the new era progresses.[1] In short, American State
constitutions at the present day strongly favor the
idea of impartiality towards all inhabitants, and the
uniform operation of all laws throughout the commonwealth to its remotest borders without preference
or privilege to any men or set of men.

If it be objected that all such hampering provisions
show distrust of the people's representatives, that
distrust is generated by a superior constituency, confident of its capacity to give instructions. A lapse

---

[1] See Wisconsin, 1871, which, among other express prohibitions
upon special legislation, names the location or change of county seats,
the apportionment of the school fund, the incorporation or charter
amendment of any town or village. The Legislature shall audit no
claim, but shall only appropriate after the claim has been audited.
New York, 1872. No extra compensation shall be voted to any public
officer or contractor. *Ib.*

in character and ability may be predicated usually of our public agents in times of peaceful routine; but all the while good citizens are vigilant and patriotic, and in great emergencies they come to the front. Public life has no great charm here with its tidal changes, and men prefer the more permanent dignity and emolument of private station. But public opinion still watches and influences; and the average community of worth and intelligence, with skilful merchants and corporate organizers, university instructors and professional men, journalists, whose power for good or evil is immense, and farmers and mechanics, trained to intelligence and self-reliance, form opinions on all public questions as they arise and determine for themselves what should be done, where once they left that determination to leaders. The morning paper keeps each in touch with affairs, and comment invites conclusion. Hence is it that the circle which legislates is itself encircled by a vaster deliberating audience, which is quick to note vicious tendencies, and brings practical ingenuity to bear upon their correction. "The longer a constitution," it is sometimes argued, "the weaker the people, and the more corrupt a community." Rather should we say that, the longer a constitution, the more complex the public interests which have to be considered, and the sounder and more confident the people that thus manifest a determination to head off corruption and to bind all lesser agencies by overmastering rules. Scarcely a change has been here recited in legislative power and procedure which is not, upon the whole, a change for the better.

VI.

THE EXECUTIVE.

THE trend of experience in American States has been since 1789 to free the Executive of the people from the trammels of subordination which the Legislature once applied. Two results have thus gradually come about: (1) that the State chief magistrate, somewhat after the example of a Federal president, brings a certain dignity and independence of his own to bear upon legislative action; (2) that the Executive, as well as the legislator, feels an immediate dependence upon public opinion, and is equally representative of the voters, though representing officially the whole State, and not a fraction or geographical portion thereof. And thus does immediate and practical representation of the people broaden greatly its original base. All this is very different from our American disposition in the Revolutionary age, for then no bulwark seemed too strong against executive tyranny, as personified in the late monarch or royal governors of Great Britain, and a legislature seemed the sole refuge of public liberty.

Now that "President" had become the style of the Federal Executive, States formerly employing that designation dropped it for "Governor" on the earliest opportunity following 1789.[1]

The first organic change noticeable in these component States after the new Union went into opera-

---

[1] *E. g.*, Pennsylvania and Delaware before 1800.

tion was inevitably to deprive the legislature of its primary choice of a chief magistrate where such a choice had formerly prevailed. Massachusetts had since 1783 furnished notably the admirable example of a State executive directly chosen by the people. The Federal mechanism, too, for selecting a president, though cumbrous and defective enough, meant at all events an escape for Federal government from the incubus of primary selection by Congress. In the new State of Kentucky, therefore, public opinion worked rapidly in the new direction. At once discarding the mother-State practice of choosing a governor by the Legislature, that State tried in 1792 the *quasi* Federal expedient of a choice by special (senatorial) electors; but by 1799 this choice was transferred to the people. Pennsylvania, Vermont, Delaware, and Tennessee, during the last ten years of the eighteenth century, concurred in the test of election by popular suffrage under their new organic law.[1] Ohio again in 1802 gave the choice of State Governor to the people; Louisiana, the next new State, making a strange compromise instead,[2] which, by 1845, gave way to popular elections conformable to American State practice elsewhere. As the nineteenth century passed its first quarter, old States, such as Georgia, North Carolina, and Connecticut,[3] in framing new constitutions, were seen conforming to this principle; Virginia, however, in 1830 still keeping to its Revolutionary mode of legislative choice of a governor. New States meanwhile were

---

[1] But Georgia, in 1798, adhered to choice by the Legislature; and so did South Carolina, 1790.

[2] A legislature fresh from the people was to ballot from the two highest candidates voted for at the polls. Louisiana, 1812.

[3] Connecticut had long pursued this popular plan under her charter government, prior to the constitution of 1818, which emanated from the people.

invariably conferring the choice of chief magistrate upon the people, under their successive instruments.

A plurality choice, moreover, by the people (which must almost invariably result in a positive selection between candidates on a single trial at the polls) found strong proselytes before the last century ended, since evidently the larger fraction of public support is the safest. Of States so committed before 1800 were Pennsylvania, Delaware, and Tennessee. Ohio opened the new century with a State constitution of 1802, which announced the same rule, since almost universal. American practice had formerly favored the idea that wherever a majority of voters was requisite, the eventual choice from among the highest candidates should revert to the State Legislature, if the people elected no one, since, in so essential a department of government, time ought not to be wasted over further trials at the polls.[1] And to this older rule some of our original States adhered during the first half of the nineteenth century, — Maine, on her separation from Massachusetts in 1820, still retaining it.

Federal example now favored an increase in length of the executive term, so as better to promote independence, experience, and stability in each incumbent of the office, formerly chosen annually. Four years was the term fixed upon by Kentucky in 1799, and in 1812 by Louisiana. Three years, somewhat earlier, had Pennsylvania and Delaware established it by way of change, while South Carolina, Georgia, and Tennessee, between 1790 and 1800, made two years their preference. Ohio, in 1802, fixed the tenure at

[1] See Vermont, 1793; *supra*, page 60. The constitution of the United States still retains this antiquated feature of eighteenth-century instruments.

two years, and various other States followed with the same limit. But Vermont, faithful to New England tradition in this respect, pronounced upon her admission [1] for annual elections; nor did Connecticut vary her ancient rule in that respect when superseding, after the War of 1812, her colonial charter. Outside New England, however, the tendency for longer terms of office and less frequent elections was soon unmistakable, New York, Virginia, and North Carolina all speeding before 1835 in that direction, and new States taking the same current almost instinctively. In short, by the present day, not a State governor can be found outside of New England whose term of office is not at least two years; while about half of our State executives are chosen rather for three or four years. [2]

Re-eligibility to supreme office was restrained by various jealous instruments of the earlier epoch; yet that restraint appears almost invariably to have been partial only, and so as to permit of one's re-election for a specified number of years out of some longer stated period, or after the expiration of so many years in retirement. Delaware in 1831, while raising the executive term from three to four years, declared the Governor re-ineligible altogether, — a constraint which appears at this day quite abnormal in the American system. [3]

Organic tests for such station were not long kept up after 1789. Pennsylvania, Delaware, Vermont, and Kentucky, among States framing new or original constitutions towards the close of the last century, dispensed liberally with both religious and property qualifications. Maryland in 1810 abolished all property qualifications, whether for executive office or the Legislature; and Ohio in 1802 entered the Union

[1] 1793.   [2] Davis, Tables, page 67.   [3] *Ib.*

free of all such impositions. Tennessee in 1834 abolished the freehold qualification for Governor. Towards the middle of the present century new constitutions and new States usually ignored both property and religious tests. On the other hand, the constitution of South Carolina had exacted property of the value of £1500; that of Tennessee a freehold of five hundred acres; that of New Hampshire, besides property, that the Governor should be of the Protestant religion;[1] while Louisiana in 1812 required landed property worth five thousand dollars. New York's constitution of 1821, with all its popular innovations in other respects, maintained for Governor the former freehold requirement. North Carolina, when revising her instrument in 1835, still disqualified atheists from the office, and required property to a moderate limit. But now in 1846 New York abolished her freehold qualification for Governor once and forever. Other old States instituted similar changes, while States newly organized one and all disregarded tests of property peculiarly unsuitable to their simple condition. New Hampshire abolished all freehold and property qualifications in 1852, and so had Massachusetts done for members of the Legislature, though for many years longer this latter commonwealth exacted of its Governor a freehold in his own right worth £1,000, and only in 1892 was this old test stricken out by vote of the people.[2] But residence remains an essential qualification in the States. The resident qualification was somewhat stringent in constitutions of the eighteenth century, aside from that of United States

[1] See State constitutions, 1790–1800.

[2] This text requirement of 1780 had probably escaped notice for many years. Governor W. E. Russell at length called attention to the anomaly, and an amendment was readily carried.

citizenship. Thus seven years' residence in the State was the test in Pennsylvania, and ten in South Carolina. A lesser term of State residence, such as six or four years, gained preference in the first quarter of this nineteenth century,[1] and the tendency has since been more liberal still. "A native citizen of the United States," following Federal precedent, several important States insisted upon early in this century, and various others embody now the same idea.[2] Disqualified classes have been announced from time to time in certain constitutions; members of Congress, for instance, State or United States officials, or ministers of religion. The Governor must not hold during his term any other office of profit.[3]

The colonial appendage of an executive privy council or directory began by 1789 to fade out in the old thirteen States; while States newly admitted and having no early custom in this respect chose to dispense quite generally with the encumbrance.[4] Special functions of the old executive sort were for the future left rather to a specific Senate, as under the Federal system. Even in New England States which retained expressly that "council" feature of the executive branch, the choice of councillors became transferred to the people by districts, in place of the early legislative selection.[5] Virginia in 1830 reduced her Revolutionary "council of State," and applied to that body a plan of rotation, but abolished the whole council finally in 1850 as Maryland had done in 1837. Maine in 1820 followed the parental example of Massachusetts in establishing a permanent executive council. Connecticut, on the other hand, merged

---

[1] Louisiana, 1812; Ohio, 1802.

[2] New York, Virginia, Alabama, Missouri (1821–1835).

[3] Maryland, 1809.

[4] *Supra*, page 61.

[5] See Massachusetts, amendment, 1840.

her council fully in the Legislature as an upper branch in 1818; while Vermont, beginning statehood with such a body, abolished it in 1836. Rhode Island's constitution of 1842 dispenses with an executive council. After 1850, therefore, Maine, New Hampshire, and Massachusetts became and since remain the only States of the Union which still maintain that old excrescence of colonial rule by Great Britain.[1]

Lieutenant-Governor was recognized in the new constitutions of Kentucky, Vermont, and South Carolina at the close of the eighteenth century; while Pennsylvania, Delaware, and Tennessee left that official out of their new or remodelled instruments during the same period, as also did Ohio and Louisiana early in the nineteenth century. During the first half of the present century new States, without sectional distinction, seem to have divided their preferences nearly evenly in respect of setting up such an office; but towards 1850 the drift set strongly in favor of lieutenant-governors, several old States changing their former constitutions to that intent. Ohio in 1851 established that office after half a century's experience without it. A lieutenant-governor, wherever recognized in State instruments, was now to be chosen by the people like the Governor; and so long as no vacancy in the chief office occurred for his advancement, his chief duty was to preside over the State Senate. Wherever, indeed, such executive functionary was dispensed with, under a State constitution, the President of the Senate supplied his place.[2] Perhaps the political convenience of a double-

---

[1] North Carolina, however, recognizes a peculiar "council," much like a Federal cabinet, and consisting of the heads of the chief departments, 1876.

[2] Delaware (1897) has just changed. Utah's constitution (1895) designates a governor, but no lieutenant-governor.

headed ticket at the polls, to attract voters and invite combinations for party support, has more to do with the popularity of this vice-executive than any solicitude over the possible vacancy that may promote him to full power. Concentration of the voting interest on an individual candidacy had, on the other hand, been thought in earlier times the surest pledge for bringing the best man into supreme office.

It became common after 1789 to adapt for new or reorganized State governments various provisions relative to the executive department which our Federal constitution had set forth in a corresponding connection. Thus the Governor's salary was not to be increased during his existing term of office. He was to take heed that the laws were properly executed. He was empowered to convene the Legislature on extraordinary occasions, and at every session of that body was to communicate public information and recommend public measures by message. He might adjourn the Legislature where the two houses could not agree. He was of course commander-in-chief of the State militia, though, as some States provided further, he should not command in the field personally save upon request of the Legislature. He might require information or advice in writing from his chief subordinates.

The pardoning power, either absolute or limited, is conferred upon the Governor by the constitutions of almost every State in the Union;[1] and the phrase of the Federal constitution (which includes reprieves) supplies the usual text in this respect.[2] But some

[1] Connecticut appears to furnish the only real exception at the present day, agreeably to local tradition.

[2] Delaware, in 1831, required the Governor to lay his reasons for each pardon before the Senate. Various States have since adopted a similar rule. He must send in to the Legislature a specific list of the

States require the advice of the Senate to such an exercise;[1] and occasional reservations are made besides the Federal exception of impeachment, particularly in the offence of State treason. In Connecticut the Governor can merely reprieve until the end of an ensuing session of the Legislature, while the Legislature alone can pardon.[2] New Jersey in 1844 set up a judicial committee on pardons to restrain the Governor's free exercise of the power; and in Massachusetts the Governor's Council takes like cognizance of his action.[3] But no remission of court fees or of a debt due the State shall be made in pardoning;[4] public notice of application shall be given before a pardon is granted,[5] and the Legislature may regulate as to the manner of applying.[6]

Among other provisions are these. The Governor shall send a message to the Legislature with recommendations at the close of his official term.[7] And having a considerable power usually to appoint, he must nominate to the Senate within fifty days after the Legislature assembles in session.[8] No person once rejected by the Senate shall be nominated again unless at the Senate's request, nor appointed to the same office during a recess.[9] Maryland in 1851 authorized the Governor to remove minor officers summarily for incompetency or misconduct. And so favorably has such provision been since regarded

pardons granted, together with his reasons in each case. Wisconsin, 1848, modifying New York, 1846.

[1] Louisiana, 1812; Rhode Island, 1854.
[2] Connecticut, 1818.
[3] See also Indiana, 1851.
[4] Kentucky, 1850; Maryland, 1851.
[5] Maryland, 1851.
[6] New York, 1846.
[7] Michigan, 1851.
[8] Maryland, 1851.
[9] *Ib.*

elsewhere that at this day the Governor in New York and various other States has enlarged power over the high officials under him, even such as the Secretary of State and Treasurer, especially where corruption or gross neglect of duty is alleged, and may examine and report to the Legislature concerning the facts, and meanwhile suspend temporarily the accused person from office.[1]

As for the veto power, this, too, is generally bestowed in the several States upon the chief magistrate, according to the Federal principle which originated in Massachusetts.[2] An absolute executive veto, to be sure, has been unrecognized in America since the days of royalty; but a qualified veto by the Governor appeals to the second thought of the Legislature, whose two houses may by a sufficiently large vote on reconsideration pass the measure in question to take effect, notwithstanding the official objections. Two-thirds of a quorum constitutes usually that sufficient vote agreeably to Federal and Massachusetts precedent;[3] but a few States set this requirement at three-fifths;[4] while a rule which has gained much favor in the Union during the present century prescribes for each house a proportion of all the members elected, in order to override a veto.[5] In four of the United States at least the Governor has no real veto power at all, but at most can only require the Legislature to reconsider its action.[6] Vermont in the last

[1] See Michigan, 1862; New York, 1846, and amendments.

[2] *Supra*, page 62.

[3] Georgia and New Hampshire (1790–1800).

[4] See Nebraska, Maryland.

[5] See *supra*, page 257; Kentucky, 1799, and many new States (1820–1835).

[6] Davis, Constitutions, Table, page 67.   Rhode Island, Delaware, North Carolina, and Ohio.   South Carolina's former constitution (1790), was to the same effect.   Ohio never granted a veto power to the Governor.

century constituted the Governor and Council a board
of concurrence in legislation with power to return a
bill or propose amendments, which, if not agreed to
by the Assembly, effected a suspension of the bill
until the next legislature. The Vermont Legislature was then a single-chambered body; and after
the radical reforms of 1836 in that State, when the
council wholly disappeared, the Governor, no longer
thus encumbered, assumed normal relations with a
legislature which consisted of two houses from that
time forward. A mere reconsideration and passage
at discretion is the practical effect of an executive
veto, under a few constitutions of this century;
that of Connecticut in 1818, for instance, which
permits the majority of a quorum to finally pass a
bill, whether before or after an executive veto; and
New Jersey in 1844 requiring a majority of all elected
in either branch to pass a bill, whether first or finally.
"Two-thirds of all elected" is the rule prescribed in
some other States for overriding a veto, though not
for original passage of a bill.[1] The "pocket veto,"
where a legislature adjourns before giving the chief
magistrate his full time to consider, is further allowed
in most States, after the Federal example; and
Massachusetts in 1822 added that feature expressly
to her organic provision of 1780, to make the veto
power complete. At the present day, under State
constitutional provisions dating for the most part
later than the Civil War, a governor may consider
and decide whether or not to veto any act of the
Legislature for a prescribed period after the session
adjourns. And in not less than thirteen States he
may also veto particular items in appropriation acts,
leaving the residue to stand unimpaired unless preferring to veto the whole act.[2] Bills thus vetoed

---

[1] Michigan, 1850; Kansas, 1859.   [2] Davis, Tables (1884), 67.

after adjournment are sent to the next session of the Legislature.

Louisiana's first constitution[1] required the Governor to visit the different counties of the State at least once in two years, so as to keep informed of the military and general condition of the State. Remnants of the ampler executive functions of Revolutionary times appeared for a while in new constitutions of the original commonwealths. That of South Carolina, for instance, in 1790 authorized the Governor to put an embargo not exceeding thirty days upon the exportation of provisions, and Vermont in 1793 authorized embargoes; while the text of the Massachusetts instrument to this day preserves unaltered the pompous enumeration of a governor's martial prerogatives, as in the old days of State sovereignty, or earlier still, of charter government.

The legislatures of the old thirteen States parted reluctantly with that public patronage of which State organic law at once began to deprive them. Lesser official appointments were before 1812 given by various new constitutions to the Governor, with perhaps the added advice and consent of Senate or Council. Secretary of State and Attorney-General were thus transferred from the Legislature for choice accordingly. But the State Treasurer was still to be chosen annually by the joint vote of the Legislature, under many such constitutions, and so was it with the State auditor, the State printer, and not unfrequently with the Secretary of State.[2] Ohio and Louisiana[3] left the appointment of all other civil officers to be directed by law. Town officers were to

---

[1] 1812.

[2] See Pennsylvania, Delaware, Kentucky, New Hampshire (1790–1800); Ohio, 1802.

[3] Ohio, 1802; Louisiana, 1812.

be chosen annually by the people. With regard to State militia, the new State of Ohio in 1802 followed New England precedent, leaving the line and most field officers to be chosen by those who served under them, while generals were to be elected by the Legislature. With a truer military instinct for emergencies, Louisiana, when admitted next in 1812, gave the Legislature full discretion for organizing the militia. Vermont's State Treasurer was required to settle his accounts yearly.[1] South Carolina made provision for two Treasurers, — one to officiate at Charleston, and the other at the State capital.[2] Pennsylvania in 1838 required the State Senate to sit with open doors upon appointments to office,[3] and to confirm or reject by yea or nay vote all nominations sent in by the Governor; which provision, approved by experience, reappeared in the later constitution of 1873.

The best-laid schemes of State organizers for thwarting the popular control of affairs, or trying strange experiments, have ignominiously failed in this country, and sooner or later the fetters of timid expediency are broken. Thus, Louisiana's first experiment in 1812 of making each popular vote for Governor a dual presentation of candidates to the Legislature and nothing more,[4] merged by 1845 into a plurality choice at the polls and popular supremacy in such elections. A governor for four years with the liberal official patronage which this Louisiana constitution had bestowed must have been sorely beset for pledges meanwhile, when a legislature had

[1] Vermont, 1793.
[2] South Carolina, 1790.
[3] Contrary to senatorial practice in Congress.
[4] A Pennsylvania device of the preceding century, but differently applied.

power to select his rival candidate in his stead. **Not** less temporary was the electoral college expedient of the last century, so far as States experimenting with it[1] were concerned, though in our Federal constitution it remains beyond the easy reach of reform. New York's absurd "council of appointment," under the instrument of 1777,[2] reached, indeed, the zenith of plunder and party favoritism in awarding the public patronage of that rising State, when the crafty convention of 1801 in that State (a convention whose work was never submitted to the people) defined that council as in effect a directory, where the Governor, like any other member, must yield to the action of its majority. The more popular constitution of 1821 in the Empire State swept out that conclave of patronage, and gave the nominating power to the Governor alone, like other commonwealths. And by that same later constitution was displaced the anomalous "council of revision" of 1777, so that the Governor's veto henceforth conformed in New York to the usual mode of making a chief magistrate solely responsible for revising the acts of a legislature.[3] Illinois, adopting from New York in 1818 this same "council of revision," dropped it not less emphatically in 1848, for the Governor's power to veto.

The Maryland convention of 1851, while raising the official term from one to four years, applied a singular expedient of rotation to the selection of chief magistrate. The State was now divided into three distinct districts, one of which comprised the area of the eastern shore, and another the Baltimore region, and it was prescribed that the Governor should be taken in rotation from each district. Once more polit-

---

[1] Maryland and Kentucky, *supra*, page 252.

[2] *Supra*, page 63.

[3] New York's constitution of 1821 was submitted to the people and ratified at the polls.

ical ingenuity for abnormal government defeated its own ends, for when the constitution of 1864 went into effect the device was dropped. So, too, did Maryland in this 1851 instrument undertake to dispense with an attorney-general, by allowing the Governor to employ special counsel instead, at a recompense to be fixed by the Legislature; but in 1864 the old public office was restored.

While the modern tendency in the United States has constantly been to give to the Chief Executive greater independence of the Legislature, greater official discretion, than in earlier times, none the less positive has been political progression towards the popular control of that great department. But for the remarkable growth of particular States in wealth and numbers, and a corresponding spread and increase of public concerns and patronage as incidental to supreme office, the dependence of the Governor upon his State constituency would by this time have become strikingly apparent. About the middle of the nineteenth century, State organic law tended clearly to submitting the choice of executive subordinates as well as principals — all, in fact, of the great officers of the commonwealth — to the suffrage of the voters at large, rather than leave such selections longer to either Governor or Legislature. New York in 1846 took a prominent lead in that direction; Massachusetts in 1855 followed. Other important States earlier or later wrought that important change in existing institutions or embodied the principle in instruments framed upon their first admission to the Union. Under such organic provisions we now find Secretary of State, Attorney-General, Auditor, and Treasurer elected by the people in most States.[1]

---

[1] Michigan, Louisiana, California (1835–1849).

Names of new subordinate officials described in State constitutions attest the expansion of government still further, — State superintendent of public education, State engineer and surveyor, and the like.[1] County as well as municipal officers were by the middle of this century chosen more generally than before by the respective constituencies concerned;[2] among them, county clerks, treasurers, and registers. But in the more populous States a great growth of public patronage is traceable, which remains subject to executive appointment under the usual limitations, on lines defined by the State constitution; and commissions or boards, with a rotating membership, have come prominently into notice.[3]

As for State elections generally to high executive honors, the people by their plurality vote decide the choice between candidates at the ballot-box. Virginia in 1850 abandoned deliberately for the Governor that time-honored method of legislative selection which had promoted to the chief magistracy such sons and patriots as Henry, Jefferson, and Monroe in less degenerate days. But South Carolina alone of American commonwealths remained aristocratic in structure down to the Civil War, unchanged by the influences about her. There an aristocratic legislature, in which planters and landowners held the preponderating force, chose the Governor, cast the votes for Presidential electors, and controlled all legislation and public patronage of the State. But to the rule of popular choice there is now no State exception.

---

[1] New York, 1846.

[2] As to judicial officers, etc., see next chapter.

[3] See canal commissioners, codifying commissioners, inspectors of prisons, etc., in New York's constitution of 1846, among the earliest organic examples.

VII.

THE JUDICIARY.

THE usual pattern for a State judiciary in these modern times may be studied in the specific requirements of each fundamental State instrument. Comparison shows that the highest State tribunal (styled sometimes a "court of appeals" and sometimes a "supreme court") is composed usually of a few individuals, often, indeed, of only three, who can so group as to supply a majority for deciding each case; and, elected each by the people at large, such members rotate, and the court changes gradually.[1] Inferior courts, arranged naturally by counties, though not unfrequently by arbitrary geographical districts, have their own judges for the burden of original litigation and appeals from the primary tribunals; while judges of municipal or police courts and justices of the peace take jurisdiction of petty matters civil and criminal in the first instance. Georgia was singularly tentative as a State for a long time on this matter of a judicial establishment; inferior tribunals shared public favor with courts merchant; nor was it until 1835 that a supreme court was recognized at all in her constitution. Legislative discretion in the erection of courts has within a hundred years been largely curtailed; and in these days a State constitution

---

[1] In some late constitutions a prospective increase of judges is provided for when the population reaches a certain limit. North Dakota (1889).

generally defines fully the judicial system. Chancery courts with special chancellors and a special equity jurisdiction prevailed largely in the middle tier of old Atlantic States; while New England cherished a dislike of such establishments. But since 1840 the fusion of law and equity in American practice, with a common jurisdiction for last resort in the highest appellate tribunal of the State, has been almost everywhere accomplished, thus unifying the two systems as England also inclines.[1]   Divorce and matrimonial jurisdiction has been taken away altogether from the Legislature; probate or orphans' courts are erected for the several counties; and the former participation of Executive or Senate in judicial business, somewhat after the English fashion of a House of Lords, has been completely excluded.

The well-established rule of the mother country, that judges should hold office during good behavior, was the usual rule in America when our Federal constitution was adopted.[2]   That constitution, as we have noticed, still preserves the English principle, well justified by the high renown of its long line of honorable incumbents, who, once promoted to the bench, have dismissed all other ambition so as to devote themselves faithfully and unreservedly to the administration of justice for the rest of their activity in life.   No rule suits so well this delicate adjustment to the whole Union.   So, too, for many years, States, new or old, kept for the most part to this same rule of judicial incumbency.   In all the later constitutions of the eighteenth century, save that of

---

[1] New York, in 1846, so reorganized the State Judiciary as to place a court of appeals above the Supreme Court, abolish the office of chancellor, and blend law and equity functions.   See page 66.

Chancery jurisdiction was similarly abolished (1851–1856) in Maryland and Mississippi.

[2] *Supra*, page 65.

Georgia alone, good behavior continued the tenure; that State of little traditional deference to judges or case law, permitting in 1789 only a three years' incumbency in its "superior" (then the highest) tribunal.[1] For a new example, Ohio entered the Union in 1802, prescribing a seven years' term of judicial office; but Louisiana, next in 1812, sanctioned the conservative rule of good behavior. The latter standard was maintained much longer; but constitutions of the next generation began formulating the theory of "a fixed term" for every public office, as though in a true democracy no citizen should claim therein a vested right. Tennessee, by 1834, and Indiana, as early as 1816, affixed accordingly a tenure of years to the judicial office. Virginia in 1850 enlarged the phrase of her famous "Bill of Rights" so as to read that "all elections" (those of judges included by inference) "shall be free."[2]

The New Hampshire constitution had fixed the rigid limit of seventy years of age for judicial capacity to serve,[3] and a few other States now adopted such a limit,[4] New York narrowing it long before to sixty.[5] But such had been the recognized need for the bench, of men upright and honest, diligent and skilled in their profession, inspiring confidence in the whole community, that property qualifications for a judge were dispensed with by general consent[6] from the earliest days of American independence, and probably earlier. Some of our more modern consti-

---

[1] Cf. Georgia constitutions, 1789, 1798, etc. Under Georgia's constitution of 1798, the inferior court judges held for good behavior; but that tenure was in 1812 reduced to four years.

[2] See page 32.

[3] And for sheriffs also, 1792.

[4] Connecticut, 1818; Maine, 1820.

[5] See page 65. Missouri (1820) set sixty-five years. Nor shall one be appointed before he is thirty. Missouri, *ib.*

[6] *Supra,* page 65.

tutions, however, declare professional qualifications indispensable, such as admission to the bar and service as a practitioner,[1] — the only real or reasonable test which a State may apply to judges.

As for selecting State judges, the choice lay originally between direct appointment by the Legislature and appointment (subject to Senate or Council confirmation) by the Executive. Towards the close of the last century, South Carolina and Tennessee in new constitutions preferred a choice by the Legislature. Vermont's peculiar constitution joined the single-chambered Legislature and the Council for such a purpose. But Pennsylvania, Delaware, New Hampshire, and Kentucky pronounced in their new instruments for appointment by the Governor with such confirmation by Council or Senate as harmonized with their several systems. This course was like that of the Federal constitution. Georgia's constitutions of this early period were peculiar;[2] and there seems little doubt that this uneasy State, where there was much undefined jealousy against law and the lawyers, led American commonwealths in point of time as to making judges elective by the people under an organic instrument. Of the two States admitted in the new century before our second war with Great Britain and Napoleon's downfall, Ohio made option of the legislative election of judges, and Louisiana of executive appointment; and so did States continue to divide in their declared preferences until 1830 or later. But Mississippi in 1832 declared that all judges should be elected by the voters, while Missouri

---

[1] Kentucky, 1850. See constitutions of North and South Dakota, Utah, Washington, etc. (1889–1895).

[2] Cf. 1789 and 1798. Under the latter instrument, "superior" court (the highest) judges were to be "elected;" but those of the inferior courts received appointment from the Legislature. By 1812 the inferior court judges were subjected to the test of popular election.

(1822–1835) worked gradually to the same doctrine. Indiana, as early as 1816, had determined upon a general judicial tenure for seven years; yet doubtful over the method of selecting judges, the convention of that new State apportioned the highest of such appointments to the Governor, the next in rank to the Legislature, and the lowest to the people voting in local districts. This compromise was a sign of the advancing sentiment; and when in 1851 Indiana's constitution was remodelled, the choice of all judges from highest to lowest was freely accorded to the people.

In short, the new political idea of limiting judicial tenure to a term of years found readier and quicker acceptance in these United States than that of electing judges at the polls. But change in this latter direction was fully ripe by 1850; and old States as well as new ranged themselves quite generally in favor of popular elections as opportunity henceforward permitted. New York, Pennsylvania, and Virginia led among the old commonwealths that now embraced the new faith; Maine and Vermont acceded far enough to permit probate and other minor judges to be thus locally elected. The last stand for the old method was made at the tribunals of final appeal and against the choice of supreme judges by the voters at large. Massachusetts resisted wholly the new departure, and Maine herself in 1876 retreated from the partial experiment. But in general the tide of innovation has swept steadily on.

Judges have been made liable to removal, after an English rule, in many States. The Governor "shall" remove (or, as many States prefer the text, "may" at discretion remove) on the address of two-thirds of each branch (or, as some States prefer, the majority)

of the Legislature.[1]   Other States leave this power
of removal to the Legislature apart from the Executive.[2] Happily, it should be said, this summary
means of purging the bench has not often been unfairly applied. In many States, on the other hand,
as under our Federal constitution, such sweeping
process is wholly ignored; while still other States
permit a summary removal under cautious qualifications; such as confining the procedure to instances
of mental or physical inability in the incumbent, or
requiring, properly enough, that the cause of removal
shall be plainly set forth of record, and due notice
first given to the judge himself, that he may appear
and defend himself.[3]   Rhode Island's constitution of
1842 had a singular provision in this respect; it made
all judges elective in the first instance by the Legislature, and each one should hold until a majority of all
elected to each house should by joint resolution declare his place vacant.   This liability of judges to a
somewhat arbitrary removal has gained of late years
such progressive approval in America that we may
consider it a remedy kept readily in reserve for the
corrupt and inefficient who have forfeited just confidence rather than to foster in judges a timid and a
time-serving dependence upon popular favor.   For
apart from the right of impeachment, which prevails
almost universally[4] in this Union, three-fourths of the
States, or more, now permit removal by the Legislature, or by the Governor on legislative address, under
constraints more or less particular, but in any event
without any formal indictment and trial, or the need-

---

[1] *Supra*, page 67.   Kentucky, Pennsylvania, Delaware, Georgia.
This New Hampshire rule results in various hasty removals, where
some new political party comes into power.
[2] New York, 1821, which is peculiar in the voting test applied.
[3] Delaware, North Carolina, Maine, etc.
[4] See next chapter, page 296.

ful production of testimony under strict rules of evidence.[1]

Obnoxious judges have sometimes been legislated out of office in a body by some act of the Legislature abolishing the court itself, and creating a new one in its place. The rigid formula of so many modern constitutions which specify and create courts, instead of trusting so largely to legislative erection, as did the early State instruments and that of the Federal Union, diminishes largely such opportunities; while the modern limited tenure and popular choice of the judges tend to dispense largely with such a need. Special directions are found occasionally in State constitutions on this subject; and Virginia, in 1830, by way of disapproval, declared that no law abolishing a court should be construed to deprive a judge of his office, unless two-thirds of the Legislature concurred, but such judges might be assigned to other duties.[2]

At the present day we find the Judiciary in the several States of this Federal Union made more efficient, more fully independent of Legislature or Executive, than ever before, and yet, like those two other departments of government, brought under the direct control and vigilance of the people. State legislatures have been stripped of all judicial functions formerly exercised, except in the procedure of impeachment; and in the mode of appointing judges the few States which still hold out against the choice by ballot at the polls prefer Federal usage in confiding the immediate selection to the Governor, with confirmation by Council or Senate. In four States, perhaps, all old ones, the Legislature still chooses. But less than one-third of the States in the entire Union

[1] Davis, Tables (1884), 70. [2] And see Ohio, 1851.

19

trust any choice of judges but that by popular suffrage; and of that small fraction, only five States in all — Delaware, Florida, Massachusetts, New Hampshire, and Rhode Island — still preserve that judicial tenure of life or good behavior which our Federal system so highly commends.[1] Whether an elective judiciary with service for a fixed term of years is on the whole an improvement in modern politics remains a mooted question; but certain is it that no inclination has thus far been shown by the preponderating States, once committed to this policy, to reverse their opinion.[2] Every impulse of the age, indeed, tends in this respect to the popular test. There is, however, a decided leaning of late towards longer terms of judicial office than were favored when the reform began, — a new proof of that watchful and corrective habit in political experiments which the Anglo-Saxon temperament so happily displays; for while, about the middle of the present century, the tenure was usually fixed at four or six years, we now find the highest judges elected for an average term of eight years, which populous and wealthy New York, where great concerns are litigated, increases to fourteen and Pennsylvania to twenty-one.[3] An incumbency like this last, which is almost tantamount to the ordinary life service, and begins with so touching a proof of public confidence, may well furnish incentive to an honorable emulation. One sees, therefore, that even the dreaded jealousy of a democracy in the State may be tempered by sober sense. Appeals for an adequate recompense to the judges do

[1] Davis, Tables, 70. In Rhode Island and New Hampshire with peculiar limits elsewhere noted.

[2] In 1873, upon the submission of a proposed amendment relating to the judges of the highest court, the people of New York by nearly two to one refused to return to the old mode of appointment.

[3] But not re-eligible. Pennsylvania, 1873.

not go unheeded; and though rich remuneration comes chiefly to those who devote themselves to private practice at the bar, the American bench has never yet failed to attract men of honor and more than average ability.

Among miscellaneous constitutional provisions relating to the judiciary in various States these may be noted. Tribunals of conciliation to which parties may voluntarily submit shall be favored.[1] State reports shall be speedily published, and shall be free for any one to print,[2] for emolument, except the judges themselves.[3] Judges shall not charge juries as to facts, but may state the testimony and declare the law.[4] Judges shall as often as possible refer in their decisions to the particular law on which the judgment is founded.[5] Judges must render decision in ninety days.[6] Judges shall have an adequate recompense by way of salary and no fees or perquisites; such salary shall not be diminished, but may be increased; they shall not act as attorney or counsel in matters to be tried before them, nor in general be interested parties in the official business transacted in their courts.[7] They must not even practise law while on the bench.[8] And for their better seclusion, as also for encouraging a devotion to the duties for which they have been set apart, undistracted by politics, judges are sometimes declared ineligible to public office elsewhere excepting judicial station,

[1] Wisconsin, 1846; New York, 1846. See also Georgia, 1789–1835.
[2] California, 1849.
[3] Indiana, 1851.
[4] *Ib.*
[5] Louisiana, 1812, with a civil code.
[6] Rather a questionable requirement so far as fixing specific limits is concerned. California, 1879.
[7] See New Hampshire as early as 1792. Recent constitutions (1889) of new States contain such provision.
[8] California, 1879.

during their respective terms of service.[1] Special provisions are sometimes found concerning the method and limitation of suits against the State.

There are still a few States of this Union in which the Governor (and perhaps, too, the Legislature) may ask in advance the formal opinion of the judges of the highest court for public guidance;[2] but usually no opinion can be procured from the judiciary of a commonwealth except through the ordinary channel of litigation and the formality of a test case duly argued.

The common practice in this country about 1789 was for a court to appoint its own clerk; and a clerk might serve, like the judge, for good behavior. A judge often bestowed the easy office upon a son or kinsman. Ohio in 1802 required sheriffs and justices of the peace to be locally elected by the voters; and this rule grew gradually into State favor. The county prosecuting officers were formerly appointed to a considerable extent by the Executive. The modern revolution, however, in favor of fixed tenure and popular elections for all officers of a State, has swept into the patronage of the voters, clerks, sheriffs, marshals, district attorneys, and registers, as well as the judicial incumbents of the courts with which such officers are connected, from lowest to highest. In States disposed to economize the offices, the county clerk has sometimes been designated to serve as clerk of a county court, while the Secretary of State officiates as clerk of the highest appellate tribunal.[3]

The increased momentum of the judicial power in the United States chiefly results (1) from the idea

---

[1] California, 1879.

[2] *Supra*, page 67; Florida, 1875; South Dakota, 1889.

[3] New Jersey, 1844.

gradually evolved in American politics that the written constitution, the local fundamental law of any State, shall be regarded as a sovereign emanation from the people, for defining and portioning out the respective functions of well-ordered government, and while confining each co-ordinate branch of such government to its own legitimate sphere, keeping all three of them from encroaching upon the reserved rights of the individual citizen; (2) as the corollary of such a proposition, from the necessity of finding some constant safeguard and exponent of such fundamental law, so that Executive and Legislature, the originators more particularly of public policy for present and future, shall be kept to the equilibrium of fundamental constraints by some force consistent with normal tranquillity. That safeguard and exponent has been found, both in State and Federal systems, in the tranquil and deliberate oversight of the Judiciary, — a tribunal devoted to revision of the past, co-ordinate as far as possible with these more active and aggressive departments, yet equally independent in fundamental theory, and equally bound to regard the will of the people as constitutionally expressed. The courts accordingly compare the acts of these other departments with the written constitution, and as to acts of legislation, most particularly, whose scope might otherwise be resistless by the individual, pronounces them invalid and of no effect, if in fundamental conflict. Foreign observers of our institutions marvel that such a mechanism of constraint can be practically applied, and they pronounce its application confusing; yet they freely admit that the mechanism works, and at this long distance of time works easily.

Such arbitrament works all the better because no violent array is brought up against Executive or

Legislature, because the test case made is that of private individuals, and because argument is heard, delay accorded, and the public mind, well prepared to doubt whether the act complained of were really consistent with organic law, learns in due time the decision and its reasons. The test case comes to judgment; the particular judgment is enforced; and the people, and they, too, of co-ordinate departments of the government whose pride is not wounded, and whose agents have perhaps already changed, concede that the judgment for one individual contestant ought to prevail equally for all other private contestants similarly situated. Cheerful acquiescence in the decision of the highest appellate tribunal becomes doubly the policy of fairness, — a maxim like that of acquiescence in the political will of a majority; and even were resistance continued, the court's process is available to all other individuals in turn who feel aggrieved, and disobedience to the law-makers becomes obedience to the State. Thus does wrongful and despotic legislation become sapped of its mischief.

The idea of a power thus overriding the enactment of a legislature was not wholly new to American citizens in 1789, but existed to some extent in colonial and Revolutionary times; and in the national era which has succeeded that date, the Supreme Court of the United States simply exerts on a new and more comprehensive scale, and with a more imposing fundamental operation, what States independent of Great Britain had severally begun to exercise in the intervening years through their own highest tribunals.[1] Perfect government is gained in this inherent operation of fundamental law of the land, when general acquiescence is peacefully given

[1] See "Atlantic Monthly," November, 1884.

both by the people and the public departments, so that the Executive desists from enforcement, and the Legislature repeals the devitalized statute without further controversy. For even supposing the court to have registered an unrighteous decision (which is seldom), it is better that the people, who make and unmake judges and other public servants, shall defer to the decision until their own peaceful opportunity comes to reorganize and reconstruct.

The field of the American Judiciary becomes thus immensely enlarged as appellate judges in a State become thus the conservators of organic law. The judges represent, as a recent writer has well expressed it, "the deeper and more abiding popular sense of order and justice;" and the court, no less an instrument of the people than the Legislature, reflects the public sentiment in a deeper, calmer, more lasting form, embodying popular aspirations after an ideal of perfect order.[1]

[1] Horace Davis's American Constitutions, 61.

VIII.

MISCELLANEOUS; CONCLUSION.

IMPEACHMENT by the Legislature for the removal of
public officers is a process still sanctioned almost
everywhere in our American States, Oregon long
constituting the sole exception. Impeachment provisions in the Federal constitution furnish, with some
local variations, the usual model in this respect. But
the cumbrousness and uncertain result of all such
political trials have induced contempt for the procedure; so that in consequence some States are now
disposed to extend the summary removal of public
officers by address or joint resolution as a legislative
substitute; [1] while others empower the Governor,
whenever charges are preferred against subordinates,
to suspend or remove the culprits from office, and
to institute criminal prosecution against them in the
courts. Elections at frequently recurring intervals
and the popular test for all high officers of State,
judges included, must largely dispense with the
necessity of impeachment. Some modern State constitutions expressly confine impeachment by the
Legislature to high officials, making all the lesser
public servants liable to indictment and trial in the
courts, and even to judicial removal, in case of conviction, as part of the punishment. [2]

[1] See Louisiana, 1812; Indiana, 1851; page 288.
[2] Tennessee, 1834. And see California, 1848; Oregon, 1857.

We have observed in the States of this century a growing insistence upon geographical residence as a test of the right to vote or hold office. Qualification, or rather clear definition, of this rule finds occasionally an organic recognition; thus absence from home on business of the State or Union shall not deprive one of such residential rights.[1] The chief officers of State are specially required under various constitutions to reside at the seat of government,[2] and to keep the records there, while county officers are similarly enjoined. States, while seldom liberal, have sometimes been parsimonious respecting public salaries; as when Tennessee's constitution in 1796 prescribed a maximum limit for such recompense in specific instances, yet named no minimum. "All salaries and fees shall be moderate," enjoins Delaware in 1792, "and receipts which specify particulars shall be given for all official fees."[3] The Legislature shall determine what deductions shall be made from the salaries of public officers for neglect of duty. Among citizens specially enumerated as ineligible to State office we find ministers of the gospel,[4] army and navy contractors, persons in the service of the United States, and those, moreover, convicted of bribery or infamous crimes. Plurality of offices, State and national, is frequently forbidden in State instruments. Virginia in 1850 disqualified every salaried officer of a bank or attorney for the commonwealth from sitting in the Legislature. Delaware has been the latest

[1] Kentucky, 1799.

[2] Michigan, 1835; Indiana, 1851, etc. Louisiana's early constitution of 1812 declares that all civil officers for the State at large shall reside within the State; and all district or county officers within their respective districts or counties, and shall keep their respective offices at such places therein as may be required by law.

[3] Delaware, 1792.

[4] *Supra*, page 68.

State in the Union, apparently, to retain a property qualification, somewhat as in the last century.[1] Religious qualification was ignored so generally in new State constitutions early in this century that it seemed a relic of. old times when Arkansas, as late as 1836, declared upon admission to the Union that no atheist should hold office nor be an admissible witness in the courts.   But North Carolina as late as 1876 renewed the atheist disqualification of her earlier constitution; and a few other instruments of old States are of the same purport.[2]

Following the traditions of her colonial age, Connecticut, far into the nineteenth century, maintained two State capitals, Hartford and New Haven, where the Legislature was required to hold alternate sessions; but since 1873 Hartford has absorbed the honor of State residence.   Rhode Island, with a similar colonial history, still pursues that old custom of double headquarters at Providence and Newport. In all other States of the Union one capital city has always sufficed, and from the very outset of the nineteenth century we see the Federal rivalry of 1789 reproduced, and the strife of local settlements emulous for selection as the seat of government, shaping the expression of conventions, under whose guidance Territories were ushered into the Union as full-grown States.   Thus Ohio in 1802 declares Chillicothe the seat of State government until 1808, and forbids money to be raised until 1809 for erecting any State House.   Louisiana in 1812 orders the State capital to

[1] For the Senate.   A convention has (1897) ordained a new constitution for Delaware.   A peculiarly obstructive method of calling a State convention under the old organic law (namely, the vote of an average representative majority of the people) hindered the needful popular assent earlier.

[2] See *supra,* page 230.

continue at New Orleans until removed by law. By the middle of this century the location of the seat of government in a new State had become a prize for keen and speculative competition; so that the convention which framed the organic instrument for submission to Congress would often evade the choice of more than a temporary capital, leaving the permanent one to be fixed later by the Legislature, under the proviso that a State or even a county seat of government once deliberately selected should not be changed again at discretion. Oregon in 1857 made the majority vote of the people indispensable to every proposal for capital removal, — a wise precaution, since schemes of the kind turn usually in the Legislature upon local jobbery and debasement. State boundaries are defined, and the fundamental conditions with Congress concerning admission are seen set forth in the constitutions of most new States of modern times; and a schedule is conveniently affixed to new constitutions in general for temporary details connected with the new establishment.

The revision and codification of State laws, at once or at some later specified period, is found a feature of many State constitutions in modern times; and commissions for that purpose, or for devising improvements in the penal and practice codes, are sanctioned accordingly.[1] Indeed, commissions of three or more have multiplied much as the drudgery of State business increases; and boards of commissioners, gradu-

---

[1] See this idea emanating early in the southwestern region, as in Alabama, 1819, and Missouri, 1820. By 1846 New York set an example in that respect since largely followed. But Michigan, in 1850, forbade all general revision of laws in the future, pointing out a simpler method of reprinting, in the government publication, by way of substitute. Whatever State legislatures might have ordered in such States as Virginia and Massachusetts without constitutional direction, Georgia's constitution of 1798 is seen directing that within five years the body of laws of that State, civil and criminal, should be digested.

ally rotating, came into vogue by 1850, to supplant single heads for bureau service of a commonwealth.

The old thirteen States, once colonies, received no liberal gifts for education from the Federal Union of 1789, such as endow common public instruction so liberally in States west of the Alleghanies from the proceeds of the Federal public lands. Some of these original States, however, have had public educational funds of their own creation; that, for instance, of Connecticut, known as the common-school fund, and excellently managed; and New York had a similar endowment.[1] Knowledge, virtue, literature, and the common schools — the latter free from sectarian control — are all repeatedly commended in the organic law of these United States, superintendents of State education being specially provided. Asylums for the poor and feeble gain provision also; and the State almshouse, and State institutions for the insane, blind, deaf and dumb, are seen by 1850 among the public institutions recognized by the fundamental law of the people. Humane sentiments make constant advance, and organic prohibitions multiply against duels and lotteries,[2] as well as the older offences enumerated. The evil practice of duelling, which had cost so many distinguished lives, was by 1850 not unfrequently denounced as a disqualification for office; and Texas in 1845 required an oath to be taken by every State officer and member of the Legislature that he had not fought nor been second in a duel since the State constitution was adopted.

Tennessee's constitution at the time of her admis-

[1] Connecticut, 1818; New York, 1821; *supra*, page 228.

[2] See Maryland (1851) and other States (1851–1860). Previous to 1800, lotteries had been widely recognized in America as a suitable mode of raising funds on behalf of charity, religion, and public improvements.

sion to the Union in 1796 contained a protective clause, exempting from taxation all articles manufactured from the produce of the State. During the era of this century that State internal improvements made an absorbing issue in national politics, some of our local constitutions exhorted the Legislature to encourage such projects, while others forbade or restrained all expenditures of the kind.[1] By 1860 the condemnation of such costly enterprises at the expense of the State had become general. New York's constitutions have taken special concern in protecting and developing the salt springs of the State and the Erie and Champlain canals,[2] ordaining in 1846 that these public sources of wealth should never be sold. Indiana has enclosed as a sacred precinct the Tippecanoe battle-field; and Maryland her State House square and grounds at Annapolis, while New York seeks to rescue from private waste or depredation the Adirondack forests and the water supply of the Hudson and Mohawk valleys.

The increasing tendency of an American population to swarm at central points of the commonwealth, to the detriment of town representation and the old uniform local government by selectmen and town meeting, drew general notice before this century had far advanced. New York in 1821 ordained that mayors of all cities in that State should be chosen by the respective common councils, but in 1833 permitted the mayor of New York City to be elected at the polls. Massachusetts in 1822 by a constitutional amendment authorized the Legislature of the State to incorporate cities wherever there were twelve thousand inhabitants, and the local voters desired such

[1] Cf. Missouri, Tennessee, Alabama, Mississippi, Michigan, Florida, and Texas (1819–1845).
[2] New York, 1833, 1835.

change of government. Since the Civil War, State
constitutions, having large cities within the jurisdiction, are seen devoting much detail to that increas-
ingly difficult subject of municipal self-government.
Thus, Maryland in 1867 makes lengthy provision
regarding the government of Baltimore. One municipal change which the recent New York convention
of 1894 favored is that of separating such municipal
elections from those of State or national officers, and,
by making them local and distinct, concentrate the
voter's attention to candidates detached from other
issues. In comprehensive schemes, however, for
municipal government, States are still confessedly in
the experimental stage of a most gigantic problem;
it may be said that of divided responsibilities, multiplied checks and balances, and varying terms of civic
servants, the present age seems heartily sick; and
dispensing with councils or mimic representative
assemblies, the remedy of the hour, which may or
may not prove finally effective, is that of establishing
a business man's government, controlled essentially
like a private business corporation, with powers concentrated in a commission or single executive whom
a board of aldermen can but slightly restrain.[1]

The political tendency has been in many States
for the legislative majority, on behalf of rural constituencies, to take a great metropolis in hand, med-
dling in its morals by a State board of police, and
regulating and experimenting with its municipal government; but some late constitutions react a little in
favor of that home rule and local influence which all
good citizens must cherish while republics endure.[2]

[1] The mayor of any city may make official objection or "veto"
within fifteen days to bills of the Legislature which affect the city's
domestic affairs. New York, 1894.

[2] New York's 1894 amendments classify the cities of that State
according to relative population; and as to cities of the first class

We have elsewhere traced the growth of that fundamental doctrine which required the submission of constitutions and of constitutional amendments to the voters. Towards the middle of this century such convenient reference to the people became a resort for relieving a State convention of various troublesome decisions upon such fundamental propositions as granting suffrage to the colored race in a free commonwealth; and thence the further advance was easy for a convention to authorize a legislature to frame other specific issues of a like perplexing kind for the voters. Thus the Wisconsin convention in 1848 permitted a popular reference by the Legislature of "bank or no bank," the creation or non-creation of such corporations to depend upon the will of the popular majority as expressed at the polls. The creation of public debt for certain purposes was so referred in various instances. The liquor question, too, where those who would prohibit in a State altogether conflict with the promoters of a license, became about 1850, as it has been ever since, an issue for popular *referendum* under State constitutions,[1] with later a "local option" application as between the two plans in the various towns and cities. Taxation and other provisions are seen framed in the modern organic law of several States never to be changed without a *referendum* to the people. In many States a *referendum* is regularly made to the people at specific periods, such as twenty years, on the question of calling a constitutional convention. And States are already agitating a new and final advance in the same direction which shall require the submission of all enactments by the Legislature to

empower a mayor to guard as chief executive the interests of the community against injurious legislation.

[1] Ohio, 1851.

the same final sanction of the people at the polls. Ancient experience shows the unfitness of a plebiscitum for framing and originating measures in a free republic of more than moderate population, but not, in matters of general concern, for considering the adoption of what some representative body has proposed in concrete form.

The Anglo-Saxon temperament has held sway thus far throughout the Union; and, whether in the old French and Spanish annexations of territory and inhabitants, or that incongruous immigration from abroad which pours in so constantly over the whole area, foreign elements have been easily assimilated. To this predominance of the primitive race and character through all such admixture, the stability of our institutions is immensely owing. New States have spread the influence of English ideas in law and literature, and the mother tongue is the language of this continent. Louisiana, on her admission in 1812, ordained that all laws of the Legislature, and all judicial and legislative proceedings, should be promulgated, preserved, and conducted in the same language as that of the constitution of the United States.[1] California, more yielding to her native element, announced in 1849 that all laws or decrees requiring publication should be published in English and Spanish; but the former style has gained the mastery. The genius of republican free government on this continent is Anglo-American.

In conclusion, we are impressed by the progressive strength of the two great forces of this American

[1] It was conceded, however, in the Louisiana constitution of 1845, that the Secretary of the State Senate and Clerk of the State House of Representatives should be conversant with both English and French, and that members might address the Legislature in either language.

Union, the centripetal and the centrifugal, in their constant relation to one another, as the whole undivided people advance to continental empire. The Federal government, now fitly styled national, stirs best the spirit of public pride and love of glory, because of its splendid historical achievements, and, since the Civil War, its sure foundation in the American heart. Exercising with energy such paramount functions of sovereignty as those of war, peace, foreign relations, commerce, territorial acquisition and development, the post-office, immense resources of taxation which are exclusive as respects tariff and the customs; symbolized in the national flag and controlling the only active and permanent army and navy of the people; regulating the mutual intercourse of States and their inhabitants in essential particulars, — the United States government with its continuity of administration is at length easily paramount. But in the several States, — prosaic by comparison, whether in area, population, or the scope of ostentatious action, — we see the multiplying nurseries of self-government, the abodes where public spirit and confident experience in free institutions must still be generated while generated at all. Here originate constitutional reforms and the inventions of democracy to curb and regulate all rulers; and in these jurisdictions will popular liberty maintain its last stand, should the Union, ages hence, fall asunder. Corruption that corrodes, despotism that oppresses, vice that unnerves, need only be feared when poisoning such fountain-heads.

Humble as may be the field of local achievement in this Union, material as may appear State ends and inconsequential State public routine, the study of republican institutions is an exceedingly interesting one which these several commonwealths furnish.

Political geography reckons usually by nations alone and their chief cities; and of State political divisions in America the outer world makes scarcely more account than would we of the counties or provinces which make up England, France, or Germany; all the more so that while homogeneousness continues in a national sense, States with merely artificial boundaries multiply. Yet, while the Federal constitution has yielded but little to structural reform for more than a hundred years, State instruments abound in improved ideas of government which deserve to be nationalized.

Our first impression, perhaps, as we approach the study of these documents, is unfavorable. So much constitutional detail seems needless. We object that something ought to be left to the discretion of the governing power, that the closest ligature of parchment offers no adequate guaranty of good government. But when we have well studied and compared State constitutions, such prejudice softens; we discern that the modern governing power in the American commonwealth is not the agent, but the principal, not individual ambition, but the general opinion. We realize that a constitution becomes the most imperative of written law, because the enactment of the people. Breadth, not intolerance, characterizes these later schemes of State government. Dislike of monopolies, of class and money-making privileges, though visible, is not destructively manifested. If some impertinent or niggardly constraint can be pointed out in a State constitution, it is only on rare occasion. If rulers seem now and then hampered in action, it is because the ruled are "subjects," in the old-world sense, no longer; because American citizens are keenly sensitive to public shortcomings, and apprehend the temptations which beset those placed temporarily over them by their own suffrage. Sooner or later the best thought of each community, of business men, of journalists, of university scholars, of literary writers, of those who make a comparative study of politics and government, of professional men and philosophers, as well as of recognized political leaders, has gone into the marrow of these State constitutions. Republican home government finds here the widest scope and expression; experiments bring results; and expedients for reform soon develop vital principles. The whole outlook of such progression is hopeful, since the salvation of self-government lies in a continuous sense of honor and patriotism among the people, and in the courageous determination, moreover, of the majority to correct whatever practical mischief public administration may at any time bring to light. The American people, as a mass, are far from being hasty and capricious in ordering fundamental changes. Even in the great mass of statutes churned out periodically by the several State legislatures, those who explore inform us that the really important changes of written law are few and unfrequent; and our present study of institutions convinces us that in organic political reforms as well, the conservative instinct of the American people is very great. The inertia of the mass opposes those who are actively pushing for new results.

The grandeur of our American example in the world's history seems well assured, if only two dangers be well guarded against. One of these, which is fostered by the exceeding laxity of the Federal power originally given in that respect to Congress, or assumed, concerns the future territorial expansion of this Union; and it might be well if a constitutional amendment should guaranty in this respect a better constraining right to the people. The new and remote annexation of a people unfitted to mingle in self-government, and of a foreign country not contiguous, may imperil the experiment of the fathers in some future era of "manifest destiny." The other danger lies in the excrescent growth of political agencies for organizing the voters, massing cohorts for the candidates, and making selfish spoils of the public patronage. Against this latter evil should be set the best mental and moral enlightenment of the people, so that citizens may grow up good patriots, able to combine and co-operate for noble ends without arrogance or class spirit. That virtue which has well been pronounced by Montesquieu the animating spirit of a republic is in its essence patriotism, — a burning passion for one's own country, and a desire to advance always its true good and greatness. Though latent in commonplace times, such patriotism, when intelligently directed, becomes an overwhelming force for the general good in times of danger.

CONSTITUTION

UNITED STATES OF AMERICA.

WE the people of the United States, in order to form a more perfect union, establish justice, insure domestic tranquillity, provide for the common defence, promote the general welfare, and secure the blessings of liberty to ourselves and our posterity, do ordain and establish this CONSTITUTION for the United States of America.

ARTICLE I.

SECT. 1. All legislative powers herein granted shall be vested in a Congress of the United States, which shall consist of a Senate and a House of Representatives.

SECT. 2. The House of Representatives shall be composed of members chosen every second year by the people of the several States, and the electors in each State shall have the qualifications requisite for electors of the most numerous branch of the State Legislature.

No person shall be a Representative who shall not have attained to the age of twenty-five years, and been seven years a citizen of the United States, and who shall not, when elected, be an inhabitant of that State in which he shall be chosen.

Representatives and direct taxes shall be apportioned among the several States which may be included within this Union, according to their respective numbers, which shall be determined by adding to the whole number of free persons, including those bound to service for a term of years, and excluding Indians not taxed, three fifths of all other persons. The actual enumeration shall be made within three years after the first meeting of the Congress of the United States, and within every subsequent term of ten years, in such manner as they shall by law direct. The number of Representatives shall not exceed one for every thirty thousand, but each State shall have at least one representative; and until such enumeration shall be made, the State of New Hampshire shall be entitled to choose three, Massachusetts eight, Rhode Island and Providence Plantations one, Connecticut five, New York six, New Jersey four, Pennsylvania eight, Delaware one, Maryland six, Virginia ten, North Carolina five, South Carolina five, and Georgia three.

When vacancies happen in the representation from any State, the Executive authority thereof shall issue writs of election to fill such vacancies.

The House of Representatives shall choose their Speaker and other officers; and shall have the sole power of impeachment.

SECT. 3. The Senate of the United States shall be composed of two Senators from each State, chosen by the Legislature thereof, for six years; and each Senator shall have one vote.

Immediately after they shall be assembled in consequence of the first election, they shall be divided as equally as may be into three classes. The seats of the Senators of the first class shall be vacated at the expiration of the second year, of the second class at the expiration of the fourth year, and of the third class at the expiration of the sixth year, so that one third may be chosen every second year; and if vacancies happen by resignation, or otherwise, during the recess of the Legislature of any State, the Executive thereof may make temporary appointments until the next meeting of the Legislature, which shall then fill such vacancies.

No person shall be a Senator who shall not have attained to the age of thirty years, and been nine years a citizen of the United States, and who shall not, when elected, be an inhabitant of that State for which he shall be chosen.

The Vice-President of the United States shall be President of the Senate, but shall have no vote, unless they be equally divided.

The Senate shall choose their other officers, and also a President *pro tempore*, in the absence of the Vice-President, or when he shall exercise the office of President of the United States.

The Senate shall have the sole power to try all impeachments. When sitting for that purpose, they shall be on oath or affirmation. When the President of the United States is tried, the Chief Justice shall preside: and no person shall be convicted without the concurrence of two thirds of the members present.

Judgment in cases of impeachment shall not extend further than to removal from office, and disqualification to hold and enjoy any office of honor, trust, or profit under the United States: but the party convicted shall nevertheless be liable and subject to indictment, trial, judgment, and punishment, according to law.

SECT. 4. The times, places, and manner of holding elections for Senators and Representatives shall be prescribed in each State by the Legislature thereof ; but the Congress may at any time by law make or alter such regulations, except as to the places of choosing Senators.

The Congress shall assemble at least once in every year, and such meeting shall be on the first Monday in December, unless they shall by law appoint a different day.

SECT. 5. Each House shall be the judge of the elections, returns, and qualifications of its own members, and a majority of each shall constitute a quorum to do business; but a smaller number may adjourn from day to day, and may be authorized to compel the attendance of absent members, in such manner, and under such penalties, as each House may provide.

Each House may determine the rules of its proceedings, punish its members for disorderly behavior, and, with the concurrence of two thirds, expel a member.

Each House shall keep a journal of its proceedings, and from time to time publish the same, excepting such parts as may in their judgment require secrecy ; and the yeas and nays of the members of either House on any question shall, at the desire of one fifth of those present, be entered on the journal.

Neither House, during the session of Congress, shall, without the consent of the other, adjourn for more than three days, nor to any other place than that in which the two Houses shall be sitting.

SECT. 6. The Senators and Representatives shall receive a compensation for their services, to be ascertained by law, and paid out of the Treasury of the United States. They shall in all cases, except treason, felony, and breach of the peace, be privileged from arrest during their attendance at the session of their respective Houses, and in going to and returning from the same ; and for any speech or debate in either House they shall not be questioned in any other place.

No Senator or Representative shall, during the time for which he was elected, be appointed to any civil office under the authority of the United States, which shall have been created, or the emoluments whereof shall have been increased, during such time; and no person holding any office under the United States shall be a member of either House during his continuance in office.

SECT. 7. All bills for raising revenue shall originate in the House of Representatives; but the Senate may propose or concur with amendments as on other bills.

Every bill which shall have passed the House of Representatives and the Senate shall, before it become a law, be presented to the President of the United States; if he approve he shall sign it, but if not he shall return it with his objections to that House in which it shall have originated, who shall enter the objections at large on their journal, and proceed to reconsider it. If after such reconsideration two thirds of that House shall agree to pass the bill, it shall be sent, together with the objections, to the other House, by which it shall likewise be reconsidered, and, if approved by two thirds of that House, it shall become a law. But in all such cases the votes of both Houses shall be determined by yeas and nays, and the names of the persons voting for and against the bill shall be entered on the journal of each House respectively. If any bill shall not be returned by the President within ten days (Sundays excepted) after it shall have been presented to him, the same shall be a law, in like manner as if he had signed it, unless the Congress by their adjournment prevent its return, in which case it shall not be a law.

Every order, resolution, or vote to which the concurrence of the Senate and House of Representatives may be necessary (except on a question of adjournment) shall be presented to the President of the United States; and, before the same shall take effect, shall be approved by him, or, being disapproved by him, shall be repassed by two thirds of the Senate and House of Representatives, according to the rules and limitations prescribed in the case of a bill.

SECT. 8. The Congress shall have power, —

To lay and collect taxes, duties, imposts, and excises to pay the debts and provide for the common defence and general welfare of the United States; but all duties, imposts, and excises shall be uniform throughout the United States;

To borrow money on the credit of the United States;

To regulate commerce with foreign nations, and among the several States, and with the Indian tribes;

To establish an uniform rule of naturalization, and uniform

laws on the subject of bankruptcies throughout the United States;

To coin money, regulate the value thereof, and of foreign coin, and fix the standard of weights and measures;

To provide for the punishment of counterfeiting the securities and current coin of the United States;

To establish post-offices and post-roads;

To promote the progress of science and useful arts, by securing for limited times to authors and inventors the exclusive right to their respective writings and discoveries;

To constitute tribunals inferior to the Supreme Court;

To define and punish piracies and felonies committed on the high seas, and offences against the law of nations;

To declare war, grant letters of marque and reprisal, and make rules concerning captures on land and water;

To raise and support armies, but no appropriation of money to that use shall be for a longer term than two years;

To provide and maintain a navy;

To make rules for the government and regulation of the land and naval forces;

To provide for calling forth the militia to execute the laws of the Union, suppress insurrections, and repel invasions;

To provide for organizing, arming, and disciplining the militia, and for governing such part of them as may be employed in the service of the United States, reserving to the States respectively, the appointment of the officers, and the authority of training the militia according to the discipline prescribed by Congress;

To exercise exclusive legislation, in all cases whatsoever, over such district (not exceeding ten miles square) as may, by cession of particular States, and the acceptance of Congress, become the seat of the government of the United States; and to exercise like authority over all places purchased by the consent of the Legislature of the State in which the same shall be, for the erection of forts, magazines, arsenals, dock-yards, and other needful buildings; and

To make all laws which shall be necessary and proper for carrying into execution the foregoing powers, and all other powers vested by this Constitution in the government of the United States, or in any department or officer thereof.

SECT. 9. The migration or importation of such persons as any of the States now existing shall think proper to admit, shall not be prohibited by the Congress prior to the year one thousand eight hundred and eight, but a tax or duty may be imposed on such importation, not exceeding ten dollars for each person.

The privilege of the writ of *habeas corpus* shall not be suspended, unless when in cases of rebellion or invasion the public safety may require it.

No bill of attainder or *ex post facto* law shall be passed.

No capitation or other direct tax shall be laid, unless in proportion to the census or enumeration herein before directed to be taken.

No tax or duty shall be laid on articles exported from any State.

No preference shall be given by any regulation of commerce or revenue to the ports of one State over those of another; nor shall vessels bound to, or from, one State, be obliged to enter, clear, or pay duties in another.

No money shall be drawn from the treasury, but in consequence of appropriations made by law; and a regular statement and account of the receipts and expenditures of all public money shall be published from time to time.

No title of nobility shall be granted by the United States; and no person holding any office of profit or trust under them shall, without the consent of the Congress, accept of any present, emolument, office, or title, of any kind whatever, from any king, prince, or foreign state.

Sect. 10.   No State shall enter into any treaty, alliance, or confederation; grant letters of marque and reprisal; coin money ; emit bills of credit; make anything but gold and silver coin a tender in payment of debts; pass any bill of attainder, *ex post facto* law, or law impairing the obligation of contracts, or grant any title of nobility.

No State shall, without the consent of the Congress, lay any imposts or duties on imports or exports, except what may be absolutely necessary for executing its inspection laws; and the net produce of all duties and imposts, laid by any State on imports or exports, shall be for the use of the treasury of the United States; and all such laws shall be subject to the revision and control of the Congress.

No State shall, without the consent of Congress, lay any duty of tonnage, keep troops or ships of war in time of peace, enter into any agreement or compact with another State, or with a foreign power, or engage in war, unless actually invaded, or in such imminent danger as will not admit of delay.

ARTICLE II.

SECT. 1. The executive power shall be vested in a President of the United States of America. He shall hold his office during the term of four years, and, together with the Vice-President, chosen for the same term, be elected as follows : —

Each State shall appoint, in such manner as the Legislature thereof may direct, a number of Electors equal to the whole number of Senators and Representatives to which the State may be entitled in the Congress : but no Senator or Representative, or person holding an office of trust or profit under the United States, shall be appointed an Elector.

[The Electors shall meet in their respective States, and vote by ballot for two persons, of whom one at least shall not be an inhabitant of the same State with themselves. And they shall make a list of all the persons voted for, and of the number of votes for each ; which list they shall sign and certify, and transmit sealed to the seat of the government of the United States, directed to the President of the Senate. The President of the Senate shall, in the presence of the Senate and House of Representatives, open all the certificates, and the votes shall then be counted. The person having the greatest number of votes shall be the President, if such number be a majority of the whole number of Electors appointed ; and if there be more than one who have such majority, and have an equal number of votes, then the House of Representatives shall immediately choose by ballot one of them for President; and if no person have a majority, then from the five highest on the list the said House shall in like manner choose the President. But in choosing the President, the votes shall be taken by States, the representation from each State having one vote ; a quorum for this purpose shall consist of a member or members from two thirds of the States, and a majority of all the States shall be necessary to a choice. In every case, after the choice of the President, the person having the greatest number of votes of the Electors shall be the Vice-President. But if there should remain two or more who have equal votes, the Senate shall choose from them by ballot the Vice-President. — *Repealed by Amendment XII.*]

The Congress may determine the time of choosing the Electors, and the day on which they shall give their votes; which day shall be the same throughout the United States.

No person except a natural-born citizen, or a citizen of the

United States at the time of the adoption of this Constitution, shall be eligible to the office of President ; neither shall any person be eligible to that office who shall not have attained to the age of thirty-five years, and been fourteen years a resident⁻ within the United States.

In case of the removal of the President from office, or of his death, resignation, or inability to discharge the powers and duties of the said office, the same shall devolve on the Vice-President, and the Congress may by law provide for the case of removal, death, resignation, or inability, both of the President and Vice-President, declaring what officer shall then act as President, and such officer shall act accordingly, until the disability be removed, or a President shall be elected.

The President shall, at stated times, receive for his services a compensation, which shall neither be increased nor diminished during the period for which he shall have been elected, and he shall not receive within that period any other emolument from the United States, or any of them.

Before he enter on the execution of his office, he shall take the following oath or affirmation : — " I do solemnly swear (or affirm) that I will faithfully execute the office of President of the United States, and will, to the best of my ability, preserve, protect, and defend the Constitution of the United States."

SECT. 2.   The President shall be commander-in-chief of the army and navy of the United States, and of the militia of the several States, when called into the actual service of the United States ; he may require the opinion, in writing, of the principal officer in each of the executive departments, upon any subject relating to the duties of their respective offices, and he shall have power to grant reprieves and pardons for offences against the United States, except in cases of impeachment.

He shall have power, by and with the advice and consent of the Senate, to make treaties, provided two thirds of the Senators present concur ; and he shall nominate, and, by and with the advice and consent of the Senate, shall appoint ambassadors, other public ministers, and consuls, judges of the Supreme Court, and all other officers of the United States, whose appointments are not herein otherwise provided for, and which shall be established by law ; but the Congress may by law vest the appointment of such inferior officers, as they think proper, in the President alone, in the courts of law, or in the heads of departments.

The President shall have power to fill up all vacancies that may happen during the recess of the Senate, by granting commissions which shall expire at the end of their next session.

SECT. 3. He shall from time to time give to the Congress information of the state of the Union, and recommend to their consideration such measures as he shall judge necessary and expedient; he may, on extraordinary occasions, convene both Houses, or either of them, and in case of disagreement between them, with respect to the time of adjournment, he may adjourn them to such time as he shall think proper; he shall receive ambassadors and other public ministers; he shall take care that the laws be faithfully executed, and shall commission all the officers of the United States.

SECT. 4. The President, Vice-President, and all civil officers of the United States, shall be removed from office on impeachment for, and conviction of, treason, bribery, or other high crimes and misdemeanors.

ARTICLE III.

SECT. 1. The judicial power of the United States shall be vested in one Supreme Court, and in such inferior courts as the Congress may from time to time ordain and establish. The judges, both of the Supreme and inferior courts, shall hold their offices during good behavior, and shall, at stated times, receive for their services a compensation, which shall not be diminished during their continuance in office.

SECT. 2. The judicial power shall extend to all cases, in law and equity, arising under this Constitution, the laws of the United States, and treaties made, or which shall be made, under their authority; to all cases affecting ambassadors, other public ministers, and consuls; to all cases of admiralty and maritime jurisdiction; to controversies to which the United States shall be a party; to controversies between two or more States, between a State and citizens of another State, between citizens of different States, between citizens of the same State claiming lands under grants of different States, and between a State, or the citizens thereof, and foreign states, citizens, or subjects.

In all cases affecting ambassadors, other public ministers, and consuls, and those in which a State shall be party, the Supreme Court shall have original jurisdiction. In all the other cases before mentioned, the Supreme Court shall have appellate jurisdiction, both as to law and fact, with such exceptions, and under such regulations, as the Congress shall make.

The trial of all crimes, except in cases of impeachment, shall be by jury; and such trial shall be held in the State where the said crimes shall have been committed; but when not committed within any State, the trial shall be at such place or places as the Congress may by law have directed.

SECT. 3. Treason against the United States shall consist only in levying war against them, or in adhering to their enemies, giving them aid and comfort. No person shall be convicted of treason unless on the testimony of two witnesses to the same overt act, or on confession in open court.

The Congress shall have power to declare the punishment of treason, but no attainder of treason shall work corruption of blood, or forfeiture, except during the life of the person attainted.

ARTICLE IV.

SECT. 1. Full faith and credit shall be given in each State to the public acts, records, and judicial proceedings of every other State. And the Congress may by general laws prescribe the manner in which such acts, records, and proceedings shall be proved, and the effect thereof.

SECT. 2. The citizens of each State shall be entitled to all privileges and immunities of citizens in the several States.

A person charged in any State with treason, felony, or other crime, who shall flee from justice, and be found in another State, shall, on demand of the executive authority of the State from which he fled, be delivered up, to be removed to the State having jurisdiction of the crime.

No person held to service or labor in one State, under the laws thereof, escaping into another, shall, in consequence of any law or regulation therein, be discharged from such service or labor, but shall be delivered up on claim of the party to whom such service or labor may be due.

SECT. 3. New States may be admitted by the Congress into this Union; but no new State shall be formed or erected within the jurisdiction of any other State ; nor any State be formed by the junction of two or more States, or parts of States, without the consent of the Legislatures of the States concerned, as well as of the Congress.

The Congress shall have power to dispose of and make all needful rules and regulations respecting the territory or other property belonging to the United States; and nothing in this

Constitution shall be so construed as to prejudice any claims of the United States, or of any particular State.

SECT. 4. The United States shall guarantee to every State in this Union a republican form of government, and shall protect each of them against invasion; and on application of the Legislature, or of the Executive (when the Legislature cannot be convened), against domestic violence.

ARTICLE V.

The Congress, whenever two thirds of both houses shall deem it necessary, shall propose amendments to this Constitution, or, on the application of the Legislatures of two thirds of the several States, shall call a convention for proposing amendments, which, in either case, shall be valid to all intents and purposes, as part of this Constitution, when ratified by the Legislatures of three fourths of the several States, or by conventions in three fourths thereof, as the one or the other mode of ratification may be proposed by the Congress; provided that no amendment which may be made prior to the year one thousand eight hundred and eight shall in any manner affect the first and fourth clauses in the ninth section of the first article; and that no State, without its consent, shall be deprived of its equal suffrage in the Senate.

ARTICLE VI.

All debts contracted and engagements entered into, before the adoption of this Constitution shall be as valid against the United States under this Constitution as under the Confederation.

This Constitution, and the laws of the United States which shall be made in pursuance thereof, and all treaties made, or which shall be made, under the authority of the United States, shall be the supreme law of the land; and the judges in every State shall be bound thereby, anything in the constitution or laws of any State to the contrary notwithstanding.

The Senators and Representatives before mentioned, and the members of the several State Legislatures, and all executive and judicial officers, both of the United States and of the several States, shall be bound by oath or affirmation to support this Constitution; but no religious test shall ever be required as a qualification to any office or public trust under the United States.

ARTICLE VII.

The ratification of the conventions of nine States shall be sufficient for the establishment of this Constitution between the States so ratifying the same.

Done in Convention, by the unanimous consent of the States present, the seventeenth day of September, in the year of our Lord one thousand seven hundred and eighty-seven, and of the Independence of the United States of America the twelfth. **In Witness** whereof we have hereunto subscribed our names.

[Signed by]
G⁹: WASHINGTON,
Presidt. and Deputy from Virginia,
and by thirty-nine delegates.

ARTICLES

IN ADDITION TO, AND AMENDMENT OF, THE

CONSTITUTION OF THE UNITED STATES OF AMERICA.

ARTICLE I.

Congress shall make no law respecting an establishment of religion, or prohibiting the free exercise thereof; or abridging the freedom of speech, or of the press, or the right of the people peaceably to assemble, and to petition the government for a redress of grievances.

ARTICLE II.

A well-regulated militia being necessary to the security of a free state, the right of the people to keep and bear arms shall not be infringed.

ARTICLE III.

No soldier shall, in time of peace, be quartered in any house, without the consent of the owner, nor in time of war, but in a manner to be prescribed by law.

ARTICLE IV.

The right of the people to be secure in their persons, houses, papers, and effects, against unreasonable searches and seizures, shall not be violated, and no warrants shall issue but upon probable cause, supported by oath or affirmation, and particularly describing the place to be searched, and the persons or things to be seized.

ARTICLE V.

No person shall be held to answer for a capital, or otherwise infamous crime, unless on a presentment or indictment of a grand jury, except in cases arising in the land or naval forces, or in the militia, when in actual service in time of war or public danger ; nor shall any person be subject for the same offence to be twice put in jeopardy of life or limb; nor shall be compelled in any criminal case to be a witness against himself, nor be deprived of life, liberty, or property, without due process of law ; nor shall private property be taken for public use without just compensation.

ARTICLE VI.

In all criminal prosecutions, the accused shall enjoy the right to a speedy and public trial, by an impartial jury of the State and district wherein the crime shall have been committed, which district shall have been previously ascertained by law, and to be informed of the nature and cause of the accusation ; to be confronted with the witnesses against him ; to have compulsory process for obtaining witnesses in his favor, and to have the assistance of counsel for his defence.

ARTICLE VII.

In suits at common law, where the value in controversy shall exceed twenty dollars, the right of trial by jury shall be preserved, and no fact tried by a jury shall be otherwise re-examined in any court of the United States, than according to the rules of the common law.

ARTICLE VIII.

Excessive bail shall not be required, nor excessive fines imposed, nor cruel and unusual punishments inflicted.

ARTICLE IX.

The enumeration in the Constitution, of certain rights, shall not be construed to deny or disparage others retained by the people.

ARTICLE X.

The powers not delegated to the United States by the Constitution, nor prohibited by it to the States, are reserved to the States respectively, or to the people.

ARTICLE XI.

The judicial power of the United States shall not be construed to extend to any suit in law or equity, commenced or prosecuted against one of the United States by citizens of another State, or by citizens or subjects of any foreign state.

ARTICLE XII.

The Electors shall meet in their respective States, and vote by ballot for President and Vice-President, one of whom, at least, shall not be an inhabitant of the same State with themselves; they shall name in their ballots the person voted for as President, and in distinct ballots the person voted for as Vice-President; and they shall make distinct lists of all persons voted for as President, and of all persons voted for as Vice-President, and of the number of votes for each, which lists they shall sign and certify, and transmit sealed to the seat of the government of the United States, directed to the President of the Senate; — the President of the Senate shall, in the presence of the Senate and House of Representatives, open all the certificates, and the votes shall then be counted; — the person having the greatest number of votes for President shall be the President, if such number be a majority of the whole number of Electors appointed; and if no person have such majority, then from the persons having the highest numbers not exceeding three on the list of those voted for as President, the House of Representatives shall choose immediately, by ballot, the President. But in choosing the President, the votes shall be taken by States, the representation from each State having one vote; a quorum for this purpose shall consist of a member or members from two thirds of the States, and a majority of all the States shall be necessary to a choice. And if the House of Representatives shall not choose a President, whenever the right of choice shall devolve upon them, before the fourth day of March next following, then the Vice-President shall act as President, as in the case of the death or other constitutional disability of the President. The person having the greatest number of votes as Vice-President shall be the Vice-President, if such number be a majority of the whole number of Electors appointed, and if no person have a majority, then from the two highest numbers on the list the Senate shall choose the Vice-President; a quorum for the purpose shall consist of two thirds of the whole number of Senators, and a majority of the whole number shall be necessary to a choice. But no person constitutionally ineligible to the office of President shall be eligible to that of Vice-President of the United States.

ARTICLE XIII.

SECT. 1. Neither slavery nor involuntary servitude, except as a punishment for crime whereof the party shall have been duly convicted, shall exist within the United States, or any place subject to their jurisdiction.

SECT. 2. Congress shall have power to enforce this article by appropriate legislation.

ARTICLE XIV.

SECT. 1. All persons born or naturalized in the United States, and subject to the jurisdiction thereof, are citizens of the United States and of the State wherein they reside. No State shall make or enforce any law which shall abridge the privileges or immunities of citizens of the United States; nor shall any State deprive any person of life, liberty, or property, without due process of law; nor deny to any person within its jurisdiction the equal protection of the laws.

SECT. 2. Representatives shall be apportioned among the several States according to their respective numbers, counting the whole number of persons in each State, excluding Indians not taxed. But when the right to vote at any election for the choice of Electors for President and Vice-President of the United States, Representatives in Congress, the executive and judicial officers of a State, or the members of the Legislature thereof, is denied to any of the male inhabitants of such State, being twenty-one years of age and citizens of the United States, or in any way abridged, except for participation in rebellion or other crime, the basis of representation therein shall be reduced in the proportion which the number of such male citizens shall bear to the whole number of male citizens twenty-one years of age in such State.

SECT. 3. No person shall be a Senator or Representative in Congress, or Elector of President and Vice-President, or hold any office, civil or military, under the United States, or under any State, who, having previously taken an oath, as a member of Congress, or as an officer of the United States, or as a member of any State Legislature, or as an executive or judicial officer of any State, to support the Constitution of the United States, shall have engaged in insurrection or rebellion against the same, or given aid or comfort to the enemies thereof. But Congress may, by a vote of two thirds of each House, remove such disability.

SECT. 4. The validity of the public debt of the United States, authorized by law, including debts incurred for payment of pensions and bounties for services in suppressing insurrection or rebellion, shall not be questioned. But neither the United States, nor any State shall assume or pay any debt or obligation incurred in aid of insurrection or rebellion against the United States, nor any claim for the loss or emancipation of any slave; but all such debts, obligations, and claims shall be held illegal and void.

SECT. 5. The Congress shall have power to enforce, by appropriate legislation, the provisions of this article.

ARTICLE XV.

SECT. 1. The right of citizens of the United States to vote shall not be denied or abridged by the United States, or by any State, on account of race, color, or previous condition of servitude.

SECT. 2. The Congress shall have power to enforce this article by appropriate legislation.

INDEX.